Reviews

I have really enjoyed the book you both wrote. I love the cover which is luxurious and glossy, and it was a real adventure story, with thoughtful research and scholarship.
Eveline Ashbee

A fascinating read – especially for the many fans of The Lord of the Rings – but written in a living, modern context. Very thought provoking – I couldn't put it down.
Julia Hunter

Well, I started to read the book and enjoyed every moment. Well done to the authors for expanding The Lord of the Rings to encompass today's world, and that we are all on a quest as mentioned in the book. It was wonderful that someone has taken the time to record the unfolding events as they happened, and then to put them into a book that many people will read and enjoy, and will bring about a happy ending to the Ring.
Robert Light

I found this book very difficult to put down. It is very easy to read and at points invokes the same levels of dread that Tolkien's classic achieves. If you have an open mind and a stout Hobbit heart then you should definitely read this book.
Elfed Williams

I found 'Ring Quest' a most enjoyable book to read. It held my interest from start to finish. Truly a book all should read.
Frank Trim

Between two worlds, an amazing feat of merging dimensions: a link between 'here' and 'there' – awesome!!!
Linda Williams

Website. www.ring-quest-book.co.uk
Link to http://truthteachings.blogspot.com

Caroline Milton and Cassie Martin are mother and daughter. Caroline was educated at several convents, subsequently attending university where she read English. She worked for a short time in London before marrying a soldier and spending the next two decades travelling and living abroad in the Far East, Africa and Europe while bringing up a family of three. On returning to England, she worked as P.A. to a Member of Parliament during which time she became interested in esoteric subjects.

As an army daughter Cassie had a childhood of travel, sun and warm seas. A year was spent at university studying history after which she worked in London where she met her husband. For six years she worked as a secretary for the World Health Organisation in Geneva, where she developed an interest in astrology and spiritual books at the same time as Caroline. She returned to the UK to bring up her two daughters.

RING QUEST

The Continuing Story of the Ring

❖

Cassie Martin and Caroline Milton

This book is dedicated to Robert Light
without whom it would not have been written.

Acknowledgements

We give a big thank-you to our family and friends who, over the years, when the quest was underway and the book being written, gave us their support and encouragement. We would also like to thank Darren Bowden for his inspired design of the book cover and Maria Burns for her elegant illustrations of the Signs of the Zodiac. Grateful thanks also to Alice, Toni and Victoria.

Contents

Illustrations of Astrological Signs in London

Introduction

In the early hours of the morning a lorry drove slowly up the hill in the village of Badby, Northamptonshire. It was a spring day and the light was still dim. In the middle of the road stood a white horse. As the lorry driver drew closer he could make out a woman in an old-fashioned white dress mounted on the horse and she just stared at the lorry. It was only when the vehicle was 15 feet away and the driver had just opened the door to get out and ask the lady to move that the horse suddenly jumped over the hedge. There was no sound of horse's hooves, just the rustling of bushes. So real was the apparition that, instinctively, the driver got out of the lorry and climbed on some bricks to get a better view over the hedge of the horse and rider. But there was nothing to be seen.

He later discovered the woman to be the ghost of Mrs Fitzgerald who had been murdered by her husband as she returned home on her white horse from an illicit meeting with her lover. Her husband was waiting for her in the servants' quarters with a shotgun and shot her dead. Such traumatic circumstances can very often result in the person being trapped at the low astral level, in that time, repeating the tragic events that led to their deaths. It is moving to speculate that when her horse died it chose to remain with its mistress out of love and because of the mistress's need for companionship. Her faithful horse must have been of great comfort to Mrs Fitzgerald in her desolate state.

As so often in such examples of ghostly re-enactment, the person who saw the ghostly pair thought they were real. The story implies that at another, finer level people are still caught up in events that took place a long time ago and should by rights have ended. Yet these souls appear trapped and hopelessly bound to repeat them in order to try and change the outcome. We are affected by the emotional imprint of past events left in the ether around us, even to the extent of it adversely affecting our health.

As many know, there is an interaction between our physical world and those other dimensions on certain anniversaries. Laurence Gardner (author of the well-known

1

Bloodline of the Holy Grail) says in his book Lost Secrets of the Sacred Ark that modern scientists have '....confirmed the existence of parallel dimensions..' and that these scientists have '..expressed their particular concern that the public are kept in the dark about such matters.'

Our story pushes out the boundaries of our understanding a little further. In 1997 a man called Robert Light entered our lives. He has extraordinary powers, of which there are many examples throughout this book. He sets us off on a quest, in which he himself plays a vital part, to change a story - a true one - that has been repeatedly re-enacted at that finer level at the end of every Age, where we once again find ourselves. Those events are then bound to be played out at the dense physical level because of the old saying: 'As above, so below'. The story we were to work with was J.R.R. Tolkien's trilogy, The Lord of the Rings. It can be no coincidence that the book has now been turned into an epic film, catching the attention of many millions of people throughout the world.

A group of us was told by Robert that by consciously earthing the Story at the dense physical level, we have the ability to clear the ether of the ghosts of our past. Those energies of good and evil, of great deeds and battles fought, swirling around us at other dimensions, would then be cleared to the benefit of humankind. That change can only be made from the physical level where we are not trapped within those events. We were also told that through our ability consciously to interact with those events, we can change the Story and so bring about a satisfactory resolution.

Why should we need to change the story, we wondered and, for that matter, why has the saga continued to be recycled? The answer came from Robert that humanity had not learnt its lessons and has continued to repeat the same mistakes. Had the Evil Ring of Power made by the Dark Lord truly been destroyed when it fell into the fiery abyss of the volcano? And if not, what would have been the consequences? Apparently, we are at a unique time in our history where we have the opportunity to get the Story right at those higher levels. Everything is coming together – the past, present and the future. We are at the End Times.

There is a belief in some circles that our planet is undergoing great changes and that its vibrations are rising, as well as the vibrations of all life on the planet including ourselves, if we choose. If this is the case, would we not get a nasty shock if the veil that presently separates us from unseen worlds were suddenly removed? There might be horrors that we would rather not see. In this light, the work that our group and others are doing to clear those levels first, suddenly makes a lot of sense. Also, in order for the planet to raise its vibrations, it is necessary to clear the enveloping black miasma which some books have described and which prevents the light penetrating.

The authors of The Green Stone, Graham Phillips, Martin Keatman and others were also involved in a story which connected with evil at the astral level in a very real way, just as ours does. They enter a tale whose origins go back in time to Egypt and the Pharaoh Akhenaton. It centres round a stone of great power and a direct confrontation with the Evil One.

With the benefit of hindsight, we can see that both groups had a period of preparation so that our minds were open to ideas which many would have dismissed out of hand. Some of the participants in the story of The Green Stone came to their experiences via research into UFO's, which took them straight into their amazing adventures.

We began in a small way, some seven years before the start of this story. After picking up the idea from a book in January 1991, we decided to test our possible powers of dowsing. This soon led on to clearing areas of negativity, particularly churches on energy lines in and around Northampton. Cassie lived in Northampton with her husband and two small daughters. Caroline, Cassie's mother, was in London at the time but used to travel regularly to Northampton to help out with the two girls. Later, a book on ghost stories of Northamptonshire led us to focusing for a while on releasing trapped souls such as the lady at Badby.

We found the free flow of energy at churches along the energy lines was often blocked. There were varying causes for this and one was a new discovery due to the practices of the pagan cult of the worship of the Goddess. Cassie had been researching the pagan cults and she discovered that their focus

3

was the supposed life-giving powers of the semi-divine King. This resulted in his twice-yearly sacrifice at mid-summer and mid-winter. The idea was that the community would benefit from those life-giving powers in a most gruesome manner. With tragic consequences for women, he was sacrificed in the name of the all-powerful Queen who was considered the Goddess's representative on earth. We discovered that successive sacrifices took place at the same place which were more often than not at energy centres on where several energy/ley lines cross over underground water. It was on such sites that many pre-reformation churches and cathedrals were subsequently built.

The negative energy began to build up with such sacrifices so that the souls of the young men became trapped at these power points. How Cassie came to find out about the existence of this forgotten Cult does not come into this book. Suffice it to say, we were so moved by the cruel end of so many young men that we began travelling the country visiting cathedrals, churches, hill forts, abbeys and castles, which are on sites of former pagan worship, releasing these trapped souls and cleansing the area.

We were blithely unaware that such work involved very real dangers as we were drawing attention to ourselves from what you might call the 'evil forces'. It is from such centres of polluted energy that they draw much of their power. To see that energy being transmuted into positive energy was not to their liking. At this point, in the summer of 1998, through a friend of Caroline's who lives in the Wye valley, we began attending self-awareness workshops in Gloucestershire given by Robert Light. He astonished us with his knowledge of our activities without our having mentioned them to him. He pointed out that we were working at a more powerful level now which took us beyond his protection and that we had gone into some very dangerous places. Caroline remarked that we must have gone where angels fear to tread and Robert, smilingly, agreed. We needed to learn to protect ourselves.

Unfortunately, mention of active forces for evil in the world today can have the effect of making some people automatically consign any such book to the realms of science fiction. Yet it has to be acknowledged that we live in a world of polarity – of light and dark, masculine and feminine, East and West, good and evil. In fact, the one cannot exist without the other. In C.S. Lewis's book The Screwtape Letters the senior devil tells the junior devil that their supreme weapon is that nobody believes they exist.

The adventures and experiences in this book are real and we, as a group, have as our guide a most remarkable man. We were made aware that we would encounter opposition and we needed to be alert to this. We also knew that the worst thing was to have fear. For this reason we thought it best not to dwell on the danger. The downside to our approach sometimes meant, unfortunately, that we were negligent in protecting ourselves and in picking up the signs around us which link the two worlds. It was easy enough to be aware when we were very deliberately stepping into the Story but less so when immersed in our everyday lives.

Tolkien

In bookshops Tolkien's books are put on the "Fantasy" shelves. However, it cannot be denied that The Lord of the Rings has profoundly affected many people the world over and has sold in its millions. If Tolkien's writings were just fantasy would they have drawn such responses as the one from a college student: "The Lord of the Rings was and will probably be the most significant book of my life."? Patrick Curry, a great admirer of Tolkien's work, wrote a book called Defending Middle Earth based on the idea that the Story is relevant to us today. He writes that on first reading The Lord of the Rings at the age of sixteen, "I was overcome from the beginning by the unmistakable sense of having encountered a world that was more real than the one I was then living in .....Accompanying this feeling was the equally odd one of inexplicable familiarity with that world."

Many new ideas have come 'out of the blue' and have not been the product of the logical, deductive process. Einstein said that his ideas on Relativity came suddenly to him out of nowhere. Composers will hear the music in their heads, perfectly formed, and all they have to do is write it down. This can be called 'inspired' or, dare one say it, given to us from a higher level from whatever benign source.

Later, Tolkien himself came to believe that the saga he had written was true. He says that he 'was drawn irresistibly' to certain things and that 'discovery' felt much more the case than 'invention' and that 'the story unfolded itself as it were'. The American writer, Clive Kilby, who spent three months in the summer of 1966 working closely with Tolkien, writes in his book Tolkien and The Silmarillion (1976) of an extraordinary incident when a Member of Parliament visiting Tolkien in his home declared, ' ..."You did not write The Lord of the Rings," meaning that it had been given him from God. It was clear that he (Tolkien) favoured this remark.'

If such is the case, the question arises, 'for what purpose?' Could such an involved story, which many find so gripping and powerful, be anything other than the true history of Man? When people say Tolkien derived his tales from the Teutonic, Celtic and Norse Mythology, could it in fact be the other way round? Legends, mythologies and fairy stories have come down to us from the tales Tolkien relates and are but windows on our remote past. With Tolkien, we get the original story.

Then in 2002 a friend sent Cassie an article dated 26 February 2002 that had appeared in the local paper for the West Country: *The Western Daily Press*. It was about the forthcoming sale by auctioneers, Dominic Winter, of a letter from Tolkien of 8 September 1955, to a youthful fan enquiring when the third book was going to appear. The telling passage in the letter states: "*I have not myself any doubt that things went just so, but that does not say that my attempt to record them is successful.*" Documents expert, Richard Westwood Brookes stated: "*It certainly seems to suggest that Tolkien really believed the events of The Lord of the Rings actually took place and that he was merely setting them down on paper.*"

The Cult of the Goddess and the Sacred King

A brief outline of this Cult is necessary for a fuller understanding of our Quest. In the pagan religious cults, it was the Queen who ruled in the name of the all-powerful Goddess on whose fertility the community's very survival depended. Her consort, the semi-divine Sun King, was the embodiment of the sun and for her continuing abundant fertility both she and the earth had to be fertilised by the Sun King. It was believed that the power of the sun built up in the very body of the King as the sun ascended to its zenith at midsummer, when he too, like the sun was at full power. On that day he was sacrificed, in the name of the Queen/Goddess, on a high place – a hill or mountain - and his body and blood were used to bless and fertilise the land and the people. There were two Kings, one for the Waxing Year and one for the Waning Year. Upon the sacrifice of the first, his 'twin', or 'King-in-waiting' took his place. As the sun began its descent in the skies, the King's strength likewise was perceived to decline. Finally, at midwinter the sun was seen to 'die' and the King of the Waning Year was also put to death. His sacrifice at that time of year took place in a sacred grove of trees, marshland or underground. The sun had returned to the very womb of the Goddess from whom he was reborn as the 'New' Sun King as, once again, the sun began to ascend the sky and the grisly cycle was repeated.[1]

Grotesquely, for all its seeming emphasis on the life-giving qualities of the semi-divine Sun King, the cult was, in reality, a Death Cult, as the focus of the religious year was the sacrifice of the Kings at mid-summer and mid-winter.

Cassie's source also makes it absolutely clear that this practice was worldwide. Perhaps the reason for this is that the original, uncorrupted ideas on which the Cult was based, came out of Atlantis and were taken to the different corners of the earth by refugees fleeing the destruction of that island.

However, it was to be many years before we realised that the Cult was an integral part of our Quest.

---

[1] See historical research in Appendices

The Road goes on forever following the Ring

Chapter 1

The One Ring Reformed

"The One Ring has remade itself and is exerting an evil influence in the world today"? we repeated incredulously to Robert who had just made this outrageous statement. He was referring to none other than the Ring of Power forged by the Dark Lord, Sauron, in J.R.R. Tolkien's book The Lord of the Rings. Naturally, we were aghast at such a suggestion, but not disbelieving because we had come to know Robert over the past year and knew that he was quite capable of making such a statement in all seriousness. We were also in no doubt as to the truth of this extraordinary idea.

We had been attending Robert's self-awareness workshops held near the Forest of Dean, making the long journey from Northampton. For some time before that a group of us used to get together at the weekends at the house of a friend of Caroline's nearby. We had similar 'New Age' interests, as they were then called, in such subjects as hands- on healing and self-awareness. It was Ellen, a member of this group, who first went to one of Robert's self-awareness workshops and strongly recommended them to us. We found his teaching to be different from anything we had experienced before - it was simple, yet at the same time, mind-stretching, a sort of 'back to basics' spirituality that had existed before man forgot his interconnectedness with the living world.

To begin with, his teaching focussed on simple things like being grounded and balanced for which he used the image of a daisy. The daisy is a beautifully simple, yet effective, idea. The white petals and yellow centre represent the principles of feminine and masculine so that balance is quickly acquired, and the roots of the flower give the necessary grounding. You then draw energy up through the roots and down from the sun where they mingle in the centre that is the solar plexus. He would ask us to visualise our daisy. Cassie can remember how she visualised hers the first time as a tall, thin-stemmed version and how it drooped easily. He used to go round advising everyone in the circle in turn. He looked at her, when it came to her turn, and told her somewhat tersely that a daisy was a hardy flower and close to the ground. Thereafter, she saw it as short-stemmed, sturdily taking the buffeting of any winds. Caroline, much to her surprise, was told that she was floating a foot above the ground and, obviously, needed to 'ground' herself.

For emotional well-being we were to visualise a rose. Robert's comment, when it came to Cassie's turn, was uncannily accurate. It was clear to her that he was able to see the image she was holding in her mind. She realised with a shock just how accurate her own subconscious mind was in throwing up a rose in that particular state of bloom. For physical strength we were asked to visualise a tree. We could then draw up energy from the roots and energy down from the sun, as with the daisy.

From such experiences, we realised that Robert had extra-ordinary gifts.

It was July 1998 and five of us were sitting in Ellen's house when Robert dropped his bombshell about the Ring of the Dark Lord exercising an evil power in our world today. He had arranged this particular meeting saying it was important. However, only a few people were free to attend. Several topics were discussed but all we have recorded and can remember now is what was to set us all off on an extraordinary adventure.

Robert quite suddenly changed the conversation and asked us about the history of the planet and of Man and what life had been like on this planet in the remote past. We did our best to answer these unexpectedly profound questions and finally suggested that life had been at the etheric level. The etheric is still part of the physical world but vibrating at a higher level, which we cannot yet see until such time as we are able to raise our own vibrations. He went on to say that the story of The Lord of the Rings was a true one that had taken place about sixty thousand years ago and that Tolkien's book had been 'inspired'.

The Ring of Power had not been completely destroyed when it fell into the fiery abyss with Gollum; it had only been destroyed in one of the elements, that of fire. Sauron had made the One Ring in <u>all</u> the elements – earth, water, air, fire and ether so that it might have power in the land of the living. When it was thrown into fire, therefore, it was not fully 'unmade'. This meant it could reconstitute itself at the end of an Age when its master, Sauron, re-emerging from the Shadows, began to grow in power once again and bend his mind and will to finding the lost Master Ring. This 'awoke' the latent malice of the Ring, which in turn began actively seeking its Master.

We learnt that the Story has been repeated many times at the end of every Age because "Man had not learnt his lessons." We were only vaguely aware of what those lessons might be. It seemed to us that Tolkien himself tells us humankind's weaknesses. One is that we are easily enamoured of the Dark Arts and many people worshipped the Dark Lord then - as they still do today. Another, was that men's wills quickly submitted to the power of the other Rings forged by Sauron. Nine of these were given to proud and powerful kings who became the 'living dead', called the Nazgul or Ringwraiths (also the Black Riders) in the story of The Lord of the Rings.

Even Frodo and Samwise's Quest to throw the One Ring into the fires of Mount Doom is already a second attempt to destroy the Ring. The earlier attempt had failed due to Man's weakness of will.[1] The opportunity is missed and therefore Sauron is incompletely defeated, only to rise and, once again, attempt world domination at the end of yet another Age. The customary way evil lures people into its service is through greed and the lust for power. There is evidence aplenty of this in our present world. These must be some of the lessons that we have not yet learnt.

Later on at home, when we were still trying to work things out, we telephoned Robert and he told us that we had to think harder about Man's journey to the present day. This made us realise that we have to go back the way we came, which means we must return to the etheric level of existence. The fall in the earth's energy level, or slowing down of the vibrations, which occurs at the end of the story in The Lord of the Rings, is a subtle current throughout the book.[2] Sauron's defeat at the end of the Story means that he will sink so low that he will not be able to take form again in the world of the living. But, if Robert is to be believed, Sauron is still trying to exercise a malevolent power over us from the lower astral levels, or the Regions of Hell, as the Christians would call them, as the replay button is pressed once again.[3]

This time around, we are being made aware of the wider reality we live in, although some may deny such truth. If we can detect the signs of the Story of The Lord of the Rings interacting with our world we can, uniquely, ground it through being consciously aware of what is taking place at that other level. This gives us the opportunity to change it, get it right and clear it from that level once and for all.

Chapter 2

The Eye of Surveillance

What evidence is there to suggest that the Ring of Power is influencing our world? And what evidence is there that the story in The Lord of the Rings is being played out again at another level, as Robert has suggested?

Walking down the street in any town in the country in May 1999, it wouldn't take long to come across a poster of the latest Star Wars Film. Cassie found herself staring with growing disbelief at the image of Liam Neeson, a member of the elite fighting force known as the Jedi. He holds up a light sabre as if it were a shining sword. She took in his long brown hair, the plain brown clothes, the eagle-like nose and the grim expression. Here was a man who fitted the description of Aragorn, the King-in-waiting in the story of The Lord of the Rings, in a most uncanny way. He also held a great sword: Aragorn was the wielder of the great sword Anduril, Flame of the West. There were other posters advertising the film Godzilla, which showed just one large, menacing eye. If Liam Neeson was Aragorn, this was the Eye of Sauron. Later, when re-reading the description of Sauron's Eye in Tolkien's book, the comparison was confirmed: it was an exact description of the Eye of Godzilla - yellow with a black slit for a pupil.

Most amazing of all was the timing. These films were being shown at the end of a millennium to coincide with the original Story being re-activated once again at other levels which means, according to the law of 'as above so below', that those events will impress themselves upon our world. Here was proof that this was already happening.

The ever-watchful Eye of Sauron is present in many ways. It occurred to us that television, cinema, computer screens and CCTV cameras all share characteristics of The Eye. They even have the optic nerve, which is the electrical wiring. The moving, watchful eye of surveillance cameras can be directly compared with the ranging Eye of Sauron as he monitored developments in the world far and wide.

Television creates an artificial world and in recent years we have increasingly been fed an artificial diet of sex and violence. Video games have taken the violence to new extremes. Even the expression for the internet as 'the worldwide web' aroused our suspicions, as it brought to mind the giant evil spider, Shelob, in the Story. She very nearly killed and devoured Frodo, the Ringbearer, on his seemingly hopeless quest. The Web, of course, is a very useful resource but it can also be put to evil use through the misuse of 'chat rooms' and exchange of pornographic material. Again, it can create an artificial world cut off from social interaction and relationships, and the real world.

Sauron's powers of surveillance can partly be attributed to possessing one of the Seven Stones of Seeing which resemble the gypsy's crystal ball.[4] Only Saruman and Denethor, Steward of Gondor, in addition to Sauron, possessed this powerful but dangerous tool. The other Stones had been lost during the many wars. Both men, in their different ways succumbed to the will of Sauron. When Denethor looked into the crystal ball, he only saw what Sauron wished him to see, which was the military strength of the Dark Lord, beyond count. This slowly poisoned the mind of Denethor and he succumbed to the evil of despair and hopelessness. To a large extent we have no control over what is fed to us on television and many of us are alert to this and protest about the foul language and violence. More recently, people have been concerned with the 'dumbing down' in the programmes on offer. In other words, we are being given a distorted view of world affairs, just as Sauron gave a distorted view to Denethor.

Robert told us of how, when asked to see if he could help a family which was having problems, he walked into the house and removed the television. A week later, peace had descended on the household. Instead of watching television constantly, which made them subtly bored and irritable, and was the cause of outbursts of violent temper, they had been forced to find something creative to do with their free time. Most of us do manage to be selective and have a balance. But are many of us, like Denethor, endlessly shown selective scenes of violence in the trouble spots of the world, in danger of succumbing to a feeling of helplessness?

We can remember the moment when the significance of 'ring' roads struck us. There has been a proliferation of these in recent years in order to remove traffic from town centres. When Cassie next looked at a map she noticed that these 'ring' roads, such as the M25, actually resemble gigantic spiders: the roads leading into them looking remarkably like the legs of a spider. The extra large spider sitting over London could be likened to Shelob in the Story, and the smaller ones, crouching over the lesser cities, are her offspring. It is therefore not surprising that we get 'road rage' if we think that these black, tarmac 'rings' and roads are being used to channel evil energy from another level. The One Ring was created to control all the other Rings and all, therefore, became evil.[5] The powerful men who wore them were subverted and eventually controlled by Sauron's will, all except for the dwarves. Only the three Elven Rings were free. They had been forged in secret without Sauron's knowledge.

In a telephone conversation with Robert in the summer of 1999 Robert said something rather staggering, which shows in the most graphic way that history repeats itself. He said that the White House in the United States of America is Minas Tirith with its white tower, and Mordor is Afghanistan. However, the major players are not yet in place. Just as in Tolkien's story there is the division of East and West, so is it the case in our times. He identified The Fens with the Dead Marshes, which Frodo and Samwise crossed with Gollum as their guide. The Forest of Dean is the Shire – not so far from our meeting place - and the New Forest is the Forest of Fangorn.

In The Lord of the Rings we learn of the superior Numenorean race of men. They were exceptionally tall, black haired and grey-eyed. Their superiority also lay in their exceptional abilities – they had bright eyes with particularly acute eyesight, great physical strength and endurance, exceptional hearing and the gift of foresight. Aragorn, the future king, was of this race of men and one of his names was Thorongil, which means 'eagle-eyed'. Has anyone ever given a

15

thought as to the origins of Superman? He clearly belongs to a superior race of men. But why is he always dark haired and blue eyed and never blonde and blue-eyed? We realised that his origins are most probably Numenorean. For us this was yet further evidence of the truth of Tolkien's story.

As if to press home the difference between the races in the story of The Lord of the Rings, among the television presenters at Ascot this year (2006) was the extraordinary sight of ex-jockey, Willy Carson, who is extremely short, standing beside the statuesque model Jodie Kidd. There is a spectacular difference in height: they really do look like representatives from two different races. Willy Carson resembles a hobbit or 'halfling', not only in height, but he has the round face and is unquenchably cheerful and talkative – just like Tolkien's description of hobbits.

Most profound of all is the description of the Ring itself, as a plain, gold band without a gem. It suddenly dawned on us that this exactly describes the wedding ring. Can this be mere coincidence? Wouldn't it be fair to say that the married state, for women certainly, has often been a source of cruelty and tyranny? This has been truer the higher up the social scale you go. It was not so long ago, even in the West, that a husband had absolute jurisdiction over his wife, and his wife's property became his on their marriage. The absolute power a husband wields over his wife still persists in many countries today. Nor was it uncommon for men to change character for the worse on becoming married. We have all heard stories of how some husbands will start to ill treat their wives, having given no indication of being capable of such behaviour during the period of courtship. There are examples in literature such as in Charles Dickens' David Copperfield. Does it suggest that the evil power of the One Ring is operating through those plain gold wedding bands (the word 'band' implies restriction)?

We then realised with amazement that the engagement ring, with its gem, so often either of sapphire, ruby or diamond, exactly resembles the Three Elven Rings in The Lord of the Rings. Elrond wore the Ring with the blue stone - sapphire, Gandalf, the red stone – ruby, and Galadriel the clear stone of adamant - diamond. The period of courtship seems to reflect the good energy of those rings, being a period of happiness, excitement and hope for the future.

This difference between the two states – that of being engaged and that of being married – is reflected in astrology. The love planet, Venus, is said by astrologers to cast her beneficent influence during the period of betrothal. On becoming married, the relationship then comes under the harsh rule of Saturn, with its qualities of duty, cold reserve and restriction, not to mention criticism.

Chapter 3

St Dunstan's Church and Two Templar Forges in the City of London

It is not Robert's way to tell us very much: he expects us to work things out for ourselves. If we flounder for too long he gives us further clues. However, in retrospect, we were often too passive, which is one of the dangers in the teacher/pupil relationship. So, first of all we understood we were to 'destroy' the Ring, then we found out later from Robert that our actions would in fact be cleansing it, rather than destroying it.

How were we to accomplish such a cleansing? First we needed to locate the One Ring. This much we did understand: that Sauron's Ring is operating from the etheric level. The answer was to find a place of power. Because of the interaction between the two dimensions – physical and etheric – we would be able to call the One Ring to us. Our understanding was that, because we were the ones at the dense physical, we had the greater power. We are not trapped in the Story, so we are in a position to change it. Incidentally, Robert said something rather interesting. There are other stories, which other people are involved in, but this is the Story we are working with.

The idea of places where there is a concentration of energy is not a new one. In the course of dowsing two major energy lines in Britain, the authors of The Sun and The Serpent, Hamish Miller and Paul Broadhurst, write about special energy sites where two or more energy lines cross. As mentioned in the introduction, for a number of years we had ourselves been involved with clearing pre-reformation churches and cathedrals, as well as hill forts which, as many people know, are built on power points and energy lines.

All we had to go by was that the Ring needed to be thrown into a fire, that the site would be somewhere near Holborn in London, and that twelve people would be involved. Caroline had just moved back to London and so was able to launch herself into the research.

Unfortunately, Robert was obliged to furnish us with more information. We had got nowhere as we were being too literal. Caroline had drawn up a list of all working glaziers in London from the local library but it turned out that the fire was an ancient forge no longer at the gross, physical level, but still existing at the etheric, and that it would be at the centre of a six-pointed star, the Star of David. The connection between the six pointed Star of David and kingship set us thinking that this was also the Star of Elendil, symbol of the Royal Line of Numenor, and that the Line of David was none other than its continuation. In Tolkien's Story it was foretold that the Line of Luthien (which became the Royal Line of Numenor) would never die out. Aragorn was the proof of this, stepping out of obscurity to claim the kingship in direct line from the last King, despite a lapse in kingship of over a thousand years when the stewards ruled in the king's stead

Robert also told us that it would be located in one of the signs of the Zodiac, which was to be found in the centre of London, in the same way as the twelve signs of the Zodiac are arranged around Glastonbury Tor in Somerset, and that we should look for the outline in the roads and landmarks of the old City of London. We decided that of the three Fire signs in the Zodiac it was most likely to be Leo whose planetary ruler is the Sun and connected with kingship. As for the twelve people, we discovered that they did not need to be there in person as long as they were with us in spirit. To do this we just needed to name them, which we did, choosing from friends and relations.

Caroline visited the Guildhall Library in the City, the British Library and the British Museum, taking copies of old maps and notes from various books on the history of London. Cassie had a book on the ancient mounds of London and, with its help, we were able to draw the Star of David locating its six points at places of power, three of which are ancient prehistoric mounds. Two of the Sacred Mounds are on the banks of the River Thames and are entirely artificial. One of them is the famous Tower of London with its moat, originally known as The Bryn Gwyn, or White or Holy Hill. There is a plan afoot to refill the moat in honour of the London Olympics. Two miles away on Thorney Island was the Tothill in Westminster not a trace of which now remains. However, the memory of the ancient "Place of Assembly" survives in the names of Tothill Street and Tothill fields ('Tot' means a sacred mound).[6] The third is a natural hill called the Penton ('pen' means head and 'ton' also means a sacred mound) although nothing remains of it today.

The centre, as Robert suggested, was on or near St. Dunstan's church in Fleet Street and Caroline's research revealed that two forges had formerly stood on either side of this church. They had originally belonged to the Knights Templar who possessed a field known as Ficket's Croft on the north side of Fleet Street by Temple Bar. The field was used for training, jousting and exercising of the horses and the forges were, specifically, armourers' forges. Smithies and blacksmiths have always been magical and there is a connection to be made here with Freemasonry, the Philosopher's Stone and the higher spiritual and mental vibrations anciently attributed to kings. Aragorn is a good example. His lifespan was three times that of mortal man and he possessed healing powers and insight into the future.

As Caroline researched and measured, she wandered through the courts and gardens of the Temple and surrounding areas and had a frugal lunch of rice cakes and grapes in Fountain's Court. She felt out of Time, and the rice cakes became the Waybread or Lembas of the Elves. She discovered that popular house signs were preserved in the names of the warren of courts leading off Fleet Street pointing to the masculine and feminine principles representing both Sacred Kingship and the Goddess: names such as The Three Kings, Apollo Court, Crown Court, Hind Court and Hare Place, the latter two being animals sacred to the Goddess. Since the dawn of time this had been a centre of masculine power, later usurped by worship of the Goddess although it is commonly thought that the female principle was the first gender to be deified by Man. Worship of the Goddess evolved because Man, having sunk down the levels and become childlike in his ignorance of who he was and where he came from, felt the need of a protective and all-powerful mother figure.

At this point Cassie came up to London for a week's visit and we started doing things together. Poring over several maps, ancient and modern, we discovered a reasonable outline of a lion running along streets with names such as Kingsway, Worship Street, Apollo Street and Sun Street, indicating the symbolic connection between the lion, kingship and the sun and the 'worship' of the glorious Sun King as a semi-divine being. It is interesting to note that the roads Sun Street, Worship Street, Apollo Street and Old Street are all within the head of the lion. The head of the Sun King was deemed particularly sacred as it represented the sun itself. Old Street alludes to the Sun King becoming 'old' as the sun sank ever lower in the skies and 'died' at midwinter.

How the sign of the Royal Lion came to be corrupted by the energy of the Cult of Sacrifice of the King and why some Kings became cruel tyrants, ties in with that cult because those souls who were so cruelly and unjustly treated reincarnated with a great hatred for all those who conspired in the spectacle of his torture and death. In particular, his hatred was especially reserved for the man who supplanted him who, in the earlier stages of the Cult, was his son, and then later became a brother or son of one of the noble families. Here is to be found the root cause of the hatred and rivalries we see through history amongst the ruling elites. The King's hatred and desire for revenge were also directed towards his wife, the Queen, who might also have been his mother, such was the perversion of relationships that resulted from this Cult. In fact, there were few whom a reincarnated King did not fear, distrust or hate at the subconscious level. To an extent the structure of society came to be shaped by the King's need to create mechanisms whereby he might cope with these powerful emotions. For example, one such mechanism was to create a way of life which would minimise his interaction with women of his own class and when forced to do so, for that contact to be in a controlled and formal setting.

The Lion faces due East from where the 'new' sun will rise (the name of the road forming the profile of the lion's head is Great Eastern Street). Most extraordinary of all was that the generative organs of the outline of the Lion were exactly at the site of the two forges either side of St. Dunstan's Church - which symbolism obviously needs no explanation. St. Dunstan, as well as being Abbot of Glastonbury, is also the patron saint of goldsmiths and gold is symbolically connected with kingship.

We can also expect to find the masculine emblems of power in an area permeated with the energy of the Lion, such as institutions connected with Law and Order. The Royal Courts of Justice, the highest Court in the land, is located there, as well as other Inns of Court nearby. The Nation's gold reserves are to be found within the golden Lion beneath The Bank of England. However, in the past, these institutions have been used to oppress the people. The royal power was often unjust and cruel so we find in the vicinity such notorious prisons as Fleet Street and Newgate. We had noticed that the qualities, or energy, of the four Signs of the Zodiac we had discovered, spread beyond their outlines. Just outside the shape of the Lion, to the south and east, is the Tower of London - a Royal Palace, place of torture and imprisonment, and site of execution. But these were no ordinary prisoners: they were high ranking and often royal: Queen Anne Boleyn was beheaded there. It is interesting to note that beheading was reserved only for the nobility. It was the Sacred King too, who was beheaded so that his head might be worshipped at shrines for its prophesying powers, or sent rolling down the hill after his midsummer sacrifice.[2] The Mount, on which now stands the Keep, known as The White Tower, was clearly a former energy centre, which has been polluted by the Cult of Sacrifice of the King and the memory has lived on with beheadings continuing to take place at the site long after the Cult came to an end. Are we also to connect it to the White Tower of the City of Minas Tirith in the Tolkien's tale, home of the Kings of the West?

Traditionally, the King is a healer. To touch but the cloak of a Merovingian King of France of the Dark Ages, was considered sufficient to bring about a healing. Aragorn was also a healer. So it comes as no surprise to find a hospital right at the

---

[2] See historical notes in the Appendices

LEO ~ *the Lion*

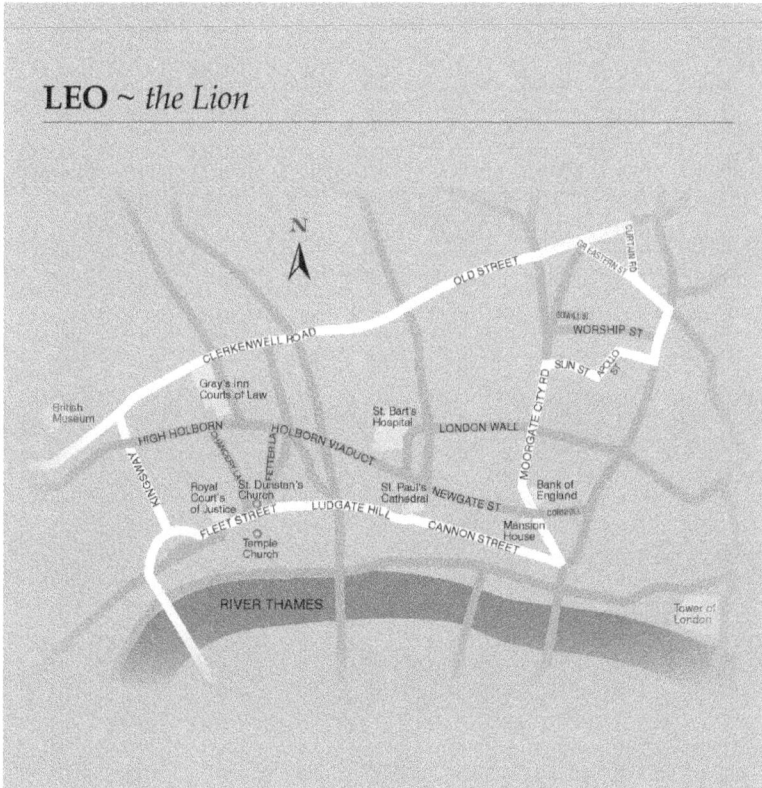

centre, or heart, of the Lion, which is the very source of life and health.

Chapter 4

'Smith Bernal Intl'

We were stirred into action when Robert suddenly said that things were getting to a critical point in the world and it was time to find the Ring. We started getting some quite startling coincidences or synchronicities. We visited Watkins's Bookshop in Charing Cross and our eye fell on a book by Hamish Miller. It was called Its Not Too Late and on the cover was a huge and fiery ring. Towards the end of the story, when Frodo and Samwise are toiling across the parched wasteland surrounding the volcano, Frodo says his whole mind is filled with the image of a 'fiery Ring'. That evening there was a programme on television about volcanoes. In fact there were two programmes on television running at the same time called, respectively, Savage Earth and Raging Planet and it seemed that whenever we switched on the box there would be violent pictures of exploding mountains and fiery lava flows. Everywhere we went in London we again saw posters of a large and grizzly eye on the buses and in the shops advertising the film Godzilla: the unsleeping Eye of Sauron.

All that week the affairs of the world continued to deteriorate rapidly: the economic situation in Russia affecting the whole world economy, the Arab Fundamentalist attacks on US embassies in Kenya and Zambia, followed by the retaliatory attacks by the US on targets in the Sudan and Afghanistan inflaming the whole of the Muslim world, including Pakistan with its nuclear arsenal, all culminating in the horrific bomb incident in Omagh.

It was the forge to the East of St Dunstan's, which turned out to be the right one and a most unpromising location it appeared to be when we went to check it out. We could see from behind the church from a raised level, a rather evil-looking, derelict house, blackened by soot, exactly like something out of Victorian London or a novel by Dickens. It was a strange sight in a built-up area in twentieth century

London. To the East of this building was a tallish block of flats with what looked like a court between it and the derelict house. Our hopes lifted. We decided to try and reach it, if necessary, by getting into the block of flats. We walked into Fetter Lane and were relieved to find an archway leading into the court where there were a few parking places for cars from nearby firms. This was obviously the place and we rather desperately wondered where the exact spot of the furnace could be when Caroline noticed a plaque on the far wall. She walked across and there were the words 'SMITH BERNAL INTL', in other words, 'Smith, burn all internationally'. In this case, we knew that Smith was referring to a blacksmith, who would have worked in such a foundry hammering and welding the armour for the knights. The international part was referring to the worldwide effect it would have for reasons given below.

Underneath the plaque was a large, oblong slab of stone, like a hearthstone. We knew we had found the location of the forge's furnace at the etheric level where the fire was strong enough to cleanse the One Ring in the element of fire.

But what fairly took our breath away when we first saw the church was that the 'spire' was like a beautiful and delicate crown. It was as if someone in the Middle Ages knew the significance of this site when building the church. The only candidates who came to mind were the Templars. Even when they outgrew the site in High Holborn, they did not move far away, as evidenced by the Round Temple church just across the road about a hundred yards away. The Temple Church was consecrated in honour of the Blessed Virgin Mary on 10 February 1185 and was the chapel serving the London headquarters of the Knights Templar.

The power point we had decided upon where we would be able to summon the Ring, was the Royal Hospital Chapel, Chelsea. We had dowsed, as was our wont, to check that the chapel was on an energy centre, which it proved to be, and we cleared it of any negative energy. Robert had informed us over the telephone that we would have a guardian when we went to collect the Ring and that he would be wearing red.

May 2006. As we began to revise Ring Quest three years later, right on cue there appeared two programmes on television, within six days of each other, on two major natural disasters. The first one, Krakatoa – The Last Days (BBC1 on Sunday 7 May 2006), described the days leading up to the eruption of Krakatoa in Indonesia in 1845, which was the largest volcanic eruption in recent history. Sea levels were affected worldwide. The second, on BBC2's Timewatch, examined the story of the San Franciscan earthquake on April 18, 1906. It is described as America's biggest natural disaster: six thousand people were killed and the city all but completely destroyed.

Chapter 5

Link to Energy Centres Worldwide

Probably realising that we were not going to work it out for ourselves, Robert mentioned that the energy centre at St Dunstan's was linked to other places of power around the world. We surmised that they would also be masculine energy centres, as was St Dunstan's, and would therefore be sited on high places such as mountains. We also decided to match the number of sites with the 21 Rings of Power mentioned in Tolkien's books, which includes the Ruling Ring belonging to the Dark Lord. He had given seven rings to the dwarves, nine to men and three rings, made by the Elves, had been hidden from Sauron so that he knew nothing of them, although he suspected their existence.

Robert added that, when drawing the line from the centre in London, we had to take into account the curvature of the earth's surface! What a blow - our maths/geometry was not up to such calculations. We felt rather despondent but thought our best chance of finding out about these power points would be on the Internet. However, we drew a blank. Robert had given us a few places in England through which one or two of the energy lines would pass. We felt a great reluctance to go down that route, as the task felt too great. Much later it dawned on us that Robert knew all along that we wouldn't. Rather, he was providing the masculine balance, which is a more scientific approach whilst we provided the feminine, intuitive approach. In his talks he has stressed the need for this balance. We therefore started trying to find the places of power first and then working from the outside into the centre, thereby obviating the need to take the earth's curvature into consideration – something that was never going to happen!

We spent Sunday looking at a map of the world, which, curiously, mentioned the names of quite obscure mountains, which were to prove most helpful to us. We each began suggesting sites and were astonished at how many were well-known. We should not have been, as extra powerful energy sites such as these would have acted as a magnet. We finally had our twenty in a surprisingly short period of time, dowsing for confirmation: the Kremlin, the Vatican, the Potala Palace in Tibet (no wonder the Chinese want, or rather need that country), Mount Fuji, Ayers Rock, Mount Kilimanjaro, Glastonbury, the Parthenon, Golgotha in Jerusalem, Krak des Chevaliers in Syria, Angkor Wat, the Great Pyramid of Giza, the Royal Palace in Baghdad, Mount Whitney in California, Mount Teotihuacan in Mexico, Machu Picchu in Peru, the Buddhist Temple at Kandy, Ceylon, Jotunheiman in Norway, Montcalm in the Pyrenees and, finally, London at the centre. It is interesting to note that England has two sites, the other being Glastonbury, whereas the continents of North and South America have only one site each (if you count Mexico as Central America). Australia also has only a single site and the continent of Africa two. The vast majority, fourteen, are in Asia and Europe, seven in each.

Chapter 6

"Don't Forget the Ring"

We had one last synchronicity just the night before setting off to cleanse the One Ring for the first time. Caroline's husband turned on the television to watch the Bond film 'Licence to Kill' and the first words we heard were 'I hope you've remembered the ring'. As if we could forget it! Whoever, or whatever is creating these synchronicities – the universe responding to us most likely – has a sense of humour.

The sun was shining as we set off the following morning, 25th August 1999. We took a bus to the Royal Hospital and made our way to the Chapel and there we met our guardian. He was a Chelsea Pensioner and of course he was dressed in the traditional red frock coat. His name was William West and, after we had chatted to him for a while, he told us that he was the Pearly King of Chelsea and that we should bow to him! Here was our King. He pointed out a beautiful wooden panel above the altar on which was carved a sun with rays shooting from it. It is supposed to have been rescued from a church after the Great Fire of London. He then showed us a chair, which at the request of the Queen Mother was reconstructed from the debris of the panelling where a bomb had hit the Chapel. It was called 'The King's Chair'. Here then were the themes of the sun, fire and kingship, which were so fitting.

After talking to our Pearly King for a while longer we began to wonder how we would ever be able to call up the Ring in private, so Caroline rather desperately said: 'Now we would like to say a little prayer,' to which he replied, much to our consternation: 'You're joking'. Staunchly showing him we weren't and wondering if any visitors ever prayed in the Chapel, we walked towards the Choir stall, knelt down and shut our eyes hoping for a miracle. One duly happened. The telephone rang and he went to answer it. Feeling slightly silly, Caroline got out the white handkerchief (we thought white would be a counterbalance to the evil vibrations of the Ring) and placed it over the palm of her hand. We called three times, as planned, not too loudly, for the Ring to materialise on the handkerchief. Nothing happened and at that point our guardian reappeared. Stupidly, Caroline kept her hand out with the handkerchief still on it until she suddenly noticed that our King was eyeing it rather suspiciously. Hastily, she put it in her pocket and a second miracle happened: the telephone rang again. We then rather desperately repeated the performance and still nothing happened. With a sudden flash of inspiration Caroline realised that it would not materialise as a physical object, it would be present on the palm of the hand at the etheric level. Quickly she whipped off the handkerchief and this time felt a distinct tingling on her palm. She carefully tipped it onto the handkerchief, wrapped it up, and then placed it in the bag. With that we made a hasty exit before our guardian could reappear, feeling sorry that we were unable to say goodbye.

As we left, Caroline began to wonder if she would suddenly be overcome by the power of the Ring and refuse to relinquish it. Luckily, she felt reasonably calm. We made our way to Sloane Square and took the Circle Line to the Temple. From there we walked through the gardens, into Fleet Street, through the courts and alleyways of The Temple, until at last we were in the small parking area to the side of St Dunstan's church. Standing in front of the plaque and the hearthstone Caroline tossed the etheric ring into the air while we asked out loud for it to be cleansed in the fires of the furnace. We also sent the purified energy down the energy lines to the masculine centres of power worldwide so that they too would be cleansed. In her mind's eye Cassie saw a flame leap up, confirmation that we had been successful. Feeling both deeply satisfied and elated we decided to celebrate by going to the nearest café for coffee and croissants.

In the days following, events in the world took an upturn. Gerry Adams renounced violence – the negative side of the fiery energy - and then agreed to decommissioning of the IRA's arsenal, the Muslim world remained calm and the US and UK stock markets rallied. A week later the Real IRA renounced violence and there was an historic meeting between David Trimble, Northern Ireland's Prime Minister, and Gerry Adams, leader of Sin Fein. The week after that, Basque separatists in Catalan sought reconciliation with the Spanish Government and ETA called for a ceasefire. On the 20th September Iraq dropped the Fatwa against Salman Rushdie.

Synchronicities continued. In the American sit-com Friends two of the young men, Chandler and Ross, are expecting a visit from an old college friend whose nickname is Gandalf, the 'party wizard', and one of the characters says, 'You remember Gandalf from the book The Lord of the Rings'? On a more sinister note there was a huge eye on the cover of one of the Sunday paper's magazines.

There was also a strange sequel. We had promised Cassie's two girls an outing the following day and two places had been suggested, Kensington Palace and the Zoo. However, at the last minute we changed our plans and decided on Madame Tussaud's and the Planetarium. It was a warm and sunny day but later it became overcast. We all had an enjoyable time, although the room full of severed heads of those who had been decommissioned was weird, for it reminded us of our research into the pagan Cult of the Goddess. On leaving we walked along Euston Road intending to get a bus down Baker Street. As we passed Baker Street Underground station one of the girls said, "Shall we go on the Underground"? However, we decided that a journey by bus would be more fun. That evening we heard on the news that a man carrying a bomb had been apprehended at Warren Street Underground station which just happens to be the next station along from Baker Street. We felt glad that we hadn't after all taken the Underground and thought nothing more of it.

At our next meeting and workshop with Robert two months later, Caroline happened to mention this incident in passing as we felt there was some connection with us having been in the area when the man with the bomb was found. Robert gave her a strange look and replied, 'The bomb was intended for you'. We were stunned. We had had no idea that the Forces of the Left could work in this way, i.e. that the energy of evil could manipulate people for its own ends.

We also realised that Robert kept quiet about a lot of things, trusting to our own common sense but also providing a lot more protection than we knew. He later said that he might be on the beach walking the dog and he would tune in to us to see how we were getting on. So we could be mentally influenced by the Other Side to change our plans if we did not protect ourselves adequately. In retrospect, we can remember feeling mentally confused as we kept changing our minds about where we were going to go for the day. We had even lingered in the area longer than we intended but, fortunately, had not been influenced to take the Underground.

We now had to wait until the Ring reformed itself. It seemed to us that what we were doing was both destroying and cleansing it at the same time. Each time we destroyed/unmade it, its evil vibrations would be lessened, thus purifying it. In the meantime we set about finding the shape of the crab in the streets and landmarks of London for the astrological sign of the water sign, Cancer.

Chapter 7

Red Eyes in the Night

Although Cassie had been in Salisbury for a year, she had still not found a permanent home and was 'camping' in a cramped flat with most of her furniture in storage. Moreover, it was close to a ring road <u>and</u> a roundabout, both of which we later found can be used to channel the energy of the evil Rings of Power which are still in existence at the astral levels. It was the end of September 1998 and we were still blissfully ignorant of the roles we had already begun to enact.

One morning Cassie had a flash of black in her mind's eye as she went about her daily business and then it was gone. It happened a second time during the course of the day and she wondered what it meant. That night in bed, she suddenly saw several black-cloaked figures descend upon her with fierce, glowing red eyes. She was so frightened she hid her head under the pillow to shut off the terrifying images. Not knowing what to make of it, she thought no more about it but from that day on she would wake every morning to find that her left arm had gone dead.

This had continued throughout the month of October 1998 when, at the end of that month, we made a trip to Wales to see Robert for private consultations. Robert has his own therapy business which includes crystal healing, Reiki healing and counselling. Our private sessions were on the Saturday and we were spending the night at a Bed and Breakfast so that we could attend a workshop he was giving the following day.

During Cassie's appointment she remembers the conversation turning to the story of The Lord of the Rings and hearing Robert telling her that she was in the role of Frodo. Unfortunately, she was 'stuck on Weathertop' and he was trying to get her off! Naturally, she was aghast. He went on to say that her shoulder had been hurting, which was true. We had both of us, unsurprisingly, read The Lord of the Rings not long ago since our memorable meeting with Robert so she understood how dire was her situation. It was on Weathertop that the four hobbits, guided by Strider, were attacked by five of the dreaded Black Riders, or Nazgul, and Frodo was stabbed in the shoulder. He was now in grave danger of becoming a wraith just like them and falling wholly under the power of the Dark Lord if he did not receive healing for his wound in time.

Suddenly, she remembered her experience of a month ago when she had been attacked in her bed at night. She noticed that Robert had begun to give healing to her shoulder with a crystal, even though she had not mentioned this experience to him. It occurred to her that she had received a real stab wound that night to one of her lighter 'bodies' that surround the physical body, hence the reason for her arm going dead. He then sat to one side of her and placed the palm of his hand on the middle of her back, and looked as if he was about to put a lot of effort into the hand. At that precise moment Cassie felt warmth spread through her whole body. He explained that he was now in the role of Glorfindel who gave Frodo healing, briefly, before he and his companions reached the safety of Rivendell. At this point in the Tale it says that Frodo felt a warmth come into his shoulder and travel down his arm and the pain eased as Glorfindel gives him healing, just as Cassie experienced.

Robert went on to explain that Caroline was the tall, grim Strider, who turns out to be Aragorn, the rightful heir to the throne. Without her, Cassie/Frodo would go round in circles, just as the hobbits would have done in the Story without Aragorn to guide them. Cassie commented that he, Robert, had to be Gandalf, to which he agreed but also said that he would be stepping in and out of different roles in the Story, as necessary.

He asked her where Rivendell might be and she offered some geographical places without much conviction, so that Robert eventually said that it was a 'timeless place'. When she reached it, in her role as Frodo, she would be healed of a wound to her heart. This was where he was trying to get her and where other people would appear who would make up the Fellowship of the Nine to set against the Nine Black Riders. These people would slip in and out of different roles but that hers and

Caroline's roles would remain the same. He said it was useful for us to have prior knowledge of the unfolding Story having re-read The Lord of the Rings since Robert first mentioned it earlier in July.

As for the wound to her heart, this must be referring to the knife wound to her shoulder. When Frodo reaches Rivendell, he receives healing from Elrond, Master of Rivendell, who discovers that a splinter from the deadly dagger is slowly working its way inwards towards Frodo's heart.

It was important to be aware that Gollum was also out there somewhere. Gollum was the pathetic but dangerous creature who had possessed the Ring or, rather, been possessed by the evil power of the Ring for many years. To be without it was a torture to him and he was driven to try and reclaim it for his own, as it was 'his Precious'. Cassie remembers feeling genuinely frightened at the thought of Gollum seeking the One Ring and therefore herself.

Chapter 8

The Olives Court Guest House

For our weekend with Robert in South Wales, Caroline had booked us into The Olives Court Guest House, just off the roundabout on a ring road which, as we now knew, were used to channel the evil energy of the One Ring. It was a substantial house with a large wide hall so we were surprised to be shown our bedroom on the ground floor, immediately to the left of the main entrance where you would have expected a reception room. Our bedroom didn't have a proper window but there was a narrow conservatory-like room between the window and our bedroom, which seemed a bizarre arrangement. This room was full of junk. With our heads buzzing with Robert's astounding revelations and the story of The Lord of the Rings somewhat uppermost in our minds, we both immediately thought the same thing when we noticed that we had a red, emergency exit light actually in our bedroom. Surely, this was the Eye of Mordor which appears red on the distant horizon.

As many people know, Sauron's Eye is actively seeking the One Ring, which Frodo is carrying. Its recovery is uppermost in Sauron's mind since he learnt of its rediscovery by a hobbit, a certain Bilbo Baggins, as it contains a great part of his evil power. We couldn't help noticing that there was a particularly intense spot of red in the light, slightly off-centre, which was 'looking' directly at Cassie's bed. We thought of covering it up but decided that would be a fire risk so all we could do was ignore it. We neither of us liked what appeared to be Cassie/Frodo's exposure to this red eye, particularly at night, when the Nazgul/Black Riders drew greater strength.

Nor had it escaped our attention that we were sleeping on the ground floor, just as hobbits did in their sandy holes. It occurred to us that we were re-enacting that part of the Story when Frodo and companions had reached the Inn of The Prancing Pony with the Black Riders in hot pursuit. Special ground floor rooms with round windows had been built just for hobbit travellers and it was these rooms that Frodo and his companions were given for the night, just like us!

They were in great danger at this point in the Story, as news of their arrival at the inn was taken by spies to the Black Riders. Soon after, two of the dreaded Nazgul turn up at the inn. It was therefore no coincidence that this B&B was close to a 'ring' road <u>and</u> a roundabout and it would explain the presence of the Red Eye in our bedroom for the Black Riders were directly under the control of The Eye.

Coming out of the bedroom Cassie happened to look at the picture in the hall close to our bedroom door and was stunned to see that it was an old photograph of a woman dressed in Victorian clothes standing in front of a home cut into a sandstone bank and reminiscent of a hobbit home. She had never seen such a thing before.

It had been raining rather heavily in recent days and the landlord was having difficulty with the electricity in the house, which meant that our television kept cutting out, as well as our bedside lights and the bathroom light. Unfortunately, the red emergency light was unaffected by these vagaries and shone very brightly red when we turned off our lights to go to sleep.

We told the proprietor about our lighting problem and he was most apologetic and bustled about trying to fix the problem, talking all the while. He offered to make us sandwiches for our workshop the next day to make up for it, which we gladly accepted. Suddenly he reminded us of the bustling, talkative landlord of The Prancing Pony, Barliman Butterbur, who had been extremely apologetic to Frodo for failing to pass on a letter to him from Gandalf. He was also most generous to the travellers in supplying them with a pony and provisions for their onward journey!

By the end of the workshop the next day, after the initial excitement of being told about the roles we were playing had died down and we realised that a difficult task might lie ahead of us, we thought the inevitable question "why us"? We therefore, before setting off for home at the end of the workshop, asked Robert when had we agreed to take these parts. The answer came back, "A long time ago". Cassie added that she felt it had been touch and go whether or not she would be up to the job, and Robert agreed. She was referring to the clearing work we had done on ourselves over the past six years. Past life traumas, which lay in our subconscious, had been brought to our attention and we had had to deal with the ensuing emotions.[7] This coincided with her discovering the trauma of the Sacred King and how it lived on in subsequent lives buried in the subconscious mind.

Chapter 9

A Silver Ring

At the end of the workshop, Cassie suddenly remembered that she possessed a ring, which could be said to resemble the One Ring. It was a plain, quite thick, silver band but for a raised line running sinuously all the way around, crudely resembling the famous words inscribed around the One Ring which read: '*One Ring to rule them all, One Ring to find them, One Ring to bring them all and in the darkness bind them.*'

How Cassie came by it also curiously resembles the manner in which Frodo came by his Ring. It happened about a year prior to her leaving Northampton in 1998. A friend suggested they go to a crafts exhibition being held in a private house in an outlying village. One of the items which caught her eye was the silver ring just described, only the silversmith who had made it said she couldn't have that ring as it was for show, but that he could make her a similar one. Unusually, the silversmith delivered the ring, personally, in an envelope to Cassie at her home. Frodo also received his Ring in an envelope placed on the mantelpiece in his home. We were struck by the close comparison. Another thought: because the ring was specially made for her, it is unique, just like the One Ring.

Frodo was warned by Gandalf to keep Bilbo's ring safe and not to wear it, as he had begun to suspect that it could be the One Ring made by the Dark Lord himself. If it were to be recovered by its evil master, then there would be no hope for the free peoples of the West and all would fall under The Shadow, so Gandalf knew he could take no chances. Strangely, just like Frodo, Cassie hardly ever wore her ring as she found the silver tracery on the band dug into the sides of her fingers. However, she had started to wear it regularly at about the time this Story begins, and was wearing it on that fateful trip to Wales when Robert told us we were characters in the Story. She only ever thought hers to be a symbolic 'copy', although in this, she was later to discover she may have been mistaken.

Chapter 10

The Kernel of the Story

We had much to think over on the journey home across the Severn Bridge. There were too many 'proofs' for us to be able to deny the truth of what Robert had told us at our private sessions. There was the Ring, which Cassie came by so curiously, the fierce red-eyed attack by dark figures one night and subsequent pain in the shoulder as well as the 'dead' arm. Caroline's present wanderings reflected Aragorn's life in the Story. Then there was the red 'eye' in our bedroom at the guesthouse.

We quickly agreed that another talk was necessary to find out more about what was involved and to try and grasp what precisely we were doing by taking on these roles. So a month later we paid another visit to Robert having decided upon a joint sitting.

He began by telling us more about himself. For one thing, he says he has an empty mind and that he is only given information on a 'need to know' basis. In this way he lives entirely in the present. In addition to his healing practice, he also clears places of negativity, including supermarkets! Because he himself never knows what clearing he will be doing next, he stays one step ahead of the Forces of the Left. This was further confirmation that our thoughts can very quickly be picked up out of the ether by those forces. Unfortunately, he criticised us for having done so little clearing work of late – not that we had discussed the subject: he just knew. He also explained that we need to take 'Them' by surprise. If we plan too much in advance, which is what we had been doing, 'They' can move out of an area before we have enclosed it in a circle of light which effectively traps them within that area. Our understanding is, that those evil ones are obliged/forced by the new energy to leave the lower astral level from where they feed off the negative energies that have built up over time.

To return to the story of The Lord of the Rings, Robert told us that we had counterparts on the Other Side, probably in physical bodies like ourselves, although he has never confirmed this and for some reason we have never asked. The more we could work out for ourselves, the better. Whenever he helps us, his opposite number is able to offer similar help to our opposites. This has meant that, throughout, Robert has only ever given us cryptic clues which, often, we could not at first understand. Only with a great deal of thought, trial and error, or with Robert eventually having to give us further clues, have we been able to go forward on this Quest.

It was an eye-opener to realise that the forces of evil are active in the world today and that we are still very much in the Saga of The Lord of the Rings. It is almost a taboo subject to talk about good and evil in stark terms, yet if we look at what is around us we can see that humanity is being manipulated so that it swings from one crisis to another to keep the energy of fear and anger flowing. In particular, we are increasingly caught up in the extreme highs and lows of the ever-growing sports industry.

The oft-repeated expression 'history repeats itself' took on a more realistic tinge. In fact the balance of power is in favour of the Forces of the Left with, Robert told us, a ratio of 67% to 33%. Our aim, Robert said, was to make it 50/50. We were intrigued that he did not talk about 'vanquishing' the forces of darkness, which has always been an unquestioning article of faith of the Christian church and, therefore, of our conditioned minds.

He also pointed out that there was no linear time in the journey and if Cassie did not learn the lessons - she believes those were the words - she could find herself back on the Barrow-Downs. This was a most unpleasant prospect. The Barrow-Downs were inhabited by evil Barrow-Wights, particularly malignant spirits who haunted the barrows where the dead were laid to rest. Frodo and his party had fallen into the clutches of one of these creatures and would have perished but for Tom Bombadil.

At this same meeting, Robert suddenly started saying that he was being shown a little boy dressed like Lord Fauntleroy and that we were being told we could draw on the power of the royal line to help us. On two different occasions Robert mentioned that we could give up at any time if we wished, but for two Sagittarians, who are naturally adventurous and like a challenge, this was not an option. Matter-of-factly, but closely watching us, he said that there were two of us in case one of us should 'go'.

We were told that we could change the story. However, we turned out to be somewhat inexpert at knowing which parts we might change and which we might not. When we mentioned that we might like to miss out the adventures in the Mines of Moria, Robert said that this was one part of the Story we had to experience.

At one time he quietly said that the 'kernel' of the Story of the Ring was the love and friendship which developed between the members of the Fellowship in the course of their Quest. A strong friendship developed between Legolas, the Elf, and Gimli, the Dwarf, which overrode the traditional mistrust between these two races. It would not be too far from the truth to say that it is just such mistrust and prejudice between nations which is still at the root of most conflicts in the world today and which makes us realise the importance of such friendship and why Robert called it the 'kernel' of the Story.

Perhaps the friendship between Elf and Dwarf and their shared adventures can be described as the first 'buddy' story! They are the classic ill-assorted pair and caused much wonder in the citizens of Minas Tirith as the odd couple wandered around the City together, the stocky dwarf muttering into his beard about the shoddy workmanship of some of the stone construction, whilst the tall, blithe Elf talked of the need for fountains and trees to beautify the City!

Interestingly, the actors who made up the Fellowship of the Nine in the recently made film of the trilogy of The Lord of the Rings, also formed a strong bond amongst themselves.

The same theme is to be found in a number of popular television series - Friends, Sex in the City and also Desperate Housewives. The main characters draw great strength from the unwavering love and support of a diverse group of friends through all the ups and downs in their lives. Inevitably, the

Dark Forces targeted our Fellowship in the hope of disrupting the Quest.

Chapter 11

The Water Sign of The Crab

From time to time, we would dowse to see if the One Ring had reconstituted itself and was exercising its malevolent power in the affairs of Men once again. And in December, the answer came back that this was the case. The earliest date we could set aside for our first attempt at cleansing it in the element of water was 30 December 1998.

The clue we had been given was 'water in Regent's Park'. We opened the map and located the lake in Regent's Park. Uppermost in our minds was the idea that the astrological water sign was most likely going to be Cancer the crab. As we stared at the outline of the lake we saw to our amazement and mounting excitement that the lake was in the shape of the female reproductive organs. On the north side the lake branches out sideways, east and west, to form the arms of the fallopian tubes. Below is the womb and the water then narrows to create a long birth canal. How fitting that the womb should be located in the sign of Cancer which represents the archetypal Mother.

Excitedly, we looked for the shape of a crab in the surrounding roads and there it was, in the roads that defined the shape of the park. There was even to be seen the hard outer shell created by the main roads, and the soft, inner body of the crab is defined by an inner path which runs parallel to the 'outer' main roads. Two roads to the north gave the crab its pincers and roads to the east, south and west, its legs and eye stalks. We knew with certainty that this was the sign of Cancer and felt awed that someone at some time had devised this.

As the site of the cleansing of the Ring in Fire had been at one of the testes, it followed that the place of power would be at one of the ovaries and, incredibly, these could be seen in the lake as small islands. We realised that it all made perfect, logical sense. Evil is the negation of life which is made by the coming together of masculine and feminine.

The next thing was to find an energy centre where we could summon the Ring. We eventually decided on All Souls, Langham Place: it was near Regent's Park and in a relatively quiet location. It also happened to be the church at which Caroline's parents were married. First we had to clear the church of any negativity. We realised that the best way to achieve all this in an afternoon on an overcast day in December, was to go by cab, which we duly did and were set down without incident at All Souls. As we had suspected, this beautiful Wren church with its rounded, feminine entrance was locked as are, sadly, a great number of London churches today. However, we walked round the side and found a quiet corner. It was Cassie's turn to call the Ring. She felt a tingling in the palm of her hand which told us that the Ring was present, if not visible.   Once again she tipped it into the handkerchief, wrapped it up and put it in the pocket of her coat. We then hailed another cab, which took us to Hanover Gate, the nearest entrance to the north end of the lake and the two little islands.

We began walking across the north end of the lake towards a bridge where we hoped we would see a way to get down to the water's edge and get close to the little island/ovary on the East side. Aware of the need for vigilance, Caroline's attention was drawn to a man with two large dogs walking towards us. As he drew level he met her gaze and proceeded to give her a look of pure hatred the like of which she has never witnessed in her entire life. Her jaw dropped; what had she done to this man? She told Cassie who thought she must be imagining it, but when she turned to see what he was doing, he had also stopped and was looking back at us, but this time he appeared to be avoiding Caroline's gaze. We continued on to the bridge. Off to the left at the side of a small building seemed hopeful, but we found the way barred and had to retrace our steps. As we did so, we caught sight of the same man who had turned back and was now quite definitely watching our movements. We enveloped him in Light as the best way we could think of to protect ourselves. Later we were to learn that there is nothing the Other Side like so much as Light! It is the same force of attraction as between magnets of the polar opposites. They then riposte with black energy, thereby perpetuating the battle between Good and Evil. Without Light they would not have a target. The thing to be is neutral, or grey, like Gandalf the Grey: nor must you feel any fear. Only then can evil find no point of entry. When clearing sites Robert would say that people who are accustomed to the dark find the light too dazzling and why don't we use neutral energy in place of light.

We didn't know this at the time but when Caroline later recounted this to Robert, he gave his usual laugh. He told us that the man we had encountered was a Viking and that he and the other Vikings were angry with us. Then we remembered that we had just done a lot of clearing work in East Anglia where, historically, many Vikings had settled. They were still there, at the lower astral dimension, and did not take kindly to being dislodged.

A ghost is one thing but a fully physical person manifesting themselves is quite another. When we were making revisions to Ring Quest we realised that we did not understand how this was possible. What process was enabling this man to materialise? So we decided to see if Robert could elucidate and this is the email he sent in reply:

> *some spirits who have intense energy and a very strong belief system can over-ride the normal limits or boundaries of inter- dimensional travel or movement - for one such as the Viking, there would have to be a number of living people here at this level for him to have enough energy to materialise in the physical. There are a small number of beings who do this, usually for their own gain, proper Time Lords - Avatars etc.*
>
> *Some spirits retain their evil ways and it is our duty to be of sufficient brightness to help them. Evil only exists within human consciousness or the levels that humans attain to i.e. spirit form.*

When we next saw him he asked if what he had sent had been helpful and that a lot more could be said on the subject. For the purposes of this book, though, he must have understood that we needed more of a sound bite than a treatise.

We leaned over the bridge again to get a better look at the other ovary, this time to the West. We noticed a spot close to the water's edge beneath some willow trees, which seemed accessible from the path running down that side. This was going to be the closest we could get to the island so we walked back along the path retracing our steps.

Cancer, being a feminine sign, we could expect to find evidence of the Goddess, and we were not disappointed. Gazing down from the bridge, we saw a pair of beautiful swans unlike any we had seen before with white bodies, a red protuberance on their beaks and black necks - the colours of the Triple Goddess in her three aspects of maid, mother and wise woman. Making our way to the willows and taking care not to slip, as the ground was rather wet and sloping, we threw the Ring into the lake asking the generative Waters of Life in the womb of our Mother to cleanse and revitalise it.

We both had a deep feeling of satisfaction at having completed our task and we looked forward to a leisurely walk south through the park alongside the lake. The sun was now shining and it seemed almost like spring. Signs of the Goddess were everywhere. There was a children's playground nearby and the crescent moon on top of the golden dome of the Mosque shone in the sun. Winfield House, home to the American Ambassador, lay to the north: the United States is a sun-sign Cancer country, Nanny/Mother to the world, and we remembered that London Zoo is in the park - the Goddess is Mistress of the Animals. As we wandered back past the lake we passed Queen Mary's Rose Garden, Mary, the mother of Jesus, being the Goddess of the Piscean Age, and the rose her emblem. A squirrel ran towards us and ate an apricot and some bread from our hands. The lake was teeming with waterfowl already paired for spring and a fresh round of new life. So ended our second cleansing of the Ring.

Caroline later realised a continuing royal theme in our Quest which had begun with our discovery of the outline of the Lion and the Star of David/Elendil and been reinforced with references to kingship at the Chapel of the Royal Hospital in Chelsea. We had left the park at York Gate having entered at the Hanover Gate. She felt it symbolised the demise of the

CANCER ~ the Crab

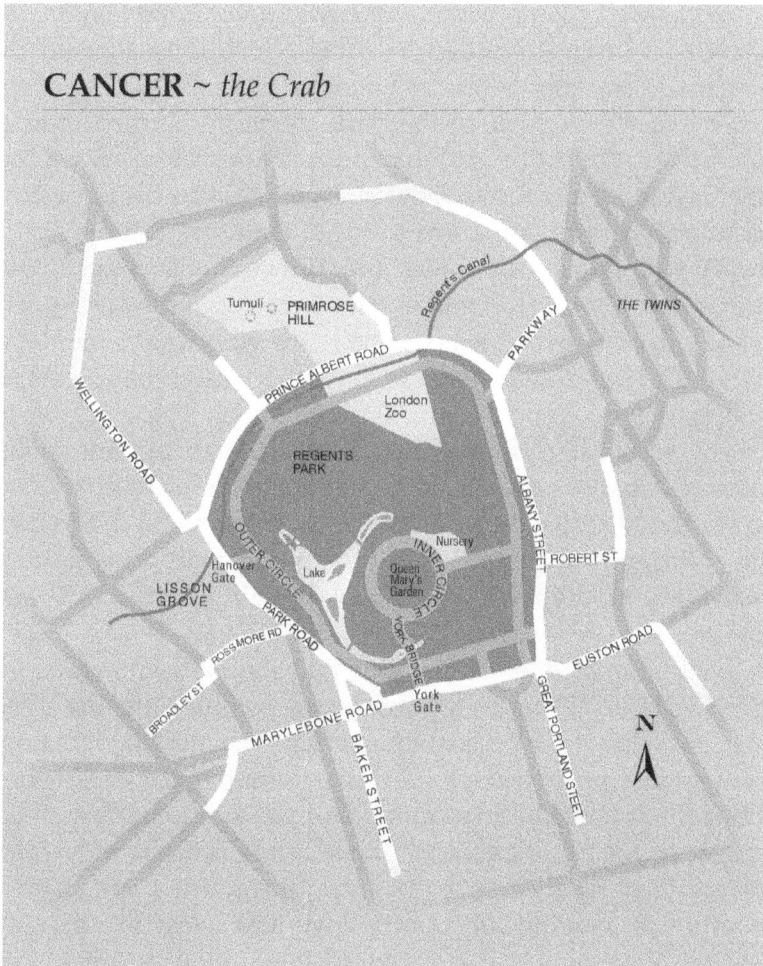

Stuarts in the figure of the Duke of York, who had become James II (he literally fled his Kingdom throwing the Royal Seal into the Thames in his haste to reach France and safety) and the entering in of a new dynasty: the House of Hanover.

Just as we began revisions on this chapter Cassie happened to look at a map of London 'on-line' which only showed the major roads. As she looked at Regent's Park, the names of the main roads which encircle the park therefore jumped out. To the North is Albert Road, to the South is Marylebone Road and to the East is Albany Street. The message was that the opposites, masculine and feminine, come together at this park and that it is a royal coupling. Albert was the Prince Consort of Queen Victoria and Mary is a name much connected with royalty, not least because she was the mother of Jesus who was of the Royal Line of David. Researchers, tracing the descendants of that Royal Line who came to Europe in the book The Holy Blood and The Holy Grail, found that it ran through the line of the Dukes of Albany – the name on the East side of the park. We also suddenly realised the significance of the name of the park itself – Regent – a word that can be either male or female. In esoteric books the One, in origin, is neither masculine nor feminine.

At the same time she realised that the path known as the Inner Circle and a small wriggly path leading into the circle called York Bridge, represented a sperm. The fact that it is huge and of similar proportions as the lake 'womb' must be showing us that the role of the masculine is of equal importance as the feminine in the act of creation. The second discovery confirmed the first. Here, anchored at the gross physical is the energy of the opposites coming together in love and harmony to create new life. We simply had not noticed this until now, nine years later, because the sperm's tail had been concealed by a word written across it on the map we consulted at that time. The royal theme was to continue in the outline of the Divine Twins in the astrological sign of Gemini.

Chapter 12

New Surroundings and the Number 44

At our last meeting with Robert at the end of October, he had told Cassie that her present living circumstances had put her in one of the most perilous places in the Story – on the hill called Weathertop. She had to move and in March 1999 she found a house on the top of a hill, where it was quiet and leafy and outside the ring road. It was also a sufficient distance from the nearest roundabout,.

The number of the house was 44, as had been the number of her previous house in Northampton. A few weeks later, quite by chance, she bought a car whose model number was 440. We suddenly became aware how Cassie was being dogged by the number 44 and wondered why. We found out from Robert that it means 'death and destruction' which, if you think about it, was the aim of Frodo's quest: to bring about the death and destruction of Sauron and his mighty Evil Empire. But this happy outcome was by no means certain. Indeed, the Quest was looked upon as a desperate venture with little chance of success. The danger was very great that Frodo and Samwise would be captured by the Enemy. The Ring of Power would then be used to bring about the 'death and destruction' of the peoples of the West.

Fascinating correspondences between real life and the story in the Lord of the Rings continued. It turned out that Cassie's new landlord was a farmer who was unusually small with curly brown hair: in short, he had to be a hobbit. Additional clues pointed to the fact that he was in the role of Bilbo Baggins. His surname, Riddle, reminded us of the terrifying riddling game Bilbo played with Gollum in the dark roots of the mountain in Tolkien's The Hobbit, which was a precursor to The Lord of the Rings. This is a great moment in the history of The Ring as it was at that moment that the Ring chose to change hands and be picked up by Bilbo so as to come into the light of day and set in train the momentous events in the Story.

Mr Riddle was a bachelor, just like Bilbo, and also like Bilbo, he had a favourite nephew (Frodo had been Bilbo's favourite nephew and he had made him his heir, leaving him Bag End, his grand hobbit hole). Indeed, so fond was Mr Riddle of his own nephew that he had bought him a house to live in during his years at university. This money had now been reinvested in a property in Salisbury to let to none other than Cassie/Frodo. It seemed that he was being Bilbo Baggins to Cassie's Frodo in providing a roof over her head, just as Bilbo had done.

As Cassie began to explore this new part of town she came across a very strange antique/junk shop in a side street, which she became fond of visiting, picking up items for the new house and talking to the owner. However, it was the shop keeper's name which made Cassie's jaw drop: his name was Bill Biggins which is remarkably close to Bilbo Baggins. Just like Bag End, you could say his shop was full of 'mathoms' as hobbits called them, or useless items! Perhaps Mr Biggins's eccentricity is also a further comparison with Mr Baggins who was thought eccentric by his fellow hobbits.

But perhaps the single most dramatic feature, which dominates Salisbury, is the Cathedral with its tall spire. Salisbury is a small, medieval, market town. Almost every vista shows the beautiful spire on the sky line. Because of its height, a red light is set on its pinnacle to alert overhead aircraft coming in to land at nearby Boscombe Down airfield. There was little doubt in our minds that the red light also represents the Eye of Sauron. This was set in the topmost part of the Black Tower of Mordor from where it kept a ceaseless vigilance over the affairs of Men.

Some years later, we remembered that the Cathedral spire, the tallest in England, is 404 feet making the number 44 again, so attracting the energy of 'death and destruction'. Was this mere coincidence? We thought not. It seemed that for the purposes of our Quest, the Cathedral represents the Black Tower of the Dark Lord. Quite simply, its symbolic fall would spell the total destruction of Sauron's Empire, as it was driven and controlled by the One Evil Will set in that Tower.

It was not long after moving into her new home that Cassie was given an insight into the nature of the silver Ring she had so curiously acquired. She was having a cup of coffee with a neighbour, who admitted that she was somewhat psychic and who made the observation that Cassie's ring was tingling with energy. The remark caused Cassie to think of a conversation she had had with Robert not long ago. Concerning her housing problems at the time, he had suggested, to her surprise and confusion, "Why don't you use your Ring"? But she had thought better of it, remembering that in the original Story this might have helped the Other Side to locate the Ring and come after it. So she had not done so. Her neighbour's comment confirmed that she was right not to have used the Ring, or was she? How were we to reconcile the One Ring of Power, which existed only at the etheric, with the silver replica which now appeared to be imbued with power as well? We were not to work this conundrum out for some years.

It must be said here that neither of us is psychic. When we commented on this to Robert he said that it was too dangerous for us to be psychic in that way as we could very easily be led to our deaths. This had already nearly happened merely through mind suggestion, which resulted in our changing our plans for a day's outing in London with Cassie's daughters. But we did have protection in this Quest. We had the equivalent of Frodo's corselet of mithril rings and precious gems, and Aragorn was watched over from afar by Arwen, daughter of Elrond, the Master of Rivendell to whom he was betrothed.

Chapter 13

The Air Sign of the Twins

For some time, we had known that the next sign would be the Air sign Gemini, the Twins. We, therefore, began looking for things connected to communication of all kinds, which is the main characteristic of that sign and includes talking, travel, education, journalism, as well as commerce and youth. Our attention was drawn to Camden Town, a young place with a market buzzing with energy. Looking at the roads we thought we could make out two almost identical shapes, side by side. The more we looked, the more convinced we became. One of the oblong shapes is clearly feminine as it is curvy and even goes in at the 'waist', whilst the other is straight-sided. Within the two outlines are a library, a health centre, Parcel Force, MTV Studios and the Royal Veterinary College. It is interesting that the Veterinary College lies within the female twin, as animals come under the protection of their Mother, the Queen, who is the Goddess's representative. Then to our wonder we noted that the Regent's Canal, which once transported goods on barges, runs through both figures. This combines the Geminian qualities of travel and commerce, as well as demonstrating the Royal Line coming from their Mother.

We noticed that the Twins lie very close to the sign of Cancer, and that the birth canal of the lake points in their direction as well. For the cleansing of the Ring in Air we had chosen to go to the site of St Paul's Cathedral to fetch the Ring, as neither of us had been to that magnificent building for some time. The date was Sunday, 14 February 1999. As usual we did our protection: grounding and balancing ourselves. We then visualise a circle of protection around us, which has to be renewed from time to time, particularly after crossing a threshold, such as entering or leaving a building or passing beneath a bridge.

The Cathedral was full of people milling around, as might be expected, but we managed to find a quiet spot and quietly summoned the Ring. We then took a cab and were dropped off in Camden at the intersection to the three straight highways, which form part of the outline of the Twins whose roads run north and south.

We had found the energy site quite easily because there were the most extraordinary clues. On either side of a green area, as shown on the map, were two streets. The one to the north was called Carol Street and the one to the south, Martin Close: in other words, Cassie's maiden name and Caroline's Christian name. Caroline was actually christened Carol as the date given for her birth was Christmas Day. It appears that the Universe already knew that we would be carrying out this quest at the energy point between the two streets and the names were there to guide us to the right spot. Many have heard the statement that there is no such thing as Time and here is the proof! Recently, there had been a programme on television demonstrating this where grid lines in space fold back on themselves showing that the present and future are the same and that there is no such thing as linear time. Other sources say that linear time was given to us to help us get back to God, as we have become separated from the true Reality.

Unfortunately, when Caroline telephoned Robert and told him that we had found the exact sites for cleansing the Ring in the signs of Gemini and Taurus, he told her that the Other Side had immediately taken it. This was because she had failed to secure the area for the forces of Light by putting her hand on the map with the purpose of protecting it. We therefore had to look elsewhere and eventually chose from the map a nearby school. However, when we reached it the atmosphere around it was so flat that we felt very disinclined to go in and wandered on down the road until we saw a recreation ground with benches. We decided to go in and ponder what to do next. After a while we noticed a War Memorial Cross and thought that would be as good a spot as any but, as we approached, we saw a man nearby so we turned away. It was then that we saw we were in what had been an old churchyard. There were tombstones round the edge of the grounds and evidence of a ruined church in the middle. Part of the ruined walls was curved and was obviously the remains of the chancel, which was shaded by a thorn tree. This was our site: a place of power, which had been enclosed and was once again open to the air, as was appropriate for the Air Sign, Gemini. Without hesitation, as we were always aware that the Other Side were trying to prevent us, we stood under the thorn tree and threw the Ring into the air asking for it to be cleansed in that element. We also remembered to send the energy down the lines to cleanse the other Rings of Power around the world. This time we did not feel too jubilant, as we weren't absolutely certain we had found the right location.

As soon as we arrived back at the house we took out the map and saw that the recreation ground was, in fact, the very spot between Carol Street and St. Martin's Close, after all, and Robert confirmed that we had been in exactly the right place at exactly the right time. Something must have happened to secure it for the forces of Light. A possible explanation is that, knowing our intention was to go elsewhere, the Forces of the Left had left the site unguarded. Being new to the area, we had stumbled unwittingly upon the original site. Caroline told Robert that we had kept an eye open for any suspicious characters but had not seen anything untoward. He laughed and said that, on the contrary, we had been followed all the way!

This time round we were also on the look out for connections with royalty within the outlines of the pair. First off, the road running down one side of the female twin is called Royal College Street. There is a B road in yellow running East West which joins the twins like a golden umbilical cord and it is called Crowndale Road. The curving road forming the bottom of the male twin's outline is called Oakley Square and, as everyone knows, the oak is connected with the King and lives on in pub signs called The Royal Oak often showing the head of the future King Charles II who hid in the branches of the tree. Perhaps you could make a case for the significance of the road forming one side of the male twin, which is Camden High Street. This king is the 'High' King, just like Aragorn. Also, they are high in the sense of being spiritually higher than the people in their care, just as were the King Elessar (Aragorn) and Queen Arwen.

GEMINI ~ *the Twins*

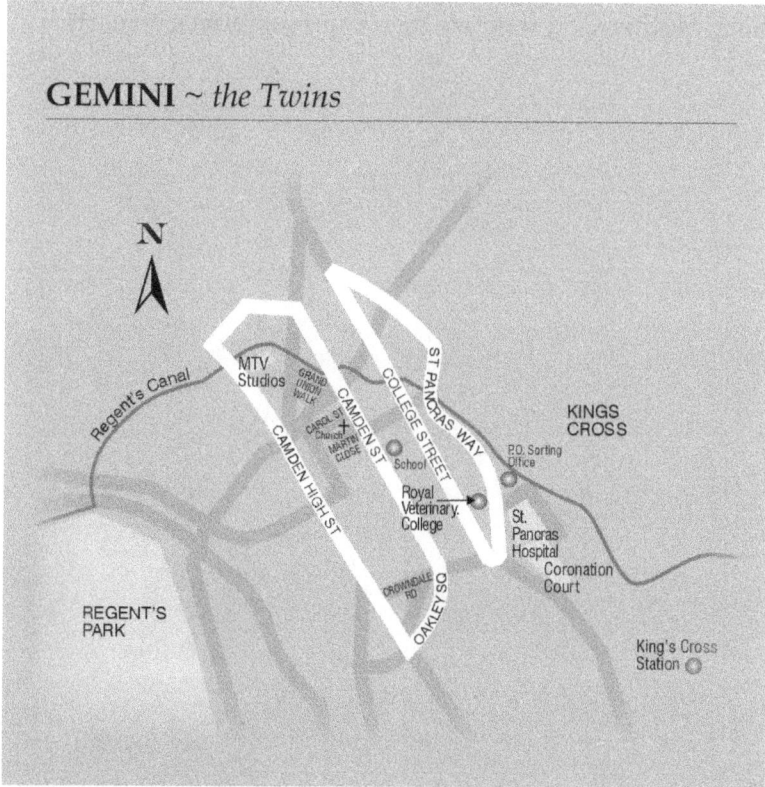

N

Regent's Canal

MTV Studios

GRAND UNION WALK

CAROL ST
Church
MARTEL CLOSE

CAMDEN ST

COLLEGE STREET

ST PANCRAS WAY

KINGS CROSS

CAMDEN HIGH ST

School

Royal Veterinary College

P.O. Sorting Office

St. Pancras Hospital

Coronation Court

REGENT'S PARK

CROWNDALE RD

OAKLEY SQ

King's Cross Station

We did not much like King's Cross Station being just to the East of the Royal Twins as we realised it was telling us how the King came to be a victim who was also crucified (he was put to death in many different ways) in the Cult of human sacrifice.

It seems to us that two royal couples are being suggested in the astrological signs – our Heavenly Father and Mother, as represented by the Lion and the Crab, and the earthly King and Queen, The Twins, who are the son and daughter of the Father/Mother God who are their representatives on earth.

Chapter 14

Enemies

On 10 May 1999, just two months after Cassie had moved to her new home, Robert and a number of friends came down to Salisbury as Robert had agreed to give a talk on crystal healing at The Salisbury Homeopathy Centre on the Sunday, with private consultations on the Saturday afternoon. It was over this weekend that Robert put forward an extraordinary idea.

Our friends from across the River Severn, Enid, Laura and Claire, plus ourselves and Robert, were having a cup of tea after the private sittings on the Saturday afternoon when Robert again brought up the subject of The Lord of the Rings. He offered Enid, Laura and Claire the opportunity to participate and they were happy to do so. He then said "What would you think of keeping the Ring? What if you could use it for Good this time round and change the Story?" This was yet a new slant on the idea of cleansing the Ring, which had not entered our heads. We were all speechless as the idea slowly began to filter through.

Leaving this new idea with us he went on to say that one of the Rings of Power was hovering over the city of Salisbury and was drawing the Other Side to the area. They were massing on the borders. Saruman was based at Old Sarum to the north (in the book the orcs called him 'Old Man'), Sauron was at the hill fort at Grovely Woods to the west - he pointed to the woods on an Ordnance Survey Map saying they made the shape of a crocodile advancing on Salisbury. Morganic, as in Morgan Le Fey (King Arthur's sister), energy was coming from the south and Merlin energy from the south west. They were all bent on snatching the Ring for themselves.

In one breath Robert was suggesting that Merlin was not the force for good that we have been led to believe, and that Morgan Le Fey, the legendary King Arthur's sister, was not just a mythical figure and was out for power for herself. We were to learn more about Merlin later. However, we were able to understand the 'Morganic energy' and its source because of the research that Cassie had been doing on the pagan cults of the Goddess and Sacred King. Morgan Le Fey was one of the cruel Queens of those times who scorned men. She was now attempting to recover her former, absolute power by drawing on a corrupted feminine energy of that forgotten period of history. As Robert has said, nothing ever goes away, it is still being recycled out there close to the dense physical, layer upon layer.

Caroline and Cassie, Robert told us cheerfully, were quite oblivious of all these different negative energies being drawn to Salisbury. Cassie had been lulled into a false sense of security by the Other Side. She had been imagining that she was safely in the Shire surrounded by comforting hobbits whom she kept meeting (this was true!), whereas she was really only approaching the Fords of Bruinen – where all nine Black Riders were lying in wait for her - and was completely unprotected.

Hence, perhaps, the timely visit of our friends. As we sat drinking our tea we realised we each represented a member of Frodo's party who were trying to reach Rivendell, and without whose help at the Fords, Frodo would not have won through. Robert was Glorfindel, as he had told us before, Enid, Laura and Claire were variously, Samwise, Pippin and Merry, and Caroline was Aragorn. So, just as the Other Side can use the negative energy for their purposes, the forces of Good can use the good energy in the Story to ensure that people of good intent appear at need.

Robert then startled us all by saying that this Ring had taken physical form and he pointed to a pink dot on the local map, which was the railway station and said, "It is south of that, on or near a wall."

Chapter 15

A Black Ring on an Island

The next day, Monday, the others having all gone home, we decided that we should take action sooner rather than later, before the Other Side were able to manipulate events at the physical level so as to acquire the Ring of Power in Salisbury. To be truthful, we felt somewhat fainthearted as we set off in Cassie's car, wondering how on earth we were going to find a Ring, what kind of ring it was going to be and how big. We just thought we had better give it a try.

We decided to make straight for the station down Fisherton Street, but Cassie missed the turning and we found ourselves driving along Mill Road to the south, where we passed on our left the river Nadder. Caroline noticed a road sign saying 'Fisherton Island'. We continued on to the station, both, curiously, (we subsequently discovered) with an idea of eliminating the area surrounding it rather than with the hope of discovery. We did, in fact, draw a blank and then remembered that Robert had said that it was near water and Caroline suggested that we try the island we had just passed.

We returned to the sign and drove over the little bridge onto the island. There was a single road with pretty houses on the one side backing onto a dyke in the water meadows and a stretch of the Nadder on the other edged with rich spring vegetation. Parking the car at the end, we wandered back up the road towards the bridge, taking in glimpses of the meadows between the houses and thinking what a peaceful place it would be to live. It could have been any lovely spring day with two people chatting away with nothing in view but a pleasant day out.

We reached the bridge and looked carefully along the top of the wall, rather late in the day remembering that we should ask the Ring to show itself to us, which we did. The gardens on the opposite side of the river were rather beautiful, and Cassie walked a little way down the bank to get a better look. We were both totally unconcerned that we hadn't yet found the Ring but suddenly, as we turned to walk back, Cassie said, 'There it is', and picked something up off the ground, quickly showed it to me, and put it in her pocket. After we had both got over our initial fear of this object, we had a closer look. It was a small, black, rubber ring the size of a conventional ring with white paint on about a quarter of the surface. It was, in fact, a rubber washer and in no way a thing of beauty, but we both knew that this was what we were looking for.

On our return to the house Caroline rang Robert and told him that we'd got it, but weren't sure what to do with it. He laughed and said, 'Put it somewhere safe'. Caroline asked him whether we could start using it for good but he said that this would come later.

We looked around for a suitable receptacle and Cassie suggested a largish Middle-Eastern cigarette box, but Caroline's eye fell on a small sandalwood box which had been in Cassie's possession for at least the last thirteen years but she could never remember how she had acquired it. It had beautiful markings all round the sides and on the top, which consisted of an inlaid ring of ivory. Inside the box was a further lid with a metal ring and then four compartments.

Caroline immediately remembered that a few days before, when looking for something to read, she had pulled out a book entitled Magic Symbols of the World. There were shown the same intricate patterns and heavily reinforced borders on cloth, boxes, etc., designed to protect and ward off evil influences. Cassie had never been able to fathom what she could keep in the box. It didn't occur to her that it was specifically for rings. Now, however, she realised that this was its purpose and that it was the perfect place for the Ring. The numerology was also right and seemed designed to keep the Ring in physical manifestation. The box had four sides and there were four compartments. Four is the number of this physical planet.

Despite the above, we began to feel apprehensive that we might be adversely affected by the energy from the Ring and Cassie suggested that we should put a small amethyst cluster on the top remembering that Robert had told us it stopped the hypnotic, circular emanations from the TV screen. By putting it on the box, it would doubtless have the same effect on the Ring.

That night Cassie remembered a curious incident on Sunday two days before, when, as everyone was taking their leave, Robert had pressed into her hand the amethyst cluster which lay on top of her television set. She put it back and a few minutes later he once again put it into her hand saying, 'I keep picking this up.' Earlier on he had put his glass down on top of Cassie's inlaid, Middle-Eastern box, which was on the chimney piece next to the small box. Seeing that Cassie looked rather horrified, he had made an amused, rueful expression as he lifted it off. Both of these actions now appeared significant. The fact that he went to such trouble suggests that it was very important to prevent the energy of the Ring emanating outward and that we must not underestimate the power of this object. The effect of the amethyst cluster also disguises the whereabouts of the Ring so that the Other Side are unable to locate it.

When we saw Robert again at the beginning of June he said that by imprisoning and neutralising the evil energy of the Ring we had protected the area around the city as far as Avebury, but that the Ring itself might be gone the following weekend. This was because there was to be a large gathering of people north of the city interested in crop circles. He asked us if we had ensured that the protective qualities of the amethyst crystals were all round the box including underneath, and we had to admit that we hadn't. We quickly proceeded to do this. Presumably the Ring could have used the energies of this gathering to escape.

A curious coincidence has just occurred as we make revisions to this chapter in September of 2006. Cassie went round to visit a friend who lives close to Fisherton Island where we found the physical Ring of Power all those years ago. Her friend asked if she had been to the special Open Day of the churchyard of the former St Clement's Church which is not normally open to the public and to which Cassie replied she hadn't. Her friend pointed across the road in the direction of Fisherton Island to a darkly wooded area, which Cassie had always thought formed the back gardens of the houses along the street. The church had been dismantled in 1850 as it had become too small for the expanding population.

When a person goes to some pains to give us information our attention is often being drawn to something we need to know. (This goes for everyone and is one of the ways the universal consciousness communicates with us but so often we don't notice). Looking at the print made in 1834 of the former church Cassie noticed that the church stood on a small 'mump' or gentle mound: in other words, it was sited on an energy centre which happened to be extraordinarily close – say 100 yards - to where we found the black ring seven years ago.

It all fell into place. This was a polluted energy site to which the evil energy of the etheric Ring of Power had been drawn. Furthermore, about the time of our finding the Ring seven years' ago, a mini-roundabout was created at the entrance to Fisherton Island and therefore close to the energy centre. Sure enough, when we dowsed, it had been a site of former sacrifice of the King and there were souls there who needed help in releasing themselves.

Chapter 16

Good and Evil

In talking about the Ring of Power and the forces of Good and Evil over the weekend in Salisbury in May, we were naturally thinking along the traditional Christian view of Good versus Evil, so we were caught off balance when Robert said carefully: 'What would you say if I were to ask you to think of Good and Evil as One', and as he said this he slowly brought the palms of his hands together. It seemed an entirely novel idea. He went on to say that you <u>cannot</u> separate light from dark, or good from evil. Where one is present, the other will be also. If we can embrace them both, balance and harmony would be ours. Certainly, we could appreciate that in this world our 'reality' is one of duality. To comprehend an abstract concept such as 'Good' or 'Light' or 'God' we have to create its opposite. But at the level of the Absolute, All is One. Shortly afterwards, Caroline and Robert happened to wander into the garden and walk over to the guinea pigs belonging to Cassie's daughters. Caroline picked out the black and white one and Robert asked her what her name was to which Caroline replied, "Twinkle". It was only the following day that the thought came to her that she had literally embraced the idea of black and white. Furthermore, in the word "Twinkle", Light and Darkness alternate as in a twinkling star.

As Caroline typed the above sentence the first time, the words spaced themselves out, firstly, with 'Light' at the beginning of the line, then nothing until the last word 'and', then the word 'Darkness' came immediately below 'Light'. Later, when she had made a few alterations to a paragraph above, these two words spaced themselves out with several spaces in between each word, and no amount of fiddling with the Word Processor would change it. Caroline thought about this for a while and then it suddenly came to her. The first instance showed that Light and Darkness are two sides of the one coin and the second had the effect of a twinkling star alternating evenly spaced black print and white paper.

At the time it was a completely new idea, at least it was for us. However, since then, others have begun to say the same thing. When one person gets an original thought, four or five others will also pick it up as it has entered the sea of consciousness, of which we all partake. There is a service held in Salisbury Cathedral, called 'Darkness into Light', which Cassie went to for the first time a couple of years later. She was struck by the fact that the service begins with the whole of the Cathedral being plunged into darkness. Gradually, hundreds of flickering candles are lit. It was a most profound experience and she could tell that everyone there felt the same way. It was demonstrating an awareness of the dark, which seemed quite new. For the most part, Christian teaching has dwelt on the light, whilst the dark has been something to be feared, suppressed, or conquered. We are told in The Lord of the Rings that the dark was not evil in the beginning but evil appropriated it for its own use. The darkness in the Cathedral was peaceful and gentle and everyone there fell silent, awed by its beauty in that magnificent setting.

At the time of going to press in May 2007 Cassie saw, coincidentally for the first time, two films in quick succession, which seemed to prove the statement that Good and Evil are One. The first was The Firm (shown on television) where it becomes evident that there is not a lot of difference between the good and the bad guys. Also, it could so clearly be seen that Evil's shadow self is Good, and Good's shadow is Evil. The outcome is unexpected by conventional standards, as the hero rejects coming down on the side of either Good or Evil. Instead, he blends the energies of both and wins back his freedom. The story reminded us of Robert's image of a coin which lies immovable when placed on one side or the other but when set on its rim, i.e. a blend of the two sides, rolls freely.

Three days later she happened to put on the video L.A. Confidential. Here, it was plain for all to see that the tactics of the Los Angeles Police Department are identical to those of the gangsters. In fact, the Chief of Police is planning on becoming the next Mafia boss! Again, the outcome is not what you might expect. The evil goings on within the Police Force are brought into the light of day and noted. Instead of revealing all to the press, the remaining Police hierarchy choose to harmonise those opposites of Good and Evil so as to maintain the morale of the people of Los Angeles and their belief in the goodness of their Police Force.

Like the Chief of the Los Angeles Police in the film, Saruman, from being on the side of good, succumbed wholly to evil. But Gandalf, being grey, a blending of Good and Evil could not be thrown off balance. There is a beautiful description in the Story when the dark-haired Prince Faramir and the beautiful fair-haired Eowyn are standing on the walls of the White City. A wind starts to blow and their hair, fair and dark, flows out and mingles in the air.

Another case in point showing that Good and Evil are indivisible, is the problem in Iraq. When America and her allies went into that country proclaiming to be the Forces of Good come to liberate the people, they acted as a magnet for the opposing forces of anarchy and terror.

Chapter 17

Gandalf Rescued

We continued to mirror the events of the Story. One sunny morning in June Cassie was hanging out the washing when in a clear blue sky she thought she could make out the shape of an eagle in the distance. Living on a hill she had a large area of sky as her view from the washing line. The more she looked at it the more convinced she became. It was most definitely an eagle but she did not link it to an episode in the Quest. When she mentioned it to Robert he grew very upset that she had been unable to connect it to the Story and that it was vital that we should do so. It was only then that we fully understood the importance of consciously linking with the events unfolding at that other dimension in order to bring them into the present and clear them from that level.

Fortunately, she had done a rough pencil sketch in her diary and realised that from the angle of the wings, the eagle was not gliding, but carrying a heavy weight. It had to be the eagle who rescued Gandalf from the pinnacle of the tower of Isengard where he had been imprisoned by Saruman who was at last revealed as a traitor. Saruman was the head of the White Council of which Gandalf was a member. The eagle, by good fortune, had come seeking him to pass on news. It was a crucial point in the Story to mark, for, without his rescue, Gandalf would not have been able to hive off four of the Nine Black Riders pursuing Frodo and friends. Thanks to Gandalf, therefore, on that fateful night on Weathertop hill, there were five and not nine of the Black Riders lying in wait for Aragorn and the hobbits. No wonder Robert had been upset.

With the benefit of hindsight, it seems to us that Robert has the ability to know what is going on in those parallel universes and he is able to help the way it interacts with or overlaps our dimension in such a way that we, in our bodies of clay, can notice - hence a cloud in the shape of an eagle. Our understanding is that Robert also has to work within certain restrictions.

Chapter 18

A Meeting in the Wye Valley

A series of meetings began to take place over the next five months in the Wye Valley, June to October, which constituted the Council of Elrond in the Story.

This momentous meeting in the Story saw the representatives of the free peoples of the West gathered at Rivendell, as if by chance, but clearly guided there by a higher purpose, for they were to form The Fellowship of the Ring. Gimli was to represent the Dwarves, Legolas the Elves, Boromir the Men of Gondor, Frodo, Samwise, Merry and Pippin were the Hobbits and Aragorn of the Dunedain – Numenorean stock unadulterated by intermarriage with lesser men and also of the royal line. Finally, there was Gandalf the Wizard.

The Council's aim was to decide what course of action those peoples should take for the safety of their realms against the massing of vast military forces by Sauron and his evil allies in the East, in clear preparation for open war against the West. At the meeting, the Council was to learn the history of the Ring of the Dark Lord going back in time, how it came into Bilbo's possession, who then passed it on to Frodo, and finally, of Frodo's flight from The Shire pursued by none other than the dread servants of Sauron, the Nine Ring Lords or Black Riders, who had, once again, grown in power and terror.

The first of these meetings was on 6 June 1999, at a house in the Wye Valley, which at that particular moment represented Rivendell. As usual, it was one of Robert's talks on self-awareness, which had been advertised in various places. There was a good attendance which included people we were meeting for the first time. It was a gloriously sunny day with blue sky and puffy white clouds.

Robert told the meeting that the battle between 'good' and 'evil' is going on around the world and where each of us lives. It is on many levels. The Lord of the Rings puts it into perspective and the writings of Paulo Coelho are also useful guidelines for our actions. There were six more people at this meeting who were hearing about the re-enacting and earthing of the events in The Lord of the Rings for the first time. He told the meeting that he was playing the role of Gandalf and he mentioned some of the people and the parts they were playing. Other parts would be given to people at further meetings.

Cassie talked about the Sacred Kings and said that they are still trapped at the astral level unless someone releases them. The balance between male and female is still not equal. The pendulum has now swung too far to the feminine and men are becoming uncertain of their role. This time round we have to find the balance, the still point in the middle. Robert asked if we could revitalise the Sacred Kings and bring in their masculine energy so that we can have balance.

Chris, one of the people who had been coming to Robert's workshops and was part of the Quest, had some very useful information about Gandalf which he had obtained from the internet and which he read out to us. Gandalf apparently had a twin, Gandolf, but they were separated at birth. This is why Gandalf sometimes appeared to be in two places at once. Robert said that if Gandalf and Gandolf had been acknowledged as one, The Lord of the Rings would have finished in a better way and Gandalf would not have had to go to the Grey Havens. However, one of them had a fear of the Ring. Robert said that if he had been Gandalf in real life, he would have played with the Ring, as it would not have affected him (just as Tom Bombadil did in the original story.)

Robert spoke of the need to find the twenty Rings, which are at large, deal with them and make them safe so that they can do no harm. We had already dealt with one, which we had found on Fisherton Island in Salisbury. The twenty rings had been given out by Sauron to the different peoples of Middle Earth so as to bring them under his control once they had been reduced, over time, to wraiths so that they lived a ghastly half-life without end. But the three Elven Rings were now in great danger of being exposed to the Eye of Sauron. If the One ruling Ring, which had so recently come to light, were ever to be recovered by Sauron, then the three Elven rings and their holders would be revealed to him and come under his power.

The year 2000 has three rings, the rings of the Elven-Kings: Gandalf's ring was Narya the Great; the Ring of Elrond, Vilya; and Nenya was Galadriel's ring. In this year, help from these three rings ceases.

Each of us is a holistic ring: body, mind and spirit. If we put all the rings together we form a greater whole. We are part of the collective life force. We are links and we should link with others to give them help. The difference between the Spirit and the Soul is that the spirit remains bright and spotless but that the light of the Soul dims as it carries our accumulated experiences in life. Thus the link between the two can weaken.

We need to clear sites permanently. We were shocked to learn that the Sacred Kings we had been releasing over many years, or so we thought, returned and settled right back. We protested that at least they had been healed and were no longer in agony. Every King had to swear an oath to his Liege Lord, the outgoing King, to protect the land. Because of this, these men had felt obliged to return to the earth to fulfil their oath. In future, we should ask the Kings to ask their Liege Lords, who had been sacrificed at the same site, to be released from this oath, then, when clearing sites, we would feel the difference.

The clearing work that we do goes back in time to the story of the Ring. An insight into Robert's rationale came when he said that we are at a unique point in history where the past can be compacted into the present and we can put history right and correct the early blunders.

Another part of the Story was earthed at this meeting. Robert referred to our hostess and her husband as being in the roles of Goldberry and Tom Bombadil at this particular moment, as they were our hosts for the day. Frodo and his companions were offered hospitality and a bed for the night in the home of Goldberry and Tom Bombadil after their perilous journey through The Old Forest.

The meeting closed with Robert asking everyone present if they wanted to go ahead. It would not be easy: we would be followed, there would be danger and we had to remember to protect ourselves at all times. Everyone said that they wished to take part in the Story.

Chapter 19

A Second Meeting

The next meeting was on 18 July and this time there were four more people present. We talked about the forthcoming eclipse of the sun on August 11 1999. An eclipse of the moon, as well as planetary alignments occur in January 2000. All these events signify the ending of an Age. The Sun and Moon and three planets, Uranus, Mars and Saturn, will form a grand cross in the sky. This is the last time this pattern at the time of a solar eclipse will be seen and it spells the end of the Era of The Cross of Suffering. Religion has killed more people than any other institution.

Penny, who takes the role of Pippin, had been looking at a bright star through binoculars. Sometimes it changed into a large snowflake and at other times a rainbow pyramid. Robert told us that the snowflake, of which there are no two alike, represents each individual soul. The rainbow pyramid symbolises many things: a focal point for energy to pass between the different levels, the marriage between heaven and earth, access to the stars. The star, of course, is the Silmaril that was cut from the very crown of the Dark Lord by the daring of Beren and Luthien and was eventually placed in the heavens as a symbol of the ending of an Age.[8] It is also the Star of Bethlehem, which, again, marked the ending of an Age.

The realignment of the planets has had an effect on the relationship of men and women. Men and women are the two opposing forces of the Chalice. In the middle is the balance where male and female come together and produce life.

Aragorn found the White Tree, a sapling of the line of Nimloth growing on Mount Mindolluin, and there is a connection here with the thorn tree on Wearyall Hill at Glastonbury, which comes into bloom at Christmas time. Robert told us that the enduring legend that Joseph of Arimathea visited Britain with Jesus and planted the white thorn tree on Wearyall Hill is true, as with so many legends. The mystic, artist and poet, William Blake, was right: those feet did 'walk on England's green and pleasant land'. The Gold Tree was destroyed, just as the Sacred King was destroyed. White and gold are spiritual colours and are perfectly balanced.

The room where we meet in the Wye Valley has pictures of Jesus and Princess Diana on the wall. Diana and Mother Theresa represented the feminine principle of the Age. Diana is the Goddess in her role of Mother, the 'Queen of Hearts'; Mother Theresa, in caring for the dying in the slums of Bombay, was the Goddess in her death aspect. The third aspect of the Goddess, the Maid, is also alive and with us today. Robert said that we can call on their energy.

At the morning coffee break Cassie mentioned to Robert that whenever she came to these meetings she developed a pain in her shoulder. He replied that this was because when Frodo arrived at Rivendell he had a wound. Of course he had! He had not long ago been stabbed in the shoulder by one of the Ringwraiths. "If I were you, I would ask Aragorn to take you a different way". So she did, and imagined the friends going south from The Prancing Pony with Aragorn as their guide, instead of northeast. The pain in her shoulder went away. Without tampering with the main patterns, we had changed the Story for the better, certainly from Frodo's point of view.

Chapter 20

The Fellowship is Formed

Robert asked Caroline to assign the various roles to people, which proved to be a delicate and difficult task. She had been canvassing people to see which roles they felt drawn to and were willing to accept. In an aside to Cassie some months ago, Robert had mentioned that Ellen was Samwise. She was a Yorkshire woman with forthright views, which also brought to mind the 'Gaffer's' decided views on most subjects - the Gaffer being Samwise's father whom he was very fond of quoting. And just like Samwise, she was stubborn, loyal and easily moved to tears. However, when the suggestion was put to her by Robert, she turned it down. Cassie chose not to say anything as she did not want to bring any pressure to bear, which in retrospect she thinks may have been a mistake. A little bit of persuasion can often work wonders!

There was another meeting on 15 August. Robert gave us all helpful insights into the Story. Galadriel, Celeborn and Elrond oversee the journey from afar and send advice and protection. We were to remember to use their energy. It is a story of losses and gains – the companions have to let Bill the pony loose, for example, to Samwise's great distress, because they cannot take a pony through the mines of Moria.

Boromir sets Frodo off on his path to Mordor. This takes place at the Falls of Rauros on the great river Anduin. Boromir is beginning to succumb to the evil vibrations of the One Ring and attempts to take the Ring off Frodo by force. Frodo understands that it is the evil power of the Ring that has turned the noble Boromir into this raving creature and it gives him the final courage to set off directly East towards Mordor with Samwise. We realised that seemingly disastrous events in the Quest have a beneficial outcome and are a necessary part of the help given the Nine on their journey. Aragorn's agony of indecision was solved for him at a stroke by the Fellowship being broken up in this seemingly disastrous manner - Frodo and Samwise are now beyond reach, Boromir is dead. He is now free, with the help of Legolas and Gimli, to pursue the orcs who have carried off Merry and Pippin. It was unsettling to be told that orcs would be represented in life as real people. Robert put Caroline in charge of the Nine just as Aragorn had been Gandalf's number two on the Quest.

In the end Cassie's choice of Samwise had fallen on Jane but she was dismayed by Robert's reaction on hearing the news. He did not think it a good choice and said that Cassie would have to carry her instead of the other way round. Frodo would not have been able to complete the Quest without the support of Samwise who deprived himself of food and water to help sustain Frodo when he was in a very bad way. At the bitter end, Samwise somehow found the strength to carry Frodo on his back up the slope of the volcano. Cassie could see the source of the problem, which was not an uncommon one. Jane had told her that she found it hard to read The Lord of the Rings and even harder to remember the Story.

This was a problem for a number of people given roles in the Story. Fortunately, it would not hinder us anchoring the energies at various times even though we might not have picked up on the clues and therefore be unaware that we were temporarily re-enacting a scene from the original Story. Robert gave an example of just such a clue by mentioning that not far from here was a street called 'Underhill'. This was where Bilbo and then Frodo lived. It was also the false name given Frodo by Gandalf under which he was to travel since, to Frodo's horror, Gandalf had told him that the name of 'Baggins' was known to The Dark Lord. The name had been given to him by Gollum under torture.

In the event, Jane was to opt out early on and to cease coming to the regular meetings that took place. Over the coming years we would often wonder who was taking the role of Samwise, as it was unclear. Only recently did we work out who, for a time, had taken on that role. Also, in February 2006, a chance remark from Robert gave us a further insight, which showed just how ingeniously the problem was solved.

Finally, the Fellowship was formed. Not all the parts had been filled and Robert said that people would dip in and out of the characters depending on which part of the Story we were attracting by our actions. Only Cassie and Caroline would remain 'in character'.

During the lunch break, we all went outside where we stood high on the hillside with its stunning views and large expanse of sky. Robert pointed to the sky asking us what we saw. To the amazement of all, a cloud could be seen forming into the shape of the Loch Ness monster with four rings looped on its arched neck. The monster rapidly changed into a horse, then a turtle, a whale and a duck. These were clues as to where we might find four Rings of Power. Strangely enough, at about this time in the 'Friends' sitcom, Joey and Chandler's pet duck swallows a gold ring. To us it seemed that the physical world was responding to the Story taking place at the etheric level because of the inescapable truth, 'As above, so below'.

At the end of the afternoon the weather had changed and become dark. Again, Robert took us outside saying that the battle lines had been drawn and told us to look at the sky. We could all see two long lines of cloud, a thicker white band above and a dark one directly below matching the dimensions of the band above, clearly showing us that the battle lines had been drawn. The Nine Walkers were leaving the safety of Rivendell and starting on their journey. We were instructed that each member of the Nine had the love of his land, devotion to his master and the desire to go home. Some would play out the scenes involving the characters they represent in the book and we would experience the difficulties and problems in real life.

Robert had pointed out that there were several working parties. We were to act as one but apart. These groups were to find Rings and not be corrupted by them. He also, confusingly at the time, said that Rings were 'proliferating' at the physical level. With hindsight we take this to mean the ever-increasing number of roundabouts throughout the country to tackle the increased volume of cars on the roads.

Time is fluid so some scenes would be repeated until the lesson was learnt. On at least three occasions over the next five years Robert was to mention at his talks that Cassie was back in Hobbiton at the very beginning of the Quest!   It reminded us of the game of Snakes and Ladders when you are at the top of the board and think you are nearly home but then land on the longest snake on the board and slither down to about three squares from the beginning. What was meant by 'lessons to be learnt', and what were the 'blunders' in humanity's history that we had to set right? We did not realise that we had to actually find out what they were so we would understand how to correct them, nor did we realise that we had to take into account the history of humanity <u>since</u> the time of The Lord of the Rings to the present day. For a long time we were doomed to go on repeating the mistakes and blunders because we did not know what they were! Therefore, for many years we were not in a position to correct them. In effect, the story told in The Lord of the Rings is a continuing one just as Samwise and Frodo realised during their Quest. Of course we had not been left totally helpless, as Robert's talks contained many of the clues we needed to recreate those lost chapters in our history.

How does the interaction between the dimensions work? If our circumstances at the physical plane become perilous then we will attract a similar energy in the Story. Likewise, if circumstances are safe and happy we will find ourselves re-enacting such scenes as those of the celebrations immediately after the battle and fall of Sauron. We suspect it also worked the other way: the interacting energy could influence us to enter or create dangerous situations similar to those being repeated in the original story.

Cassie and Caroline had already seen this in action. Cassie had been influenced to leave Northampton and set up home in Salisbury by a feeling of restlessness and the fact that all avenues appeared closed in Northampton. Caroline was temporarily without a home and had entered upon a period of wandering from place to place. This reflected Aragorn's life at this stage of the story. Many years ago Elrond, his foster father, had revealed to him his royal lineage and the 'high doom' laid upon him. If he were to fail, he and his race would disappear from Middle Earth. He therefore began a long and weary fifty year period of self-imposed exile in which he became 'the most hardy of living Men', travelling far and wide, even into the East, to learn the ways of the those people and of the Enemy. The desperate Quest to destroy the Ring was the culmination for Aragorn of all those years of preparation.

During the coming years we slowly came to understand that it was not just at one level we needed to get the Story right, but on many levels. It had become trapped on successive planes as the planet fell down the energy levels over many thousands of years.

Chapter 21

Two Wormtongues

As we were crossing the Severn Bridge on our return journey a magnificent rainbow appeared spanning the river from one end of the bridge to the other but something rather strange happened as we drove across. One end of the rainbow unmistakably kept pace with the rear of our vehicle and then finally merged with the other end and disappeared. We could find no explanation for this, so mentioned the phenomenon to Robert on the off chance that he might elucidate. The answer came that it was a sign that we were being protected by angels.

We always enjoy the return journey to Salisbury if the weather is good because the late afternoon atmosphere casts a golden glow over the countryside. It was one of those blue and white cloudy skies that draw the attention and we noticed something rather unusual in the shape of the clouds, which was quite unmistakable. It was a snake with the upper body raised and mouth wide open as if to strike. The head was disproportionately large as the body was disproportionately short. Then another, identical snake formed so that it was facing the other, also rearing up with a wide-open mouth. It was as if the two were about to fight. What did it mean? We were also very puzzled by their short bodies.

About two weeks later it suddenly came to us. One of them at least was Wormtongue. The short body was that of a worm and the open mouth suggested a snake's tongue. Gandalf refers to this traitor - chief advisor to King Theoden no less - as a snake, as he was in league with the enemy. Wormtongue had become Saruman's spy and his task, using lies and insinuation, was to undermine the King so he became confused and weak and mistrusted the very people who truly loved him.

However, we were still puzzled. Why were there two Wormtongues facing each other in such a combative fashion when in the original Story there was only one? Much later, we understood they could also represent the two Kings of the solar year fighting for the love of the Queen. At one stage in the evolution of this Cult the two kings were made to fight to the death. Also, here is to be found the origins of that potent mix called The Love Triangle. As midsummer drew near, the King knew he was about to be supplanted in the Queen's affections by the 'twin' King and his terror and fury knew no bounds.

In the meantime, we remembered the behaviour of one of the people at the meeting we had just left who, we suddenly realised, was clearly taking the part of Wormtongue.

Chapter 22

Gollum

We continued to go to Robert's workshops, which were always fascinating. He would cover many topics and we realised after a time that one of the things he did, although it was not at all apparent, was to go round every individual in turn pinpointing a problematic area of their lives and suggesting various ways they might help themselves. It was done as a general address and was interesting and helpful for all.

At a workshop, held a few months after the meetings at Rivendell had ended, Robert was, unusually, giving a talk at Susan's house. It was the lunch break when Cassie suddenly realised the person sitting next to her was taking the part of Gollum. There were unmistakable points of comparison to be drawn between the two. Both were unusually short – Gollum was related to hobbits or 'halflings' because they were half the size of a man - and both had large pale, green eyes. She was also Cassie's friend and it was through Cassie that she had begun coming to Robert's workshops. This is in keeping with the Story as Gollum was drawn to Frodo by the power of the Ring. He also becomes Frodo's and Samwise's constant companion through the dangerous lands close to Sauron's realm, as he had agreed to be their guide.[9]

We had met in November 1998 at a weekend course in the Malvern Hills. Like Cassie, she had two daughters of similar ages and they agreed to meet up after the course. She and her daughters came for a visit to Salisbury and Cassie went to their home for a weekend.

Gollum's story is a sad one. It was his misfortune to become the owner of the One Ring with a power far beyond his mind and body so he was quickly enslaved and his life became a living hell, bereft of friends, love and joy in the beauty of the physical world. Gollum also nursed a strong sense of rejection. This was because, having discovered that the One Ring made him invisible, he had taken to spying on people in his community and maliciously causing trouble. In the end, he was cast out by the matriarch of his family. Cassie's friend also lived with a sense of rejection by her family as she was put up for adoption.

The tragedy was that she began to stir up trouble and, so, experienced another rejection. She had many private consultations with Robert who showed infinite patience and, when she finally left the group, he told us all that she would eventually have to be brought back. And that we realised, was the key. One way of getting the Saga right would have been the rehabilitation of Gollum, and there had been a chance that we might have succeeded, as it had begun well.

She telephoned Cassie out of the blue after all the trouble but Cassie had mixed feelings. We had not been directly involved in all the problems as we had only attended a few of Robert's talks after the meetings at Rivendell ended and the Walkers had set out. Cassie's loyalties were being pulled in opposite directions as she still felt sympathy for this person. However, she had behaved badly towards Caroline/Aragorn. Just like Aragorn with Gollum, Caroline had little sympathy and advised Cassie against seeing this person, particularly in view of the role she had taken on. For these reasons Cassie felt unable to open the door of friendship to her again, but experienced a lingering regret.

It was also she who had been disruptive during the meeting when Caroline was trying to help people chose their 'roles'. Normally quiet and seemingly moderate, it was as if she was possessed and had turned into quite a different person. It is obvious to us now that the energy of Gollum's antipathy for Caroline/Aragorn was manifesting during that meeting because Caroline was taking a leading role.[10] At the same time we can see that she was simultaneously playing the part of Wormtongue, as mentioned above, as her underhand methods were identical.

With the benefit of hindsight we realise that the only people who were aware of the part this person was actually taking were those who had direct contact with Gollum in the original tale. These were Gandalf/Robert, Aragorn/Caroline and Frodo/Cassie. Of course Samwise knew Gollum well but at this point we did not know who had taken the part.

Cassie also had an encounter with the real Gollum. At the very first talk given by Robert, which we attended, she developed acute earache in her left ear which, thereafter, would re-occur most strongly during Robert's workshops. When she asked him what might be causing these, he replied cryptically that someone was trying to get through to her but that she was resisting. She was puzzled as she was unaware she was resisting anything.

On several occasions Cassie attempted to listen to the person who wished to communicate with her, but without success. Finally, two years later, after another bout of earache, she sat down in a particularly determined frame of mind and asked for the person who was trying to get through to her to say what it was they wished to say, and waited. To her amazement, she suddenly heard a hissing voice in her ear, which she knew immediately to be Gollum's because it was exactly as she imagined it would sound. The voice simply hissed 'Where is it: where is the Ring?' She was so taken unawares that it was hard to collect her thoughts but she does remember telling him that she did not have the Ring, that it was invisible to her, that we were cleansing it regularly, and that we had just recently cleansed it. She suggested that he visit Robert whom she felt sure would be able to help him - Gandalf had felt compassion for Gollum and had believed in the possibility of his redemption. She waited but there was no response and after a little while she could tell that he had gone.

Chapter 23

A Ring at White Horse Hill

The day was 27 August (1999), and we were setting off on a sunny day to try and find one of the Rings of Power. It was relatively easy for us to jump into the car at a weekend and set off, as Caroline had come to live with Cassie and her daughters in May of that year. It was in keeping with the Story that Strider/Aragorn should be with Frodo, as the hobbits would never have reached Rivendell without Strider as their guide.

Robert had given all of us a big clue as to the whereabouts of the Ring connected with a horse. He had previously mentioned that he wanted us to go to the chalk hill-figure of the White Horse at Uffington, with Dragon Hill nearby and Wayland's Smithy, a Neolithic long barrow, a mile and a half away along the Ridgeway. It seemed obvious that this was where we would find the first Ring.

Realising by now that the Universe would be giving us helpful hints, we kept a lookout as we drove along and the first sign was a corn-drying firm called "Gandalf".

On reaching the Vale of the White Horse we had our first view of this most graceful and ancient of the white horses believed to date back to the first century BC, or further, as it resembles the stylised horses on coins used by the Celtic Belgae tribe. We had our usual picnic with the whole of the Vale with its chequered, golden fields of late summer corn laid out before us and then made our way up the hill. All of a sudden the weather changed and white and dark clouds appeared over the horizon.

Our first walk round the outline of the horse, being careful to keep to the grass, proved fruitless so far as finding a ring was concerned. But what was significant was the sudden appearance of a youngish man dressed very conventionally in blue shirt and khaki chinos but, strangely for these days, he had a pipe stuck in the corner of his mouth, but no smoke was coming from it. He was like an actor who wishes to project a certain image but has got one of the props slightly wrong. He seemed to avoid our gaze. After a minute or so we turned round to have another look at him so that he would be aware that we knew who he was, to find him looking back at us. He turned hastily away and disappeared over the brow of the hill.

We continued to walk around looking for a clue which would suggest the point of power. We noticed a small flock of seagulls circling overhead. We hoped that one of them would come down and mark the exact spot but the flock flew away. Two more flocks appeared, circled for a while and then flew off, so at least we knew we were in the right general area. Members of the public had, meanwhile, been coming and going and we noticed a man with a black dog on whom we kept an eye. We were not having much luck, so Cassie thought she would walk over to nearby Dragon Hill. As we still had to walk a mile and a half to Wayland's Smithy and back and Caroline was feeling rather tired that day, she declined to accompany her. Cassie returned saying that it had a very unpleasant atmosphere.

After our experience at Fisherton Island where we found a physical Ring, we had again been looking for a physical object. It suddenly dawned on us that the Ring was at the etheric level and therefore invisible. All we need do was find the place of power and summon the Ring. We stood for a while just admiring the stunning view of vale and sky. Looking hopefully at the sky for a clue, one was given. The dense white clouds shifted to enclose a space of blue sky. The patch of blue grew smaller and smaller until it became rectangular in shape, resembling the head of the White Horse! We should have worked it out for ourselves, as we knew from the pagan cults that the head and the eye are seats of power. In the Cult of the Sacred King, one eye in particular was believed to be vested with great power so that a person needed to be shielded from that awesome power lest they be struck dead.[11]

Positioning ourselves near the eye we asked the Ring to come into Cassie's hand. She felt the familiar tingling in her palm, meaning the Ring had arrived, and put it safely away in her pocket wrapped in a handkerchief. As she did so, the sun came out from behind the clouds and shone down on both the hill of the White Horse and Dragon Hill, but the latter quickly became dark again. At the time we took this to mean that Dragon Hill needed clearing, but we were only partly right. This was not the only reason.

We now had to go to Wayland's Smithy along the ancient route on the top of the downs known as the Ridgeway, taking in the Iron Age fort of Uffington Castle on our way. As we walked, we noticed that the sun, which had once again gone behind clouds, was sending out rays in an exact replica of ancient Egyptian pictures from the Eighteenth Dynasty: the rays from the sun, representing Aten, the One God introduced by the Pharaoh, Akhenaten. This magnificent panorama continued for the length of our walk to Wayland's Smithy, which was beautiful, bordered by hedges of hawthorn and sloe and the late-flowering wild flowers of the chalk downs such as scabious and harebell. We saw more butterflies, mostly fritillaries, than we had seen all summer. The views over the downs were stunning, peaceful and timeless. In the hedge a wren was twittering to itself as it hopped among the twigs looking for insects. However behind us, and gradually getting nearer - eventually, to about fifty yards - was a young man in an orange and green rugby shirt. We didn't think this suspicious until, having overtaking a couple and their two children, we looked back only to find that he was nowhere to be seen. There was no way he, realistically, could have disappeared. Yet another 'person' from the Other Side taking an interest in our activities. Later, Robert told us that this person had come in through a 'time porthole' and that we must return and close it down so that it could never be used again. This we did on another occasion not long after.

We had been walking for about forty minutes and were beginning to think we had taken a wrong turning, when we finally came across the mysterious ring of beech trees, which encloses the famous barrow. The trees were surrounded by a field of ripe wheat which was in the process of being harvested. In fact, as we circled the grove of beech trees, so did the combine harvester. There was a curious atmosphere. It was as if we had been transported back to the time when it was built, a time both primitive and innocent. We walked around the barrow in the late afternoon sunshine and said a silent prayer as a preliminary to clearing the site on our return home.

On our way back, we had another reminder of the quest we were on and of the fact that everything was being repeated, all the strands of Earth's history coming together. In the evening sky was a long, thin grey cloud in the unmistakable shape of an enormous sword. In the centre there was even a dark line: it was Anduril, sword of Aragon, newly reforged from the shards of Narsil. Narsil was the sword of Elendil, leader of the faithful Numenoreans in their exile in Middle Earth after the destruction of the island of Numenor. The sword was broken in combat between Elendil and the Dark Lord, which ended the long, seven-year war. Elendil and Gil-galad both fell in battle but Isildur cut the finger with the Ring on it from Sauron's hand with the hilt-shard of his father's sword. As in The Lord of the Rings, Narsil has been reforged and given the name of Anduril, Flame of the West.

Returning to the house, we immediately put the Ring into the specially protected little Middle Eastern box in the second of the four compartments alongside the Ring we had found on Fisherton Island. As it was the weekend, we were not able to contact Robert until Monday evening and the first thing he said to us was that we had become careless and hadn't protected ourselves sufficiently. He always impressed upon us the need to protect ourselves. Luckily for us, he was still watching over us and rescuing us when we were foolish or neglectful. Had we, he asked, noticed the white clouds coming up behind us as we made our way from the car park to White Horse Hill? Those clouds had fired many black darts into us and he had spent a very long time painstakingly removing them. What might have happened had they not been removed? Doubtless, we would have fallen sick in some way and continued indefinitely in low health.

We had also brought something nasty back with us and hadn't we noticed a change in the weather and how cold our sitting room had become? Looking back we did remember thinking that the week-end in our part of the world had not been as good as forecast and feeling irritated that the sitting room was so cold and uninviting. But we had neglected to put two and two together. We immediately cleared the house and felt a great deal warmer.

We never asked, and Robert never volunteered, precisely what had attached itself to us. Nor did we ask who fired the black darts. Perhaps it was best for us not to know so that our minds would not dwell on the image and give it power. In his talks Robert has said that evil exists only in the minds of man and Shakespeare said the same thing: 'There is nothing good nor bad but thinking makes it so.' Ever in our minds were Robert's words that the less information he gave us, the less his opposite number was able to advise his helpers. In the best-selling series of books by David Eddings, which begin with The Mallorean, the set-up is identical. The reason that the task is taken up by weaker humans and hobbits is to limit the awesome power that the major protagonists might unleash should there be a direct confrontation between such as, say, the Dark Lord and Gandalf. In Tolkien's story, the Dark Lord's chief lieutenant - leader of the Black Riders - and Gandalf, come close to such a confrontation at the ruined gates of the City of Gondor. However, at the very moment of testing, they are miraculously spared by the dawn crowing of the cock and the simultaneous blowing of a multitude of horns announcing the arrival of the Riders of The Mark, who have come to the aid of Gondor.

Chapter 24

A Ring at Dragon Hill

Robert did, however, confirm that we had the Ring, but he told us that we had to return to Dragon Hill. We were rather perplexed by this enigmatic statement, but it was obviously something to do with the dragon. We had already come to the conclusion that the White Horse was, in fact, a dragon. Not least because of its forked tongue, quite apart from the fact that its long thin body and excessively long tail is quite unhorse-like. Strangely, the forked tongue is never mentioned in any of the several books we have read on the subject.

It was then that the image came to Cassie that the shape of the hill was like the vast mound of jewels, gold, armour and other precious things that dragons were wont to sleep on after their avaricious labours. She also remembered reading how the foundation of each of the dwarves' hoards of treasure was a Ring - seven of the Rings of Power had been given to the dwarf kings. The effect of a Ring of Power on a dwarf was different to that of men, who faded to become Ringwraiths, completely in Sauron's power. It intensified the dwarves' lust for gold. These treasure hoards had later been plundered by dragons, so Cassie realised that it was feasible that there was a second Ring, which was over Dragon Hill. The shape of the hill could even be said to resemble a great pile of treasure topped with a sleeping dragon just like Tolkien's Smaug in his book The Hobbit. She dowsed and found that, indeed, there was another ring at Dragon Hill at the etheric level, which was exerting an evil influence on the surrounding area.

Two days' later, on 29 August, we set off again, and this time we had protected ourselves properly. As we approached the White Horse, we observed a girl with a black Labrador talking into a mobile telephone, who looked up as we approached. Caroline made a note to keep an eye on her. We walked down to the Horse and noticed something else strange about it: the two, so-called, ears are of quite a different shape and arranged at some distance apart. One 'ear' is a thin, oblong protrusion and the other, at the very top of the head, is much larger and conical in shape - in fact, it is like a spike or a short horn. Viewed with no preconceived ideas, it is quite unfeasible as an ear. There is also a second spike on one of the front legs. We were to learn later that we were half right about it being a dragon, but there was a further insight into its full significance.

We proceeded to walk down the slope over to Dragon Hill. There were one or two people around but Caroline managed to get the Ring into her hand, again at the etheric level, and put it straight into her pocket with no trouble. As we reached the brow of the hill, we noticed that the first girl with the Labrador had disappeared to be replaced by another, older woman with yet another black dog, a very large, odd-looking poodle. It was a dog in all respects except for its eyes, which, sinisterly, were very un-dog like. In fact, they were human with a bright, knowing, aggressive stare. And stare it did. The woman, on the other hand, had her face turned away. After we had passed them Caroline turned to try and catch her eye, only to find her staring at us. Once again, as with the youngish man we had encountered on our previous visit, she turned hastily away. Later, she asked Robert why these manifestations from the Other Side seemed to be avoiding our gaze and he replied that they were frightened of us, which was good news so far as we were concerned.

We made our way back down the hill to the car park and, as we did so, we glanced up at the sky and there was the longest strip of cloud we had ever seen. It stretched from one horizon to the other like a gigantic spine. Then one of us noticed that there were distinct vertebrae, as distinct as if it were a photograph. In fact it was exactly like the spine of the dinosaur skeleton at the Natural History Museum in London, the end even thinning away like a tail. For 'dinosaur' read 'dragon' which had obviously been transported to the Great Treasure in the Sky. It reminded us of the description given of Smaug's bare bones lying at the bottom of the Lake. There he had plummeted to his ruin after being shot by The Black Arrow in the pale yellow hollow over his heart which was the only vulnerable place in his gem encrusted belly.[12]

After driving on a little way, we noticed that the cloud was still there but now it looked fatter like a rib cage, and there appeared to be a sword laid across it. At that we stopped the car and got out to have a better look. There was indeed a cloud that looked exactly like a broadsword cutting into the underbelly of the rib cage. Cassie, who had just been reading Tolkien's The Silmarillion, then realised that the second dragon must be Glaurung who appears in that book. Glaurung was killed by Turin Turambar from beneath, just as the sword was showing us. The dragon had flung its body across the chasm of a deep ravine and Turin had climbed the cliff directly underneath and thrust the Blacksword, Gurthang, up to the hilt into the dragon's soft underbelly. It is curious that the weapons which killed the two dragons were both renowned and called 'Black'. Is it an example of history repeating itself during the great sweep of time covered in Tolkien's chronicles of Middle Earth? A further example springs to mind. Both the Silmaril, which was recovered by Beren and Luthien, and the Arkenstone, were large gems beyond price: both were used as bargaining counters.[13]

It seemed that by removing the evil Rings of Power both dragons had lost their grip at the lower astral so enabling their deaths in the Story to be re-enacted. Our conscious acknowledgment of this pinned the story down at the dense physical thus clearing it from a parallel dimension.

As usual, we reported back to Robert. We told him that we thought the White Horse was really a dragon, and mentioned the forked tongue and the two spikes. He replied that although it was a dragon now, at a time in the past it had been a unicorn - that perfect symbol of purity, hence the spike, which had originally been a horn. In later times when the Earth's vibrations had become ever lower, it had been taken over by the dark forces as represented by the dragon, Glaurung, and the unicorn had gradually been altered to look more like a dragon. In fact, there is definite evidence at the site that the 'horse' was at one time a great deal fatter.

Just a week after our second visit there was a programme on television with the title 'Steve Irwin's Deadly Dragons.' The dragons in question are the Komodo dragons of Indonesia, the biggest and most dangerous lizards alive today and remarkably like the dragon of myth and legend. In a scene in the programme, as several of these creatures tear at the carcass of a deer, one only needed to magnify their size to get a picture of what dragons must have looked like when they ruled the earth, as they did at the dawn of Earth's history. There is no enduring myth that is not based on a true story.

And just as we finished going over these chapters on the deaths of the two dragons, we experience further synchronicities. On the very day, our copy of The Week (27 January 2007) arrived through the post and on the cover was a picture of an enormous, fiery, orange and yellow dragon in space (i.e. at another dimension) fiercely breathing destructive fire over a satellite. China had just successfully tested an anti-satellite missile on one of its own weather satellites. Less than a week later, there was wide media coverage of David Beckham agreeing to play the role of St George in the ancient legend of St George slaying the Dragon. And one final touch: Cassie had dinner with friends on Saturday 27 January and noticed in their room a large, serpentine dragon woven in orange and green coloured straw, which they had brought back from Thailand.

Chapter 25

The Opposition

After the last meeting at Rivendell on 15 August Robert had told us that the battle lines were now drawn. He also warned us that, as Frodo and Aragorn, we would be particularly targeted by the Forces of the Left and that we should be on our guard.

Almost immediately, on returning to Salisbury, Caroline had a curious incident. She and a friend were having an evening drink in the garden of a hotel when she became aware of a fat, squat man who had sat down fairly near her with a huge cigar in one hand and a tankard of beer in the other. She became aware of him as he emanated a sinister stillness as if he were listening to the conversation they were having. Rather stupidly, it was to do with Cassie's and her clearing work and, once again, the prop of the huge cigar looked old-fashioned and phoney. She challenged him in her mind and a minute later, to her great satisfaction, saw him jump to his feet, as if he had been stung by a bee, and lumber off as fast as he was able. However, she was puzzled when, after a few minutes, he returned, but by then she and her friend were ready to leave. Stupidly as it turned out, she looked at him as they walked away and he looked back, unlike the first one who had avoided her gaze.

When she mentioned this incident to Robert he said that the man who returned was not the same entity as the first man. He said the Other Side would send 'people' like that until there was one who was stronger than she and had she noticed a twinge of pain when he had looked at her? And indeed she had. She had felt a twinge of pain in her hip, which at the time, was a weak point. We now know that we should not challenge anyone by looking at them, only in our minds.

On several subsequent occasions, we met extremely unpleasant people in the city. They were often women invariably dressed in out-of-fashion black clothes and exuding an air of menace. We would meet them in some place, usually a shop, and then, as we left the shop, eerily, we would see them again coming in the opposite direction.

On one horrible occasion, Caroline was in an aisle in a supermarket when it suddenly emptied and she was left alone while a frighteningly tall woman, dressed all in black and walking with a stick (they were also often disabled in some way), advanced on her and stood behind her exuding menace as she dithered over a purchase, every hair on her head prickling. She asked Robert what was the point of this, and he said that she was being tested.

Chapter 26

Tom Bombadil and Crows

Around this time, late summer, we interfaced with the part of the Tale where the hobbits are twice rescued by Tom Bombadil. It is at an early stage in the Story before the hobbits reach the sanctuary of Rivendell. The Hobbits are being pursued by the Black Riders in their own country, The Shire, and are forced to take the decision to go through the Old Forest with its hostile reputation, as the only way of shaking off the pursuit. There, they fall into the deadly grip of Old Man Willow but are rescued in the nick of time by Tom Bombadil who takes them to his home where he lives with the lovely Goldberry. Robert told us that we would be visiting an orchard by a river, and to be aware of the presence of Tom Bombadil and Goldberry.

We had, in fact, already planned to go for a walk that day in the Woodford Valley alongside a river where there is an orchard and, before setting off, we called in at the pub, as we were both thirsty. There was no one else there and we were in no doubt that the publican and his wife, a lovely young girl with golden hair, were Tom and Goldberry. We duly walked past an orchard which ran down to the river and, after that, we felt that we were being accompanied. We even passed an ancient willow with a huge crack in its trunk like Old Man Willow. We stopped to look at some horses in a field who threw up their heads and stared and stared at us as if they couldn't believe what they were seeing. It was only when we eventually walked on that they returned to their grazing. Had they seen Tom and Goldberry?

Not long after this we both experienced incidents which echoed those of the first leg of the Quest shortly after the Fellowship had set out from Rivendell. The first for Caroline was the loud cawing of a crow as she left the house. It was so insistent that she looked around to see where it was coming from and eventually noticed a single crow on top of a chimney.

As soon as it saw her it flew off as if on a mission. She felt a definite unease. Then as she walked along she passed a tree full of rooks who, at her approach, flew off making a great din. Cassie also had one or two experiences involving crows. The crows, of course, were the crebains, that were flying over Hollin and spying out the land between the Mountains and the River Greyflood and which Aragorn saw as he kept watch. Aragorn knew they had come from way south, close to where Saruman dwelt. Little did he realise that it was indeed Saruman, turned traitor, who had sent the crows in the hope of intercepting the Ring and taking it for himself. The Nine Walkers now had to go without fire and travel only by night.

The next incident was on a walk when Caroline came across a young man with two Dobermans. On noticing her they raced towards her and their owner called them, as if they were out of control. Feigning complete absence of fear, which was far from the way she really felt, she held her ground and the young man eventually caught up with them and managed to put on their leads. The dogs represented the terrifying, but illusionary, wargs/wolves the company battled with one night shortly after the spying flocks of crows.

Chapter 27

An Owl in a Blossom Tree

Around this time Caroline had two dreams. She was standing by a tree with white blossom in which perched a Little Owl, a bird sacred to the Goddess, in particular, the Greek Goddess of Wisdom, Athena. A man and a woman came along and took the owl away with them. Much dismayed, she ran after them and said, 'You are not supposed to take the owl away from the tree', and managed to persuade them to return with her and place it back in the branches. When she told Robert about this dream he replied, 'So you left the Tree?' At first she was puzzled by this remark.

Later, she interpreted the dream thus: the tree is the White Tree, Nimloth (later renamed Telperion), whose seed Isildur brought with him over the waters to Middle Earth and which grew in the courts of the Kings. It was the symbol of the Royal Line of Luthien and there was a prophecy of long ago saying the Line of Luthien would never die. The Royal Line, therefore, passes through the female line, just as it did in Egyptian times and also in France. The owl, symbol of the Goddess, is Arwen who, by her marriage to Aragorn, ensured the continuance of the Royal Line through the ages of humankind. This was why Caroline/Aragorn was so concerned at the owl being removed from the tree.

It was the task of Aragorn, Isildur's heir, to keep hope, as symbolised by the White Tree, alive. By leaving it, Caroline had left it unguarded. In other words, she was placed in an impossible Catch 22 situation. If she stayed by the tree, the owl was abducted: if she went after the owl, the tree was left unprotected. It therefore reflects Aragorn's difficult position when the Nine Walkers have to decide what to do next on the journey, as The Ring, borne by Frodo, has to turn east towards Mordor. Aragorn must decide whether to go west with Boromir to Minas Tirith, which he yearns to do, or to go East with Frodo, whom he has sworn solemnly to help in his task of destroying the One Ring.

Yet another interpretation is that the Queen/Goddess has been removed from her rightful place. The reason for this is that she forfeited her position when as the Goddess's representative on Earth, she became the cruel, bloodthirsty creature of the pagan cults. She was overthrown and it was then that she was taken away from the tree. Now is the time for the Queen/Goddess to be cleansed of that cruel image, which lives on in our subconscious minds, so that the owl can be restored to the White Tree. One of Aragorn's aims is to restore the Kingship of Men and he knows he cannot do this without a Queen by his side, hence Caroline/Aragorn going after the couple and telling them they cannot take the owl away from the Tree.

A dream may have several interpretations, as do Egyptian hieroglyphs – at the mundane, the symbolic and the esoteric, or hidden, levels.

We have just had another astonishing synchronicity. The very day - Monday 22 January 2007 - we edited this chapter a large A4 size, glossy pamphlet dropped through the letterbox from one of the local estate agents. On the front page was a close-up picture of a barn owl, with its heart-shaped white face, sitting in a pine tree, with one word written in large capital letters across the page – 'WISDOM'.

The second dream, as so often, was expressed in terms of the news of the day. A certain well-known person, who was in prison at the time, gave into Caroline's safekeeping a large diamond until he should leave prison and be able to give it to the woman he loved as an engagement ring for their forthcoming marriage. It was a particularly magnificent stone and brought to mind Galadriel's ring, Nenya, which was of adamantine and one of the three Elven Rings.[14] A few weeks' later, a friend showed her a beautiful crystal, very like a large diamond. Just before leaving, he handed it to her, saying, 'I feel I should give this to you.' The following day she was choosing a bottle of wine and her eye fell on an Australian red, which she was astonished to see came from a vineyard called Nanya. It seemed that we were in Lothlorien and Galadriel's Ring, for a while at least, was protecting us, the Nine Walkers, from the harsh world outside.

Chapter 28

Giant Spiders

In the summer Caroline, who had moved in with Cassie, had a nasty encounter with a spider. She had just retired to bed when she suddenly noticed a truly enormous spider on the wall. Having thought she had conquered her arachnophobia, she suddenly realised that, at this size, she hadn't! Cassie and her daughter kindly offered to remove it and she went calmly to bed believing that it had been caught and thrown out of the house and garden. It was only the following day when she questioned her granddaughter that she learnt that the spider had actually fallen off the wall and scuttled away into a fireplace where they had been unable to catch it. They hadn't liked to tell her, as they knew she had to sleep in the room anyway. She therefore had to continue sleeping there in the knowledge that it was somewhere around.

It next turned up on its way to Cassie's bedroom. This time it was caught and thrown over the garden wall, only to be found back in the house a few days' later. This was obviously no ordinary spider. In other words, it was Shelob, the primordial and deeply evil giant spider who nearly does for Frodo and Sam as they make their way through the tunnel where she lurked at the top of the mountain pass in the land of the Dark Lord. It became obvious, therefore, that no amount of throwing out, or even killing it, would have had any effect. The only way to keep it away was to better protect the house at the spiritual level, which we were already doing, by mentally stopping up all drainpipes, chimneys, etc. This we did and Shelob, after once more being thrown over the garden wall, ceased her creepy scuttling.

A couple of months before this Caroline had visited the Serpentine Gallery in London and literally walked under Louise Bourgeois's enormous, steel spider before she realised what she was doing – in fact, something very strange for someone who disliked spiders. At the new Tate Modern art gallery at

Bankside, which opened in May, there was an even bigger spider filling some of the space in the great former turbine hall. Finally, at the same time, two truly horrific sculptures of huge black spiders came to Salisbury's Cathedral Close for the May/June Art Festival held every year. Obviously, Shelob still lives.

And, as with so many towns and cities as discussed earlier, the 'ring' road around Salisbury, and roads leading off, resemble the body and legs of a spider. On this 'ring' road are placed further 'rings' in the form of roundabouts – five in total.

As we revised the above, Caroline suddenly realised that, to have had so many experiences of enormous spiders, she must at this stage in the Story have been in the role of Samwise who engages in mortal battle with Shelob to save his beloved Master, Frodo. Then the reason she had walked beneath the sculpture of the spider in the Serpentine Gallery became clear: Samwise had finally managed to overcome Shelob by springing beneath her and, as she sank down upon him to crush him, he grasps his Elven sword holding it point upwards and she impales herself upon the blade.

In real life, Caroline had also been earthing Samwise's supportive energy for Frodo. When staying with Cassie (Frodo) and her daughters, she gave support in various ways and continued to do so after moving out of the house in May.

Chapter 29

A Ring, a Tortoise and a Maze

In early September just after the school term had begun, we were given a clue as to the whereabouts of the Ring of Power connected with a turtle. One of Cassie's children had been clearing out some of her early childhood books, including a children's version of Aesop's Fables. She passed it to Cassie, who happened to glance at the fable of the Hare and the Tortoise. It showed the race taking place round a spiral maze. As she gazed at the tortoise, she realised that it was also a turtle and that the Ring was to be found in a maze: Robert confirmed this.

We now had to locate the maze. After some thought it seemed to us that the most likely one was the famous maze at Hampton Court. We suspected that the site of the palace was a former, ancient place of power and it is to such places of energy that the Rings of Power are attracted. Dowsing confirmed this.

We set off about midday so that we could have a picnic lunch en route and break the journey. We were quite surprised at the number of cars at the service station where we stopped but realised the reason soon after we set off again. It was people returning from holiday. The traffic had slowed down from anything between twenty miles an hour and a halt. We also thought that it might be phantom road works, real road works or an accident. As it transpired two hours, two accidents and twenty miles later, it was phantom road works and accidents. At one stage Cassie, who was driving, quite understandably wanted to get off at the next junction and return home, which was doubtless exactly what the Other Side hoped would happen. However, Caroline managed to persuade her that, as we had already been crawling for more than an hour, we might as well stick it out. Caroline regaled her with some of the funnier articles from one of the Sunday papers and finally, at the junction with the M25, the traffic started to flow again and we arrived at Hampton Court three and a half hours after we had set off from Salisbury.

The gardens were looking magnificent. Surrounded by late blooming summer flowers, we made our way towards the maze, keeping a lookout for anything untoward. As is always the case, the maze seemed very much smaller than when Caroline had last visited it as a young girl. We set off to try and find the centre. After the usual false hopes, and eventually remembering Winnie the Pooh's advice to Rabbit that if you go in the opposite direction to where you really want to end up, you have a very good chance of getting there, we finally found ourselves in the middle. Quickly asking that no one else should arrive, we stood between the two chestnut trees and Cassie commanded the Ring to come into her hand. She just had time to feel it and put it away in her pocket before several people joined us. She said afterwards that, unlike the last time at the White Horse, the whole of her hand tingled and she saw in her mind's eye a particularly large and heavy Ring surrounded by gold light.

With a false sense of having accomplished our task we turned round, only to find that it was a great deal more difficult to get out than it had been to reach the middle. The maze was full of people cheerily going round and round giving advice to others on which paths not to take. We met a party of German students several of whom, as we passed them said, 'I am a potato' as if it was the greatest joke in the world. The whole expedition was beginning to take on a surreal air. Seeing a little girl in a bright orange fleece who seemed, and in fact, was, lost, we adopted her and, feeling rather like the Mad Hatter, the March Hare and Alice, we all proceeded to be lost together. Finally, on seeing a gate with a sign saying "Emergency Exit", Caroline suddenly felt like getting out and called to the ticket girl to come and rescue us. Smiling a little, she came up with a key and we escaped with a feeling of relief. The girl we had adopted declined to come with us as she had just located her real family through a hole in the hedge.

Strolling down to some willows by a canal, we wondered if we were re-enacting the hobbits' experience in the Old Forest when they met Old Man Willow, the most ancient and malevolent tree in the Forest. The branches of the trees whipped around rather more than was warranted by the slight breeze and we thought the atmosphere seemed charged and slightly sinister. Feeling a heaviness in the air, we were glad to get away and walk towards the Teahouse for tea and scones before setting off for home. On the way back we were treated to the most spectacular sunset. The sky was pure, liquid gold.

We reported back to Robert who, when Caroline told him, slightly frivolously, how we had cheated and left the maze through the emergency exit, said, 'So you escaped.' Only then did we realise that the Other Side must have been preventing us from leaving. He said that this Ring was different from the others as it belonged to one of the Ringwraiths, or Nazguls (also known as the Black Riders), which is why it felt so heavy, and that we should put it in a different box. It had to be kept separately. Luckily Cassie, who collects little boxes, had one just the right size, with a wavy pattern picked out in brass on the lid, where we carefully deposited it. We put another amethyst crystal on top and spread its energy all the way round the box so it could not escape.

Doubtless, the opposition to collecting a Ring belonging to one of the Nazgul was stronger than usual and would go some way towards explaining the traffic hold-ups we experienced en route.

Chapter 30

Rings at Avebury

In this chapter large group of us encounter dragons, fairies and giants at the etheric level. This might be difficult for some to take on board but stories about these beings have come down to us in myth and legend through the ages and many people believe that such enduring tales are based on truth.

Alison, a member of The Fellowship of the Nine who plays the role of Merry, came up with the idea that there was a ring at the Avebury stone circle in Wiltshire. Robert had told us that there were many rings which could be used by the Forces of the Left and that the group should collect as many as possible. She checked with Robert who confirmed that, indeed, there was a ring at Avebury, that it belonged to a Magus or Magician/Wizard, and it was still being used. After a little thought he said he had never been to Avebury and would like to go. He agreed therefore that it might be a good idea for some of the group, including the Nine Walkers, to meet there and would she arrange it? This she did and twelve of us plus Robert were due to meet up at Avebury on Tuesday, 5th October. In the event there turned out to be several rings.

It was a still, clear day with the promise of sunshine as we drove directly north. On meeting up with some of the others on our arrival we learnt that Robert would not be coming as two members of his family had 'flu' and he had to care for them. We were disappointed and were just wondering how to arrange our activities when, to our great relief, Robert turned up after all. He explained that his deception was necessary due to the forces ranged against him. He talked about the Michael and Mary lines which briefly merged within the stone circle and said that we needed to look for three of the Elven rings, one with a diamond, which had been hidden, never coming into the possession of Sauron. He proceeded to divide us into groups with himself, as it were, as Ringmaster, allocating a compass direction for each group to work from.

106

Guided by Robert, the different groups set off to collect rings. As we approached the outer ditch and bank Robert asked Caroline what help she would call on and, as she was thinking about this, he prompted her to remember Cassie's and her experiences with Tom Bombadil and Goldberry, which we talk about later. Feeling protected by these unseen companions, we clambered over the outer ditch to the north, turned westward and came to a grassy area surrounded by trees like a natural cathedral. We noticed a lot of feathers on the ground and followed the trail which led away until we came to a spot which we felt was the right place in a small grassy area enclosed by trees. We called the Ring into the palm of our hand and repeated this at two further sites. Meanwhile, Susan who is a psychic, was very much aware of an oppressive atmosphere. Fairies had been guarding these rings and they were not at all happy at our taking them. She could feel anger being directed towards us. To propitiate them, she left some small crystals she had with her in the area and the atmosphere lightened.

The group, who had been given a south-westerly direction, went to the field near the Great Barn Museum where there is a line of Sarsen stones. Alison collected an Elven ring near one of the stones, which she put into a box she had brought with her. Robert said that we needed to know the exact position of the planets throughout the day, and that a particular stone formed part of a yod. This is an astrological term whereby two planets in sextile aspect to one another are both inconjunct to a third forming a "finger of fate" in the shape of a long, narrow triangle. Gareth felt the different vibrations in one of the standing stones. He cleared and realigned energy lines at a subterranean level by finding bands on the stone. These energy lines go around the world. He moved on to stone no. 2 and Robert asked the group what they could pick up. They all felt a coldness round their legs and feet. Spirits of giants were present at this stone. The giants were old gods, and the group needed to ask for their permission to work at that place and use their energy. Bardic rituals had taken place there and beings were trapped in the stone. The souls were released and the area cleared. There were also white and black dragons at the site. At stone no. 3 Gareth again realigned the energy lines. At stone no.

4 Robert said fairies were trapped in the stone and wanted to escape. The group released them and they indicated that the whole area round the stone needed clearing as, again, there were trapped souls. Another group had also spent the morning collecting rings, one belonging to a Magus.

We all met up again near a courtyard opposite the Great Barn Museum. Robert invited us to cross the threshold of the courtyard but no one accepted, as the atmosphere was horribly cold and forbidding. He then reminded us of what happened in The Lord of the Rings when the Nine Walkers arrived at the closed entrance to the Mines of Moria and the cryptic message above the great door, written in an ancient elven-tongue, was finally deciphered by Gandalf as, 'Speak, "Friend", and enter'. This we did and it was then safe for us to cross. Robert told us that this was the chapel where Gawain, one of the Knights of the Round Table, had gone to meet the headless Green Knight whose challenge he had accepted at Christmas the previous year. He asked Cassie to tell us the story (See Appendix I). It was a place where many Sacred Kings had been sacrificed, and we joined hands and called on the Light to release them. Susan said that one of the kings had come and stood behind her and thanked us.

Walking to the road by the church where there were some cottages, Robert told us that bubonic plague had claimed many lives there and caused much suffering. We brought Light to the area. A black dragon had made its lair nearby and left a nasty cesspit, part of which was a place of black water. Part of the cesspool had been where the road now runs and as we walked along we felt physically ill at the precise spot. We purified the water and Robert told us to look at the sky where we just managed to catch a cloud in the process of changing quickly from the shape of a dragon to that of a lion. It was showing us that the trapped masculine energy of the sacrificed kings had been released and the rule of the king reinstated: the dominion of the dragon was at an end at last, at least at one level. So history does repeat itself. In Tolkien's The Hobbit the death of the dragon, Smaug, paves the way for the restoration of the King of Dale.

We walked on back through the village in full sunshine, passing and clearing on the way several dragon lines, which caused a marked coldness round our feet.

Reaching the village pub, we decided it was time for lunch and a break. It was a perfect autumn day, something we have come to expect when on an expedition out of doors with Robert, and we were able to eat outside. As we did we noticed a threatening bank of black cloud advancing on us from the northeast. Calling on the forces of Light to help us we exerted our power to keep the dark forces at bay. The advance halted and the clouds began to recede. After lunch the whole group crossed the road into a field of standing stones and, as we came abreast of the first stone, Susan had a strong feeling of 'protection', i.e. the outer ring was used for the protection of those within the circle. We moved towards the centre of the circle, which was opposite a small chapel, where Susan could hear children wailing and crying. Robert told us that this was a spot of great negativity where children had been sacrificed. She could feel great sorrow. We made a circle and joined hands, which we raised, and sent unconditional love to the children and prayed for them to be released. Immediately the energy started to build and Susan could see what looked like a huge diamond beginning to bury itself point first into the ground with small, sharp shafts of light flying off the surface of the diamond and away. The vision faded and we withdrew. Within the space of ten minutes Susan could hear children's laughter and the singing of nursery rhymes and knew that all was well. Afterwards, Robert told us that a Nazgul, one of the Ringwraiths, had been present.

We again split up, one group staying in the area to work with the stones and realign the energies while seven of us, directed by Robert, made our way to the outer bank to the north east to collect another ring. Robert told us to put forth all our power and, as we walked across the field towards the bank, we could see small, black clouds rising from a wood some distance away on a hill. Robert said witches were arraigned against us there and the clouds certainly appeared as serried ranks of a foe in battle formation. He then left us and returned to the others. Susan began to feel a very oppressive atmosphere and knew that there was another ring nearby. We reached the top of the bank and found the spot where the ring was to be collected. Susan felt very strongly that protection was paramount at this point, and arranged the rest of the group in a semi-circle around us. She told us that we should call strongly for the ring and she then turned away and faced a nearby wood at the bottom of the hill from where a great deal of negative energy was flowing. She asked for her light to be used as a wall to keep the negativity at bay. She called out to us that there were three rings to be collected. A strong and very cold wind began to blow until we had the rings safely in our keeping.

Robert had told us that when we had finished we should send Light down the energy line which stretched from Avebury, through Wayland's Smithy to the Wash in Norfolk and this we did, sending a golden ball of light spinning down the line to the sea. We had just started to walk away when two members called to us to return. They told us that they had noticed a black cloud, which had suddenly built up and Penny, who is a sensitive, had received a message from the Magus. The rings had been under his protection and he was not at all pleased that we were taking them away. Penny said that we did not intend to use them and that we would take great care of them. He replied that we would have to swear an oath that we would protect them with our lives if needs be. This we did and he seemed satisfied that the rings were in safekeeping. The black cloud dispersed and the sun shone again. When we met up with the others, they too swore the oath.

We repaired once again to the pub for tea, where the twelve of us gathered round Robert at a long table above which there were three lights in the form of rings, one bigger than the rest. Robert said it had been a good day's work. He talked of certain matters pertaining to the group and then went on to speak of the yod, or finger of fate, which pointed to the south-east towards Portsmouth. He reminded us that, in the past, England had been attacked along this coast line but now help was coming from the same quarter, just as Aragorn had sailed with a large force from the south coast of Middle Earth up the Anduin to the rescue of Minas Tirith, the same river up which in former times had come the enemy, the Corsairs of Umbar.

Alison then counted the rings and there were twelve altogether. Robert said that one of the rings was a Nazgul's, and had to be kept separately from the others. He designated a place of safekeeping for them. We then learnt that Gareth had merged the Michael and Mary Line along its whole length, thus bringing together the Masculine and Feminine Principles. We only hope that those dowsing the Line in the future will not conclude that it is their dowsing that is at fault when they can only find one line!

Later, Robert told us that there had been five Ringwraiths at Avebury. He also mentioned that a powerful foe, whom he would have had to confront physically, had been prevented from reaching Avebury that day. Such a meeting might have proved cataclysmic.

A couple of days later, this clue made us realise that the day at Avebury was also the scene for the re-enactment of the Battle of The Pellenor Fields which took place outside the walled City of Minas Tirith. Sauron had at last unleashed war on the West. We compared Robert's narrow escape that day with Gandalf's meeting and narrow escape from a direct battle with Sauron's Captain, Chief of the Nazgul. The Gates of the City had been broken down by a huge battering ram and finally splintered by the power of the Nazgul's evil spell. But when the black-cloaked Lord of the Nazgul enters, he finds his way barred by a White Rider seated on a white horse. It is Gandalf on Shadowfax. Just as the two are about to engage in a most terrible duel, a cock crows and, simultaneously, the horns of the Horsemen of Rohan are heard. The Nazgul realises that the time for the sacking of the City is not yet at hand, and withdraws.

It also helped us to understand Robert's cryptic remark at the beginning of the day when he turned to Caroline and said that we were only here because of her. Aragorn arrived late on the Battlefield and he brought with him two other members of the Fellowship, Gimli and Legolas, in addition to a large force from the south. This helped change the course of the battle so that victory, against all the odds, went to the West.

Robert, as he has told us, has an empty mind and can therefore be entirely in the present moment. And this is the way

111

he works – he deals with what he comes across at that moment, which explains the odd and varied assortment of tasks we encountered that day in Avebury, from dragons to sacrificed children. That was what was there, so that was what we tackled.

Chapter 31

The Last Meeting of the Year

Five days' later the whole group, together with nine further members, were foregathered once again in the Wye Valley. Fiona and Caroline had done some work on the astrological implications of our day at Avebury and today's meeting. Fiona had software with which she could plot the exact position of the ascendant and planets throughout the day, and she brought along charts for each hour starting at dawn. We all studied them and Robert, Fiona and Caroline discussed some of the implications. Robert said that the charts in time sequence matched what people did at Avebury that day. For instance, Gareth realigning the magnetic lines of the Earth matched with certain changes on the charts. He had sent spiralled loops of energy, which Robert told us was the shape of infinity, in eight directions round the earth. Caroline described a yod, the finger of destiny or fate, with Venus and Mercury, messenger of the Gods, pointing to the end of the sign of Pisces in the period before noon on 5th October. Robert asked if this was a point of change and, more from intuition than reason, Caroline suggested that it signalled the ending of the Piscean Age, and Robert concurred with this. To all those who believe that the Piscean Age ended on a different date, that too is right as Pisces is a mutable sign and slippery. The charts for Sunday, 10th October, the day of the meeting, showed certain influences we should be aware of and alerted us to certain matters to do with our work. With Saturn at the bottom of the chart, someone was trying to undermine the group and its participation in the Story in which we were all taking part.

The different groups then discussed the clearing work they had been doing. Susan, together with others, had collected a ring from a local church. Laura spoke about clearing a Sacred King site with Fiona. Fiona spoke about the Dragon lines she is finding. One is local and one in Cornwall, in or around Tintagel. Jenny and Phillipa in Norfolk had cleared Sea Henge, which had recently been very much in the news. English Heritage had removed the wood circle "in order to preserve it". Phillipa had felt a huge energy during the clearing. She saw the circle restored at the etheric level. Robert said that there were significant planetary changes after the work done at Avebury and Sea Henge. If enough people come together, they can change the destiny of Humankind and Nature.

At the meeting on 15 August of that year Robert had said we would reach the Mines of Moria - a former great kingdom of the dwarves but now abandoned and desolate - before Christmas. Five days later on Sunday 10th October, when Robert's talk had ended, the Nine Walkers congregated for a cup of tea in the conservatory, which was light and airy with magnificent views. We started to discuss the journey through the Mines of Moria when Robert stood up and walked decisively across the room, his eyes fixed on an unseen point and said: "We have just gone through the Mines of Moria".

It is hardly surprising that the terrifying journey through the Mines, through the endless dark, twisting passages, should have taken place with Robert present, in his role of Gandalf. Only Gandalf knew the way and without his guidance and the dim light, which shone from the tip of his staff as the only source of light, the Company would never have made it through. For that moment at least the conservatory had been the lofty hall of the dwarves. Robert had earlier told Caroline she was to be in charge of the Nine at the mines of Moria. This accords with the story, for Aragorn had to take Gandalf's place as leader after Gandalf was lost to them in his confrontation with the Balrog, a fiery, evil creature of great power. Long ago the mines were abandoned because the workings of the dwarves had gone too deep and disturbed this ancient evil from the Old World. So that part of the Tale had been interfaced – mercifully by Robert – and then communicated to us.

Fittingly, therefore, he then announced that this was the last meeting of the year. We all of us had plenty to be getting on with over the winter months and would carry on with our clearing work when the occasion arose, whilst at the same time continuing to be aware of our parts in the continuing story of the Ring.

Chapter 32

Fisherton Mill

Cassie suggested that we should have lunch at a rather unusual place called Fisherton Mill, a large, former mill converted to a space for artists to sell their work, and also a restaurant. There were some sculptures outside in the forecourt and, as the weather was so mild, we ate outside.

That evening, as Cassie was driving with one of her daughters to a school musical evening, they saw in the sky at the roundabout a cloud which resembled an enormous eagle with wings outstretched. Had anyone else noticed the unmistakable image of an eagle if they too had looked up whilst waiting in the traffic? Remembering that the battle of the Pellenor Fields had not long ago taken place at Avebury, she noted that it appeared to be flying west which led her to conclude that it was one of the great Eagles who came flying from the land of Mordor to Minas Tirith, bearing the tidings of the great victory of the Lords of the West. Frodo, the Ring-bearer, had fulfilled his Quest and the Ring had been cast into Mount Doom. The realm of Sauron was ended and the battle had been won.

Turning off the roundabout to go north, she received confirmation of this as she saw in the distance an immense dark cloud rising high in the sky edged with a brilliant gold light. This reminded her of the black cloud which rose from the wreckage of the Dark Tower – "a vast soaring darkness sprang into the sky, flickering with fire". It was the spirit of Sauron leaving the earth. She knew then that this was indeed the eagle, which brought the tidings of Sauron's defeat to Minas Tirith. We could hardly bring ourselves to believe this, as there were many other parts of the Story that we had not yet experienced. However, Robert had always told us that our experiences would not necessarily be in sequence and, when we contacted him, he confirmed that the battle had indeed been won, but only at one level; there were other levels at which it had to be waged. This dampened our rejoicing a little, but not much.

In the papers the following day there was the picture of an eagle, which supposedly, on its annual migration from central Russia to Africa, had landed instead in the Scilly Isles. This was due to the work our group had done on the earth's magnetic lines at Avebury the previous week, and the eagle had consequently lost its bearings. It was also, of course, the Universe echoing the flight of the great Eagle.

Two days later we both decided that, as it was another sunny autumn day, we would get out of the house, have lunch again at Fisherton Mill and then visit Heale Gardens in the Woodford Valley, which was open to the public. The gardens bordering the river Avon were peaceful and beautiful and, as we wandered over the lawns by the river, we realised we were in Ithilien where Frodo and Sam were healed of their hurts after their terrible ordeal at Mount Doom. We came across a gardener picking off the heads of the lavender, a herb with healing properties, and as we walked down a long avenue, as Frodo and Sam had done, we felt that Heale Garden was truly a place of healing.

Strangely, we had lunch at Fisherton Mill for a third time on the Saturday and realised, at last, why we kept returning. We had missed all the signs we should have been noticing. In the forecourt, where we were again able to sit outside for lunch, were two large sculptures. One was in wood and showed two men holding a plank of wood at either end, with one of the men holding the end up and the other crouching and holding it down, rather like a seesaw. The other was in metal and showed the earth in the form of a hollowed out globe lying at an angle of forty-five degrees composed of slender strips of metal and an arrow with a golden head and feathers piercing it. Round the band of metal in the middle were written various capitals of the world and the different time zones. There were also small sculptures of animals such as two cockerels in intricate metalwork.

The symbolism of the two men shows the two Sacred Kings, in their different roles, one supreme and the other as second-best, but jealously biding his time. It could also represent the 'old' King crouching, on his way out, as he gives way to the 'young' King standing over him, taking his place. The cockerel in the pagan cults was identified with the Sacred King for it was sacred to Apollo, the Sun God. The two cockerels, therefore, echo the sculpture of the men: one perched on a step looking down on the other. Cats are sacred to the Goddess and in front of the two men there was a carving of a large wooden cat: it represents the Queen who ruled supreme in the name of the Goddess during this cult.

The sculpture of the world represents many things but here, primarily, we think it shows that the cult of the Sacred King was world-wide, but the golden arrow represents hope - hope that the bringing into human consciousness of this hidden trauma will heal the wounds and enable humankind to go forward into a new dispensation, a new way of life for which every being on earth on the side of the Forces of Light so deeply longs.

In a corner of the courtyard and up some steps was a rather overgrown area. It consisted of a small pond badly in need of attention, with a few goldfish and a defunct fountain. There were a couple of sculptures: an anchor and a semi-abstract sculpture of a man and a woman representing the opposites, a construct which will cease in this new Age when the pairs of opposites, male and female, Light and Dark, will be resolved. The whole area had an air of neglect. The Piscean Age as represented by the name "Fisherton", the water, the anchor, had ended and, as we stood silently there, we realised that this corner was a symbol of something that was decayed and dead. Indeed, the end of an Age.

In this context, we then wondered about the significance of the sculpture of the two rival kings, who dominated the courtyard. We realised how the competitive spirit aroused in the two men came to taint society and we felt it was suggesting that this spirit would soon be at an end.

There was an amusing sequel to this when we returned to Fisherton Mill for a small celebratory lunch with Cassie's father on her and Caroline's birthdays in December 1999 (we were born on the same day). After looking at the menu for some time, we all chose the fish. It looked delicious when it arrived at the table and for a while we chewed away wondering if the rather strange taste was the Thai spices in which it had been marinated or, horrors, was the fish 'off'? After a little while Caroline suddenly announced, "I think this fish is definitely 'off'. What about yours?" At which both Cassie and Edwin also realised for certain that their fish was also bad. We called the waiter who kindly gave us replacements. Before leaving, we spoke to the chef who was puzzled in the extreme. He had bought the fish the day before from his usual, reliable source and it had been marinating in the refrigerator overnight before being cooked the following day. It was not until at least a fortnight later that we suddenly realised the significance of this incident. The Piscean Age had passed and the Fish was not only dead, it was decaying! The timing was immaculate as everyone was gearing up for the nationwide Millenium celebrations less than three weeks away.

As we have so often noted during the reworking of Ring Quest, when completing a particular topic, we would experienc a synchronicity. On the day we made the above revisions, in fact, minutes after writing the above, a friend called by to pick up a book Cassie was lending her for her holiday. She carried a pair of brand new, black Doc Marten boots, which none of her men folk wanted and so she was taking them to a charity shop. On an impulse she wondered if Cassie might have a use for them. Cassie picked them up and saw something shining in one of the shoes. It was a new watch. Her friend then remembered that she was also giving away the watch, as she couldn't read the face. The meaning of this singular experience is that it is confirming that the old Time/Age is dead – the shoe was black – but a new Age has been born –the new watch. The shoe is of great significance in the Cult of the Sacred King where, in some interpretations of the cult, his foot – and leg – were held to be the particularly sacred parts of his body. In some countries the King's heel was not permitted to touch the ground hence he wore heels or was carried everywhere. It was believed that the earth would be scorched should his heel/foot touch the ground for the King personified the immense burning power of the sun. It is from this memory that foot and shoe fetishism stem. A shoe or boot, which had been worn by the Sacred King, was believed to have extraordinary powers of virility and fertility. Therefore the black Doc Marten has the 'power' to give birth to the New 'Time' after the death of the Age of the Fish.

A hangover from those times is to be seen in portraits of Kings in full regalia. One stocking-covered leg is prominently revealed from the folds of the ermine cloak in an elegantly heeled shoe so that the sacred heel might not touch the ground. Or there are portraits of the King seated on his throne, exposing just the one leg but this time with the sacred foot resting on a stool so that it does not touch the ground.

It is interesting to note that the headquarters of the powerful Mayor of London are located in the leg and paw of the Lion outline in London. It further proves how the energy of kingship has been corrupted by the Cult of the Sacred King.

Chapter 33

The Earth Sign of the Bull

It was not until February of 2000 that we cleansed the One Ring in the element of 'earth' for the first time. Some months ago we had located the outline of Taurus the Bull. Studying the names of the streets we noticed the word Oseney Crescent in Kentish Town, just to the north of The Twins. We realised that the Crescent resembled an eye and that 'Oseney' sounded very much like 'oxen eye'. Could this be the Bull's eye, we wondered? Focusing now on the roads enclosing both the streets and the Crescent we could quite distinctly make out the head of the bull and we could see that the eye was located in exactly the right spot within it. We then noticed that the continuation of the road, which formed the top of the head, bent at just the right angle to form the horns of a bull. To cap it all, at the centre of the crescent eye was a church. At that point we felt we had found the site where the Ring should be cleansed. The eye was a big clue that this was an energy point and the church was further confirmation. As with the outline of the Lion in the City of London, we noticed signs of corruption at this site, as well. To us 'Brecknock' Road sounded too much like 'break neck' which linked, once again, to the cult of kingly sacrifice where the King's neck was broken at his beheading. This time we secured the site instantly.

Robert had finally suggested that we should cleanse the Ring in accordance with the seasons. Thus we should cleanse it in the element of fire in the summer, in water in spring, in air in the Autumn and in earth in the winter. Such knowledge would have been natural to the pagan peoples such as the Celts. On hearing it, it seemed so obvious and logical. Yet, as we had not thought to synchronise with the living world we are a part of, it was just another example of how, as Robert tells us, we have lost our connection with that world. We need to move away from belief systems to a living reality.

So it was on 3 February 2000, having found out that the One Ring had, once again, reconstituted itself, we set off to collect it and then cleanse it in the element of earth. It was a suitably wintry day, one of those flat, dark grey days in London. The weather was surprisingly mild but the branches of trees and shrubs were bare and stark.

We had chosen to retrieve the Ring at St Martin's in the Fields, partly because it was next to The National Gallery and we wanted to visit the Botticelli Exhibition to look at his painting of The Mystic Nativity. We duly looked round the exhibition, had lunch in the basement café and made our way to the church. Having safely summoned the Ring, we decided to take the Underground, as the Northern Line took us straight to Kentish Town from where our destination was a short walk. Caroline then had an unpleasant experience on the train so that we rather regretted this decision.

Just one stop before we were due to get off, a very bold-looking girl dressed all in black with black hair and ostentatiously chewing gum sat immediately opposite her, even though all the seats on the Other Side of the carriage were empty. Sensing that this was no ordinary person, she silently challenged her but she did not move away. Realising that the Other Side had sent someone stronger than herself, she avoided her gaze for as long as she could but suddenly found herself catching her eye, whereupon the woman gave her a nasty stare. Caroline had been meticulous in protecting herself and apart from feeling annoyed, she did not feel she had been harmed, which Robert later confirmed. Cassie had also been aware of a menacing feeling coming from the woman but had not realised she was from the Other Side.

Taurus is a sign connected to the good, solid material things of life and the area, which is once more coming up in the world, consists of large, solid Victorian houses. As we approached the church in Oseney Crescent we saw that it was almost derelict and surrounded by scaffolding which appeared to be holding it up rather than for repair purposes. We reached the gate and there, as at the lake in Regent's Park and as if waiting for us, was a grey

TAURUS ~ *the Bull*

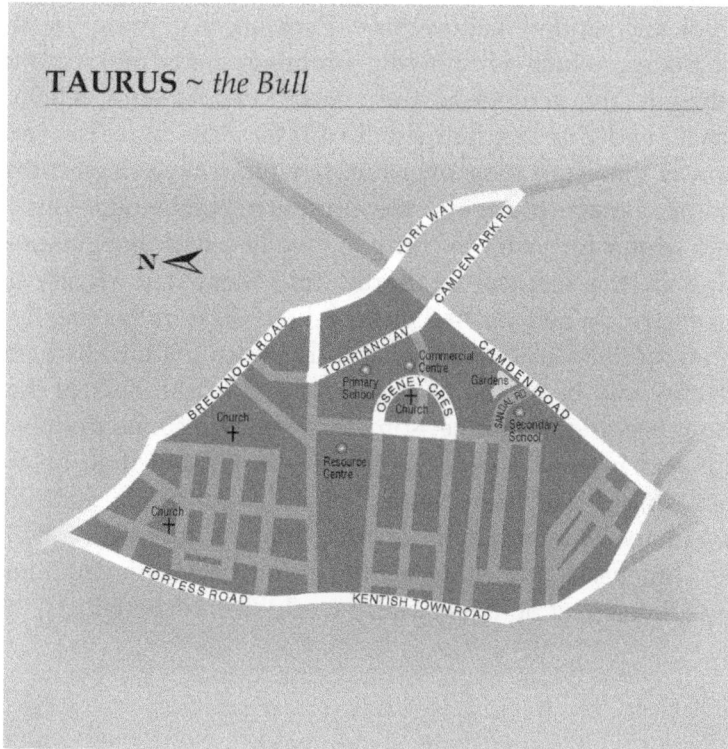

squirrel. It whisked away round the side of the church with us following, scratched a little in some earth and scampered away. We took this as indication of the exact spot where we were to purify the Ring. Opening up the white handkerchief we carefully tipped the Ring on to the earth, asking for it to be cleansed in the element of earth in the astrological sign of the Bull.

That evening there was a programme on television about a super-volcano under Yellowstone Park in Wyoming in the United States, which is showing ominous signs of erupting. According to the geologists, the volcano erupts on a 600,000-year cycle, and this last happened 640,000 years ago. The next eruption is therefore long overdue. It would have devastating effects on climate plunging the northern hemisphere into a volcanic winter for years to come. As we had that day cleansed the Ring in the element of Earth, this seemed a significant synchronicity. When we had cleansed the Ring in Air its effect had been on the realm of ideas and therefore politics. In Earth the effect would be on the natural, physical world. Fearful that, somehow, we might have set something off, we spoke to Robert about it and heaved a sigh of relief when he said that, on the contrary, things had been 'settled down'. That made us think. We began to understand more fully that by interacting with another dimension and changing the pattern at that level, it had an immediate effect on the physical world, for the better.

Chapter 34

The Royal Line

Meanwhile, experiences mirroring Aragorn's continued. Exactly a week after our visit to London to cleanse the Ring in earth Caroline had a dream, one of those 'real' dreams, where she was exerting all her power against some foe. After what seemed a very long time, the danger was over and she was able to relax. On waking she immediately thought of the Palantir, the 'Seeing' stone, which Aragorn had wrested from Sauron. She told Robert about it and he warned that she should put it safely away – at the etheric level - at once! Feeling silly that she hadn't realised this herself, she wrapped it carefully in a silken scarf and put it in a safe place.

About the same time, neighbours offered to cut the top branches of an old pear tree hanging over the garden wall. We brought two of the branches into the house, which, surprisingly, broke into white blossom a week later. It struck us that they were branches from the White Tree, Telperion, symbol of the Royal Line. The two branches represented the two 'branches' of the Royal Line,[15] which were united in the marriage of Arwen and Aragorn, thus guaranteeing the continuation of the Royal Line.

On 12 April Caroline moved house, temporarily renting a cottage. The cottage was part of a complex of converted stables and barns called King's Stables and, as she walked through the gate, she looked up at the cupola with the royal crest, the Lion and the Unicorn, and saw for the first time the inscription, 'Long Live the King 1910 – 1935', commemorating George V's Silver Jubilee. This mirrors the scene in The Lord of the Rings where Aragorn, crowned king outside the city gates of Minas Tirith, enters the city after a lapse of a thousand years to claim his inheritance as heir to the royal line of Numenor. Even stranger in its implications, and startling proof that the story of The Lord of the Rings is being re-enacted at this moment in humankind's history, was the fact that, on taking over the cottage on that day, she did not immediately move in as her furniture was still in store and could not be brought out for another six weeks. She eventually moved in the middle of May 2000. Like Aragorn, she had entered the city, but did not take up her abode there until later. A final touch - in the middle of the village there was an ancient, long distance route called Monarch's Way.

At Christmas 2000, we had a last reflection of the Story on the physical plane that year. The family had decided to attend Midnight Mass at the parish church and, on the way there, someone remembered that Madonna and Guy Ritchie were spending their honeymoon with friends, Sting and his wife, Trudie, who lived in the valley and wondered if they would be at the service. Most of us thought they wouldn't. However, we were wrong. Not long after we had taken our seats in the tiny, crowded church we noticed a group sitting in the choir stalls which, much to our surprise, included Madonna and Guy. We think it is apparent to most people that famous pop stars are the new royalty and Madonna and Guy with their daughter and newly born baby son were, at that moment, representing the King and Queen with their young family. And perhaps the word 'Madonna' is telling us that the Holy Family is of the same royal line as Aragorn and Arwen.

Chapter 35

Taking stock

The Millenium was upon us and provided a time to take stock. Tolkien's, The Lord of the Rings, is being re-enacted in the here and now. A Fellowship had been formed to match the original Fellowship and provide a counterbalance to the Nine Black Riders. We have successfully found sites with sufficient power to cleanse the Ring belonging to the Dark Lord in each of the elements in which the Ring was forged – fire, water, air and earth. Cleansing the Ring was ongoing for we had learnt that it exists at different levels, going back through time. To date, we have only cleansed it at one of those levels.

When we set out on the Quest we had little idea that the theme of royalty was going to be so important as, initially, the focus seemed to be on the One Ring and on the need to 'unmake' it. Likewise this had also seemed the major focus in Tolkien's Story. The Fellowship is formed to help Frodo fulfil the task laid upon him by The Council, which is to throw the One Ring into the fire of Mount Doom. However, the importance of the restoration of the King is revealed towards the end when, much to almost everybody's surprise, hitherto known as Strider, Aragorn turns out to be the heir to the throne of Gondor. Gandalf passes the stewardship of Middle-earth to Aragorn saying that it is now for him, as King, to order the New Age of Man. Is it any wonder that Sauron/the Dark Lord so strenuously sought the destruction of the King and the Royal Line?

Sauron's successors have continued to seek the death of the King and to undermine or destroy the Royal Line through Time. We found out just how successful 'they' have been in this aim with the discovery of the existence in our past of the Cult of Sacrifice of Kings. Much of the evidence of this terrible practice has been destroyed and/or suppressed, partly as a result of the King's own subconscious fear, but also, deliberately, by those who wished to use the powerful emotions created by these most unnatural practices, to manipulate humanity. We have only been left with the peripheral pieces and the terrible fallout. With this in mind, we should be less surprised that the Royal theme was proving to be of such importance on the Quest.

The film trilogy, The Lord of the Rings, had yet to take the world by storm. The first film, *The Fellowship of the Ring*, came out in 2001 with its successors following in 2002 and 2003 respectively. Surely, the timing of these films is a further indication of the truth of Robert's statement that The Lord of the Rings is a true story and that humankind is still in that story today as it is recycled once again.

New elements were to come into our journey of which, at this stage, we were as yet unaware. We learn more about how Man must travel back the way he came. This means raising our vibrations in order to access a higher level. To lay the groundwork for this we discovered we had to anchor the energy of the 4th Dimension here on earth and, with Robert's help, we discover how this might be achieved.

Chapter 36

The Mystic Marriage

In the middle of January 2000, Caroline decided to go away for a few days. Somewhere near Dartmoor appealed, but a friend happened to have vouchers for short breaks at The Francis Hotel in Queen's Square in Bath, which seemed like a better option. In fact, the hotel being in Queen's Square, and, 'Francis' (many kings of France were called this) was a pointer to the whole tenor of the visit which centred around the concept of marriage, and in particular royal marriage, as well as the marriage of opposites: King/Queen, Sun/Moon, Masculine/Feminine.

Her first visit the following morning was to the Roman Baths and Temple complex. This ancient, Celtic sacred site with its warm bubbling spring was taken over by the Romans, probably between 60 and 70 AD, and turned into a very large curative establishment, in fact the largest in Europe at that time, dedicated jointly to the original Celtic water deity, Sulis, and to the Roman Goddess, Minerva. Thereafter, as is apparent from inscriptions, they were considered as one and the same. This was probably because the two Goddesses possessed the same attributes of wisdom, healing and, possibly, military acumen.

One of the most striking objects found during excavations is the roundel of what is, obviously, the Sun God which formed the centre of the Temple pediment. Some archaeologists have considered this to be the Gorgon's head but the difficulty here is that the face is obviously masculine and the locks of 'hair' resemble the flames from the sun and not snakes. There is also a small star in the top right hand corner.

Halfway down the courtyard in front of the Temple and directly on an east/west axis is a stone altar where animal sacrifice took place. On either side on a north/south axis are two buildings. The one to the South is a two-way arch leading to the hot spring in the reservoir beyond with a roundel on the pediment bearing a head with a spiked crown, which is almost certainly the Sun God, Sol. The other building to the north is a monument known as the Facade of the Four Seasons, which also has a roundel on the pediment depicting the Moon Goddess, Luna.

Having completed the circuit of the whole complex Caroline felt a strong urge to return to the middle of the courtyard in front of the Temple. Enclosing the space of the Temple, the sacred spring and the two buildings depicting the sun and the moon, Caroline asked for the opposites, Sun/Moon, South/North, Warm/Cold, Light/Dark to come together in perfect balance and harmony.

Caroline had always known that her mother and father had met in Bath in the late 1920s and that it had been a fated meeting. Her father, who suffered from gout, had been given an extension of his leave to take the waters at Bath before returning to Burma, and her mother was staying there with her mother because of some quite untoward, but temporary, domestic crisis. Caroline's father had died when she was seven and she had grown up with the story of their meeting, courtship and marriage a few weeks' later, followed by her mother accompanying her father to Burma. It had been love at first sight and their marriage of just twelve years had been supremely happy. They always remained 'in love'. Because of this Caroline embarked on a quest to find out at which hotel they had been staying, her clue being that it possessed quite extensive grounds as the hotel kept their own pigs. The obvious candidate was the Bath Spa Hotel on a hill overlooking the city, which had been recently acquired and refurbished. However, people she talked to told her that it was not possible for it to have been a hotel in the 1920s, as before the recent acquisition, it had been a nurses' home. Then someone advised her to visit the Guildhall and speak to the archivist.

Caroline made her way to the Guildhall and was directed to the basement where she found the archivist talking to someone who called herself 'an aged local'. In fact, it was the 'aged local' and not the archivist who told her that it had been a hotel in the 1920s before becoming a nurses' home. Armed with this knowledge, she was just about to leave the building when the receptionist asked her whether she would like to see the

Banqueting Room on the first floor, which is the finest example of the work of Robert Adam in the country. Caroline replied that she had thought it was only open on Mondays, but he seemed to want her to see it and said that if the cleaner was still there she could just stand at the doorway and look in. However, she was delighted to find she could enter this beautiful room. It was, indeed, magnificent and as she stood in the middle under one of the chandeliers she saw that the two large portraits at the end of the room were of King George III and his consort, Queen Charlotte.

Again the pair of opposites, but, more than that, the royal line of David (through Mary Queen of Scots and the Winter Queen - daughter of James VI) and Cassie's and her ancestors, for we ourselves possess the royal gene. Caroline's maternal grandfather's grandmother was the natural daughter of William IV born of a liaison with the Housekeeper at Windsor Castle, Eliza White. This was after the Duke of Clarence, as he then was, who had separated from his life-long mistress, Mrs. Jordan, and before he married Princess Adelaide, a German princess, in order to produce a legitimate heir. Queen Adelaide was extremely kind to her husband's and Mrs. Jordan's unruly brood and, also, to Caroline's great-great-grandmother. She was raised at Windsor Castle and attended her father's Coronation, before marrying the publisher, Edward Pote Williams, printer and publisher to Eton College and, later, to Queen Victoria. William IV's wedding present to his daughter was a handsome, silver épergne - a centrepiece for a table, which was handed down through the family. Caroline then remembered that Cassie's bridesmaid lived just south of Bath and that on the way she had passed the village where the best man at her wedding lived.

The theme was one of marriage: marriage in the present day as well as through the ages, the generations signifying the uninterrupted royal line harking back to the marriage of Arwen and Aragorn.

Chapter 37

Second Cleansing of the Ring in Water

We pick up the story of the Quest with another cleansing of the One Ring of Power which is still in existence at the etheric level and, since its recent activation, once again emanating an evil energy. This has a direct impact on us here at the physical dimension. In early November 1999 we discovered Sauron's Ring had reformed and so planned a second visit to the lake in Regent's Park for 17 November. The lake is in the shape of a womb within the unmistakable outline of the astrological sign of Cancer the Crab, or the Great Mother, and we had already cleansed it once in its life-giving waters. This time we chose to materialise the Ring at the etheric level in the church of St. Martin's in the Fields in Trafalgar Square.

The National Gallery nearby seemed an ideal place for lunch after our journey from Salisbury and so it was that we learnt of the forthcoming Botticelli exhibition and saw a large reproduction of that strange painting, The Mystic Nativity, where nothing is as it appears and which is discussed in a later book. We had lunch in the café, which we carefully scrutinised for suspicious characters. After challenging the whole room, one young man sitting nearby got to his feet and left in a hurry, which made us feel a great deal safer.

From the National Gallery we crossed the road to St. Martin's where the choir were rehearsing for a mid-day service. For a while we sat in a side stall listening to the beautiful sound of the boy trebles and then quietly asked the Ring to manifest. On re-entering the busy world outside we realised that London was having one of its gridlock days and we had no alternative but to take the underground to Baker Street and, from there, a cab to the Hanover Gate.

On arrival we made our way to the same spot as before. As we approached the water's edge, we saw a squirrel sitting in the willow tree. It waited patiently as Cassie tossed the Ring into the water with the appropriate words and then ran towards us.

Luckily, we had some bread with us and, as it sat tamely nibbling, we noticed behind us a dead, black crow lying on the muddy ground under the trees about twenty feet away. It was frighteningly large as its wings were spread and we both found its presence sinister. We had the uneasy feeling that it might be a response from the Other Side. But we were puzzled as to why it was dead. However, on discussing this later with Robert he said that, this time, we had cleansed the Ring at a higher level and consequently the Other Side were not able to reach us. Hence, the reason for the crow being dead.

As before, we walked back through the Park towards the York Gate alongside the lake with its thronging bird life and, after a stop for our usual hobbit snack, home again. We waited to see if there would be any change in the mood or feelings in the outer world. Two weeks' later at midnight on 1 December the politicians on both sides of the divide in Northern Ireland agreed to sink their differences and the government of the province passed from Westminster to a power-sharing executive at Stormont. Many people will find that making such a connection with our actions hard to believe, even arrogant. But there are just as many who know that intention, strongly focussed such as at a power centre by more than one person, does have an effect. Add to that a weakening of the negative vibrations of the One Ring, and those well-intentioned politicians are given a badly needed break.

Chapter 38

Interaction Between the Worlds

We began to notice that sometimes events in the story of The Lord of the Rings taking place at another level were being brought to our attention in our dimension via the media. It was fascinating to see the interaction between the worlds.

At the end of February 2000 a great deal of fuss was made of the first pet to enter England with a passport. The pet in question was a black pug whose name was Frodo Baggins. The little dog – a fitting size for a hobbit - was welcomed at Dover by a barrage of cameras and reporters vying to interview him and his owner. Even Frodo and Sam's return to the Shire could not have attracted more attention. But there is another significance to the idea of Frodo needing a passport in order to re-enter his homeland. The hobbits were returning to a changed Shire under the tyrannical rule of 'The Boss', otherwise known as Saruman, where 'Rules', translated into our own Age as visas, passports, Customs etc, were making the lives of the jolly hobbits a misery. Tolkien himself believed England to be the Shire, so it is apt that it was to that country which Frodo Baggins the dog wished to gain entry.

On 1 March 2000 came the astonishing event of a pregnant woman, Sophia Pedro, giving birth in a tree. Because of the floods in Mozambique, she had been stranded for three days and the paramedic who came to her rescue found himself assisting at a birth. Mother and baby were then winched to safety to a waiting helicopter and thence to hospital. The baby was named Rositha, or rose, which is sacred to the Queen/Goddess, and the mother's name, Sophia, is the Goddess as the Spirit of Wisdom. The symbolism of this event, which received media coverage on the front pages of the national newspapers for two days, is absolutely clear: the baby born in a tree is telling us that, at another higher level, a child, a daughter of the royal line of Numenor whose symbol is the White Tree, had been born to Arwen and Aragorn. It is also interesting to note that the mother was dark for she and her baby represent the ancient line whose origins go back to the Dark Goddess or dark-haired Queen, Arwen, Evenstar of her people the Elves. It has continued through to the present time with the many images still preserved, carved in black stone or stained wood, of Black Isis with a baby on her lap, always known as the Black Madonna.

In March 2000 there was an article in the Home section of the Sunday paper advertising exotic holidays in tree houses resembling the 'flets', or platforms, where the Elven folk of the magical woods of Lothlorien lived.

Other events in the Story were impressed on the physical domain closer to home. We received a phone call from Judith who takes the role of Pippin, telling us of an extraordinary experience. Whilst driving through the Forest of Dean she heard in her mind someone speaking to her from the branches of a tree and she knew it must be Treebeard, the talking tree and oldest of all living creatures on Middle Earth. It was Pippin and Merry who were discovered by Treebeard when lost and hungry in the Ancient Forest. Walking in misty water meadows in the Woodford Valley by a broad stretch of the river Avon had echoes of the Fellowship's journey down the Anduin on leaving Lothlorien. Another walk in the same misty meadows reminded Cassie of Sam and Frodo's passage through the Dead Marshes guided by Gollum.

The following May in 2001, Cherie Blair, wife of the British prime minister, gave birth to a son. Two days' later we finally realised the full significance of this. In the attention that is given them, the former prime minister and his wife were treated like royalty. Consequently, the birth of their son was given royal treatment with large pictures of the infant being widely featured on the front pages of the nation's newspapers. Indeed, the baby's birth received worldwide coverage and one heading read, 'The world calls No 10 with best wishes'. With the baby being given the name of Leo, that is, the lion, which is the animal anciently associated with kingship, the symbolism of this birth became clear to us. On another level, a baby son had been born to Arwen and Aragorn as well as a daughter, and the Universe was communicating this to us.

Chapter 39

The Wasteland

At the end of Ring Quest I in early 2000 Caroline had taken up residence in the Woodford Valley near Salisbury in the King's Stables beneath the words "Long live the King" on a cupola on the roof. Two weeks' after this, as she drove up to the cottage, she was astonished to see that the large field which bordered it and which was full of thistles and more like wasteland than pasture, had turned a rusty, bloody red. On further inspection she realised it had been sprayed to kill off all vegetation. At the time she only hoped that it would eventually be ploughed up and re-sown and it was only later that she suddenly realised that this was the Wasteland of the wounded Fisher King who, we had discovered and had confirmed from Robert, was none other than the Sacred King.

A suspicion had begun to grow in Cassie's mind when she read the story of The Fisher King in Sir Thomas Malory's Le Morte d'Arthur, which is about the exploits of the Knights of the Round Table at the Court of King Arthur, that this was so. What particularly sounded alarm bells was the connection between the wounding of the King – a wound from which he could not be healed - and the subsequent infertility of the land. Caroline then supplied the information that the so-called wounding of the king's thigh was understood to be a euphemism for castration. As already mentioned, there was an intimate connection between the fertility of the land, and the virility/fertility of the King in the pagan cult of the Sacrifice of the King. And, once again, Robert Graves' research in The White Goddess revealed that the King was indeed castrated at his sacrifice. So, at a private session in Lydney in the summer of 1998 Cassie, impatient to have her suspicions confirmed one way or the other, came straight to the point: "Is the Fisher King the Sacred King?" to which Robert replied simply "Yes". As she asked the question, the sky outside grew dark and a strong wind began to blow. Cassie noticed through the French doors the tall grasses in the garden were being violently blown about. Robert commented that 'They' did not like it as she was getting too close to the truth. It was in the early days of our association with Robert and Cassie was truly frightened to think that some consciousness was out there listening in on their conversation and then showing great displeasure through controlling natural forces. No doubt observing this, Robert nonchalantly waved his hand and said "Oh be quiet" and the wind died down. Robert's calm dismissal reassured her and her fear subsided.

When Cassie was revising this chapter some years later, one of her daughters handed her a copy of the poet T.S. Elliot's strange poem, The Wasteland. For some reason her daughter was insistent she should read it! She had no idea that Cassie was writing on the very subject. The link between the Fisher King and the sacrificial Sacred King was very exciting as it was strong evidence for the existence of this forgotten Cult in Western culture. It shows that the cult of male sacrifice was still a part of our mindset at that time.

The version of the tale most widely used is that of Sir Perceval returning home to his mother having been made a knight. He is offered lodgings for the night in a castle belonging to the Fisher King. His host cannot rise to greet him because of a javelin wound through the thigh, which has rendered him lame. That evening, just before a sumptuous banquet commences, a strange procession takes place. First comes a squire carrying a spear, or lance, dripping blood. Two youths follow bearing candelabra and then a young woman holding the Grail containing a wafer used at Holy Communion. However, a Welsh version of the story called Peredur, substitutes for the wafer a severed head on a platter swimming in blood. In place of a maiden bearing the platter is a yellow-haired youth. Now all is made plain. The yellow-haired youth is the 'New Sun' King, hence the careful description of him being 'yellow-haired', and we have little doubt that his hair would have been short so as to emulate the rays of a 'new' sun. On the platter he bears the head of the recently sacrificed 'Old Sun' King.

The question poses itself, is it possible that these central elements of the cult were retained but with the author having no understanding as to their meaning? We know, after all, that the suppression of the cult when it came, was severe. The significance in the first version of the maiden bearing the platter with the Mass wafer assumes greater meaning. Many of the Arthurian Romances feature damsels mysteriously asking knights for severed heads. We came to the conclusion that these damsels represent the pagan Queen who sacrificed and beheaded Kings. In Lewis Carroll's well-known children's book, Alice in Wonderland, it is the Red Queen who, nightmarishly, keeps shrieking "Off with his (or her) head". Could it be that Lewis Carroll was tapping his subconscious memory?

The people of the pagan cult had been corrupted to such a degree that they believed the King had to die for the land to be made fertile. However, this story suggests the opposite. It suggests that the negative energy that has built up at the site of sacrifice adversely affects our physical world, resulting in less abundant crops, fewer heads of cattle and lower milk production. In other words, the land has been 'laid waste' as the concentrated negativity at the site of sacrifice - a power point on the energy grid - is then carried along the energy lines throughout the land. This raises another question - that a person involved with the composing of this Romance knew about the pagan cult, as well as how the energy system really works.

A few days after moving into the King's Stables, Caroline went for a walk along the river. A public path led down to the water's edge but, then there were notices saying, "No public right of way". This was obviously for the benefit of those who had the fishing rights but, since there were no fishermen around, she chose to ignore the signs, and continued her walk. On the way back, three fishermen, two men and a woman, walking towards her, confronted her. There was something faintly menacing about them and she knew she was about to be 'told off' for trespassing. The tallest of the men took charge, sending the other two off before turning back with her while he explained why it was necessary to keep the public away from the river as their footsteps frightened the fish. It was all very civilised and she agreed not to go there again, at least, during the fishing season.

Again the penny only dropped a few days later. Symbolically, they were keeping the people away from the spiritual nourishment of life-giving water. Anciently, the King is the champion and protector of the people and Caroline, as Aragorn, the rightful King, was being shown this injustice. Further, it would seem that this in some way connected with the Cult of the Sacrifice of the King as the three people - a woman and two men - represented the Queen/Goddess and the Two Kings of the Waxing and Waning Year.

She also remembered the fisherman's final remark after she had said that there seemed to be a path, which the public could use on the other side of the river, and he had replied, 'Yes, I think there is and it will give you the opportunity to cross the bridge'. At the time, she was puzzled by this comment thinking it was a strange thing to say as, after all, she could cross the bridge any time she liked. Afterwards, when she thought about the whole episode, she realised that he had been prompted to say this and it was a sign and a promise that there would be a coming together of the opposites.

Caroline eventually moved in with her furniture in the middle of May, 2000, not long after the time of year that Aragorn entered Minas Tirith to take up his inheritance. Aragorn may have won his kingdom at that other level but the message was that the Land is still infertile because the King is still wounded.

Chapter 40

Final Cleansings of the Ring in Earth, Fire and Air

In April, 2000 the deadlock in Northern Ireland between Sinn Fein and the IRA and the British and Irish Governments remained as insoluble as ever and it seemed as if nothing would ever shift it. We wondered if the One Ring had reconstituted itself and we discovered that it had. At this stage we were still not synchronising with the seasons and so we chose to cleanse the One Ring in the element of air in spring. It should, of course, have been water, which brings new life after winter, in the Air Sign of Gemini, the Twins. We chose Saturday 26 April for the trip to London from Salisbury.

Once again, the power point at the church of St. Martin's in the Fields on Trafalgar Square was our choice to recover the Ring but first, we planned to look around the National Portrait Gallery which had just been refurbished, as well as visit Watkins Bookshop nearby. However, by the time we had visited the NPG and had lunch in the new cafe, we found we were running a little late and, reluctantly, decided to give the bookshop a miss and go straight to St. Martins in the Fields where we manifested the Ring. Then, as we were making our way up Charing Cross Road towards Leicester tube station, we suddenly had a change of mind (something Robert had warned us not to do after our experiences after our visit to Madame Tussaud's). We decided that we would, after all, visit Watkins Bookshop and we turned instead into Cecil Court. As we approached the shop, Caroline later said that her intuition told her that we should continue straight to our destination, but to her subsequent shame and chagrin, she ignored it. Cassie was carrying the Ring on her person and never before had we not gone straight to the place where we were to cleanse it.

At first all seemed serene and we spent some happy moments browsing. It was not until Caroline reached the basement that things took a nasty turn. She had been directed to a corner to look for a certain book, which she needed for research, but found her way blocked by an Indian man who was standing reading. She politely asked him to move, which he did, but it was as she was looking for the book that she noticed a woman sitting a little way away directly opposite her. As Caroline's eye fell on her she lifted her head and gave Caroline what she can only describe as "the look", unmistakable, and terrifying. At the time, this did not have the desired effect but, nevertheless, she realised that she should get away as quickly as possible. However, once again, she found her way blocked by the Indian gentleman. Once again, she politely asked him to move but this time he took no notice. Luckily for Caroline in a way, she still did not realise she was being deliberately hemmed in and was therefore able to say in a louder, cheerful voice, 'Excuse me, I'm afraid I'm going to have to push past you again.' It was only later that evening she realised that they were both from the Other Side. We had been very foolish visiting an enclosed, public place such as a shop with the Ring actually on our person. As at Dragon Hill, we had become careless and we vowed that, in the future, we would be as careful as we had been that first time when we cleansed the Ring in Fire, which now seemed an age ago. Robert subsequently told us that in trying to hem Caroline in, they hoped to flush out Cassie who would most certainly have come to her aid. And it was she who had the Ring in her pocket. If Cassie had come to help Caroline, it would have left her vulnerable from an energy point of view, as her attention would have been solely on helping Caroline, so enabling the One Ring to 'escape'. Fortunately, Cassie was on the floor above and oblivious to Caroline's plight.

Leaving the shop, we made our way to the open green space with the children's playground in Camden between Carol Street and St. Martin's Close without further incident. As we surfaced from the underground we were surprised to find the surrounding pavements filled with young people, something you would expect to find within the youthful sign of Gemini, the Twins. Arriving at the site, we found the place full of black dogs, bounding happily around rather than staring malevolently, as one had done earlier at The White Horse of Uffington.

We walked towards the spot and realised that it was going to be tricky, as a man and woman had just settled down on a rug near the exact place where we wished to cleanse the Ring. We made a quick decision that the best thing to do was to sit on the grass ourselves. After a little while, Cassie got up in as casual a way as possible and wandered up to the thorn tree, which was growing above the low, ruined wall of the chancel. Caroline willed the couple not to look at her and they obligingly became occupied with their picnic while Cassie threw the Ring in the air with the appropriate words.

As we sat sunning ourselves for a while afterwards, we suddenly noticed two adolescent boys sitting on the top of a bench with their backs towards us wearing identical T-shirts. On the back of each shirt was a large 4. This signified both the twins of Gemini and, in numerology, the composite number 44, which means death and destruction, as mentioned earlier. We then noticed a woman on our other side wearing a T-shirt with the words, "Never Give Up" printed on the back, which we found strangely comforting. We concentrated on the impasse in the Northern Ireland peace process and linked up with the twenty worldwide, masculine power points, which have been poisoned by the forces of evil, and visualised the negative energy weakening. Air signs govern ideas, and therefore the ideology of politics, and we prayed and hoped that the politicians involved in the peace process would find a way forward. Six days' later on the evening of Friday, 5th May, the parties involved issued a late night bulletin and on Sunday morning the country was greeted with newspaper headlines signalling the long awaited promise from the IRA that they would place their weapons 'beyond use'.

Once again, in the summer of 2000 we cleansed the Ring for the final time in the fire of the forge in Fetter Lane at the power point within the outline of the Lion.

We had first cleansed the One Ring in the element of Earth on 3 February 2000 when, on a journey using the Underground, which seemed to go on forever, we had endured the company of a menacing young woman dressed all in black and with long black hair who was aggressively chewing gum. She came and sat opposite us in a completely empty carriage. For Caroline, there was no mistaking that she was one of 'Them'. We seem to be part of a curious game where certain rules apply to both Sides. In this game the Other Side are always present whenever we are involved in changing the energies because, as Robert has so often told us, you cannot separate Good from Evil: where one is present, so will the other be. We just need to be aware of them, i.e. be neutral.

A year later, on 12 February 2001, we set off for the second cleansing of the Ring in Earth at the power point at the centre of the Bull's eye called Oseney Crescent i.e. the 'eye' of an 'ox'. The derelict church was still propped up by scaffolding. Nothing untoward occurred but we noted that the next day there was an earthquake in El Salvador. The quake measured 6.2 on the Richter scale. There had been a bigger earthquake In El Salvador a month earlier measuring 7.6 in which more than a thousand people died. Perhaps our timely weakening of the evil energy of the Ring in the element of earth the day before meant that the earthquake was not as powerful as it might have been.

This proved to be the last time we cleansed the Ring at the London sites.

Chapter 41

The Fiery Demon

In early August 2000 Cassie drove down to Devon for a week's holiday with her two daughters and some friends. They had taken a house in the remote Bere Ferrers peninsula on the River Tamar, to the south of the main town of Tavistock. It was a beautiful old house perched on the hillside with a clear view down the river where the lights of Plymouth on the coast could be seen at night. On the terrace below was a small cottage, which was a reminder of the history of this part of the world for, in the garden, the relics of the silver mine at this site could still be seen. The cottage was known as the Counting House as it was where the Chief Mining Engineer had once lived and paid the workforce,and the house itself was called South Hooe Mine. For those who know the story of The Lord of the Rings the word 'mine' might have sounded alarm bells that there was a connection to be drawn with the dreaded Mines of Moria. This had once been the greatest of the Dwarf Kingdoms but, at the time of the events leading to the War of the Ring, it had long been abandoned by the dwarves due to a nameless terror which lived in the depths beneath the Kingdom. However, this big hint completely passed Cassie by.

A year later in August 2001 the same house was booked for a summer holiday, this time for two weeks, and it finally dawned on Cassie that there was a reason for her returning to the same place. It was only when she recalled that South Hooe was at the site of a silver mine that the remains of the mining shaft in the garden took on a new meaning! In fact the only really serious silver mining in England until the late 16th century had taken place in the Bere Ferrers peninsula where South Hooe Mine was situated. And the fact that it was silver ore that was mined, as opposed to copper or tin, was highly significant because it was only in the mines of Moria that the rare and highly prized silver ore known as 'mithril', was to be found.

There was yet one further staggering comparison. In their search for mithril the dwarves had dug too deep and awakened an evil creature from the Ancient World– a fiery demon known by the Elves as a 'Balrog'. Likewise, the history of the silver mining activity in the area says: 'Unlike contemporary activity in other non-ferrous mining fields, these were deep shaft mines working a rich but restricted resource.' Some of the shafts went ever deeper, even extending under the river-bed of the River Tamar until a shaft collapsed and the tunnels were flooded and mining had to be abandoned. This was exactly what happened to the deep mines of Moria and were abandoned for identical reasons. However, their delvings had also awoken an awesome terror of the deep. Did this mean there was a fiery demon to be confronted at South Hooe Mine?

The day before Cassie was to drive to Devon, we attended a talk given by Robert in the Wye valley. Afterwards, we had booked a short appointment, as it was a rare opportunity to discuss the Quest. Robert confirmed everything, adding that the fiery demon was twice as big as last year when Cassie was supposed to have dealt with him. She was terrified to learn this and her mind fairly spun in panic with the prospect of confronting this truly terrifying creature. Then Robert gave her a most helpful clue. He was silent for a moment. In retrospect, it occurs to Cassie that he was tuning into the Balrog, for he then burst out with the most surprising words said with real feeling: "Don't quench his flames". Cassie was completely taken aback by the compassion in his voice. Later, the inference of those words sank in: somehow, in some way as yet to be worked out, she would be a match for the Balrog. This was a relief and an encouragement.

You might ask, but why wasn't Robert in his role as Gandalf, the one to have the encounter with the demon, as in Tolkien's tale? It is a very good question to which we do not know the answer. At a guess, we suggest that Robert is very busy doing many things and this was something we were able to tackle ourselves. In the original tale, as the demon falls into the abyss, he drags the unfortunate wizard down with him with his whip. Gandalf has to hang on to his adversary for dear life through the deepest and darkest reaches of the earth, far beneath the tunnelling of the dwarves, for he dare not let go of the creature for fear of never finding his way out. The final stages of the battle take place on the very pinnacle of the mountain and there, finally, Gandalf destroys the demon. It is now apparent that this was not the end for, just as with some ghosts, the Balrog chose not to leave the earth but has ever sought the deep dark places to hide away from the light.

We worked out that the reason the Balrog had grown so huge was because he felt threatened, and the reason for this was due to the clearing of negative energy in the vicinity. The fiery demon would have felt the absence of its energy source and been on its guard. During her stay the previous summer Cassie had become aware that the house was built on an energy centre which had become polluted by the widespread Cult of the sacrifice of the King. Indeed, the presence of the Balrog nearby was confirmation of the proximity of a polluted energy centre to which the creature would naturally have been attracted. The abandoned tunnels of the silver mine provided a refuge from the light.

Feeling completely at a loss as to how to confront the Balrog, Cassie realised that the only way was her tried and tested method, which she had accidentally discovered in the early days of our clearing work in and around Northampton. It is commonly called 'remote viewing', the only difference being that Cassie can see at the etheric or astral levels. In turn, she can be seen by the person and even carry on a mental conversation with them. She was also able to tackle her fear when she remembered something she had recently read in the book series, The Mallorean by David Eddings. When the two forces of Good and Evil meet in combat, the hero grows to match the enormous dimensions of his opponent. At Cassie's meeting with the fiery demon, there was nothing preventing her from matching his size.

She also realised that her job was not to destroy the fiery demon but to release him from his self-imposed imprisonment and exile. The tricky task was to do it in such a way that would keep his dignity intact, for such beings are invariably proud. She decided a good plan was to go as a messenger so that her position would be neutral. Then it would be up to him whether

146

he wished to heed the message or not. It is worth noting that when doing this work, Cassie feels at one remove and is therefore unaffected by what she sees, and feels no fear. All that was left to do was to devise the message.

The moment had come to project herself to the underground place where the Balrog lived. When the children were in bed and she was ready for bed herself she went in search of him down the mineshaft. And then she saw him. He was completely black, of enormous physical power with immense shoulders and huge chest. There were black orange-rimmed flames about him. Cassie looked at herself and noted she was of the same height as the Balrog and clothed in a plain white robe. Immediately, she could tell he had lashed out at her with a whip, which of course had no effect. She told him that she had been sent as a messenger and would he hear what she had to say. Her manner was steely so as to command respect. She told him that he could not harm her as she was just a projection of her true self.

The gist of what she told him was that a new dispensation was coming and that there was one who walked the earth teaching that the Opposites are but two halves of a Whole. He and she were the same except he had chosen one path and she another. At this point Cassie was given a close-up of the Balrog's very small eyes and those eyes were sad and lonely. No wonder Robert hadn't wanted her to quench his flames! This made Cassie change tack and she went on to say that we had all fallen and that she, too, was without her twin self. She hoped that the idea of a twin, with whom he might be reunited, would act as a spur to leaving his hell. She continued that he would not be allowed to remain on this planet but would be sent to another dark place or, he could return to the Father Mother God. The choice was his. (Whether or not this was true, Cassie did not know, but she thought it sounded good). She said that 'They' longed for his return and would hear him if he called to them, which was all he had to do. Cassie then remembered her role as messenger and thought to ask him if he wished to say anything in return. He thanked her for her message and she bowed and left. On the whole, she thought things had gone rather well and hoped that she had succeeded.

The next day it began to rain heavily and there was a strong wind. It occurred to Cassie that she ought to clear the deep shafts of the mine where the Balrog had lived so long. The instant she finished, the wind dropped, the rain stopped and the sun came out. A few hours later she caught sight of a small section of a rainbow in the sky which then vanished before her eyes. Perhaps changing the energy in the mineshaft helped the Balrog with his inner struggle. Somehow she knew that the rainbow she briefly saw represented his spirit leaving the earth. As Robert later put it, she had helped him to release himself. That night a firework display in distant Plymouth could be seen from the magnificent vantage point of the terrace. Surely this was a sign of celebration at the victory over the 'Self', which the Balrog had achieved and of his return home. Fireworks are particularly associated with Gandalf – he was fond of producing fireworks for Hobbit parties in the Shire – so we felt sure we were being shown that Gandalf was also celebrating, and with good reason. The long drawn out fight with the creature had been terrible and, although he had been the victor, it had cost Gandalf his life.

Chapter 42

The New Jerusalem

Towards the end of summer in 2000 our quest took a new turn based on remarks made by Robert at the very outset of the journey in 1998. He had told us that the story of THE LORD OF THE RINGS was a true one and he said somewhat cryptically that Humanity must "return the way it came". He asked us what life had been like then. Eventually, we came up with the idea that life had been at the 'etheric level' where our bodies were less densely physical and, doubtless, less prone to disease. We need to return to this higher vibration. Legends the world over – the Indian mythological cycle of the Mahabharata, the Celtic-Irish Cycle, as well as Greek mythology – chart Humanity's fall down the energy levels. These legends all state that we began with a Golden Age where there was neither disease nor death. There followed the Silver, the Bronze, a Fourth Age called the 'Age of Heroes' and, finally, the Fifth and last Age called the 'Iron' or 'Black' Age.[16] We are now at the end of the Black Age and the only way forward, so to speak, is back the way we came.

How were we to draw down the higher energy of the fourth dimension to the dense material level to which we have fallen? Our first attempt failed because we were unaware of the scientific principles involved. Put simply, how does a higher vibration enter a world or dimension where the energy is vibrating at a lower frequency?

Our second attempt also failed and it was only at the third try that we eventually succeeded. An account of this first effort, culminating at Buckfast Abbey in Devon, can be found in the appendix. As can be imagined, when Robert told us at our next meet that we had failed at the Spring equinox of 2001 to draw the higher energy into our world, we felt deflated and confused. Apparently, the energy had 'bounced off the energy grid'. So why had we gone to such time and trouble in setting up the event? With the benefit of hindsight, and picking up clues from remarks Robert has made over the years, we have come to the realisation that Robert himself does not always know if an idea will work. He says he aims to be creative and this, combined with the fact that he has an empty mind and is given information only on a need-to-know basis, ensures that his work is never dull or routine. Moreover, he is also constantly learning himself, for nothing ever stands still or is repeated. Alternatively, it could be that we failed to work something out for ourselves and, as he has so often said, he is not able to let us know.

Never one to dwell on the past, he immediately began another attempt to bring in the higher energy mentioning, somewhat cryptically, that we would be working separately, as we would need to be in different places. We would be using two crystals – the same one which Cassie had used to unlock the gates at the three sites making up the Yod or 'Finger of God' - and one that Caroline would find. Simultaneously, we would be unlocking opposing gates.

At the same meeting the subject of the New Jerusalem of the Bible came up as Caroline mentioned that she had recently had several instances of synchronicity concerning William Blake and his poem, "Jerusalem", in which he prophesises that the New Jerusalem will be the British Isles, also known as the White Isles or Albion. She had gone on one of her usual walks and decided to look round the churchyard of the village church. The first gravestone she looked at had the name "William Blake" inscribed on it. A few days' later there was an even stranger synchronicity. She was looking up 'Jerusalem' in a Treasury of English verse and was astonished to find that it came from a book of Blake's poems entitled Milton. Later still, on 9 August, 2000 there was an item in all the newspapers about a couple who were marrying in church and wished to have "Jerusalem" included in the hymns sung at the marriage service. However, they were told by the vicar that he couldn't allow it, as it was too "nationalistic". In the following days this provoked a positive storm of controversy in the press, the debate moving to the question as to what William Blake actually meant by the notion of "building Jerusalem" in "England's green and pleasant land". One broadsheet actually printed in colour Blake's painting, Jerusalem, The Emanation of the Giant Albion.

'Where is the exact place you think the New Jerusalem will be located?' Robert asked. Thanks to William Blake's poem, we knew it would be in the former industrial heartland of England. He also dropped a heavy hint by saying that our idea of the New Jerusalem was 'primitive'! Doubtless he was alluding to the concept we had in our minds having just read the description of the New Jerusalem as given in Revelations in The Bible. The Golden City descends to earth from on-high:

> 'And the city had no need of the sun, neither of the moon, to shine in it: ...And there shall be no night there; and they need no candle, neither light of the sun; for the Lord God giveth them light: and they shall reign for ever and ever.'

This much we understood: it was describing life at the fourth dimension where the opposites have been reunited and the physical body no longer decays. Robert's remark made us realise that it was much more scientific and esoteric than the notion of a golden city gently descending to Earth.

In order to actually enter our reality, the higher energy first has to divide in two. This is because our illusory world is made up of opposites – light and dark, male and female and Good and Evil. By creating opposing entrances we could see it would result in the energy being pulled through by the Law of Attraction of the Opposites. You only have to think of the irresistible pull between two magnets of opposite poles. The energy would then meet at the halfway point and merge again. Immediately, we understood how much more scientifically effective this would be.

There were to be two pairs of opposing gateways and Robert gave us some clues as to the location of three of the sites – in the Wash in Norfolk, a place near Leeds and somewhere in the south. He gave us quite a lot of factual details about the latter, i.e. that it would be not far from Oxford, on a hill near a mausoleum and surrounded by two rings of trees. He said that

151

"They" (the Other Side) would scatter "crumbs" to lead us astray, which, in due course, they did.

A few weeks after this we decided to visit Glastonbury with the express purpose of finding Caroline's key. We wandered through the bookshops and shops selling crystals in particular, of which there were many. In one of them there was a lucky dip and, thinking that this might be how Caroline would find her crystal key, she dipped her hand into the bran and came up with a small package. Inside there were several pretty pieces of crystal and a small fossil. None of them looked anything like a key.

It was only when we had a chance to really study the crystals, all of which were quite small, that we were drawn by the fact that one crystal consisted of a larger, darkish-coloured piece, attached to a small, translucent piece, symbolising the opposites becoming one. Then we both knew that, despite its smallness, this was the key. The following day Caroline read in a book by Linda Goodman that the keys of the kingdom are 'very small' and the day after that she saw in one of the Sunday papers the statement that Prince Charles, in acquiring the Queen's Keeper of the Privy Purse, had acquired 'the keys of the kingdom'.

Chapter 43

A Diamond and Two Pyramids

As soon as we were able, we got together to think over all that had been discussed. We realised that the opposing points formed a cross which, when linked together, made the shape of a diamond. It was then that the significance of our two 'keys' occurred to us. They were the 'Cross Keys', the image of which can be seen in pub signs around the country. There is a 'Cross Keys' shopping arcade in Salisbury where we are living at present. Perhaps, the subliminal meaning of this potent symbol is to remind humanity that the keys to the Kingdom of Heaven are within reach and that 'heaven' is the higher vibration of the Fourth Dimension brought to earth. As John Lennon put it so well in his song 'Imagine' below:

Imagine there's no heaven
It's easy if you try
No hell below us
Above us only sky

The diamond is nothing less than two pyramids, the lower one reversed. In fact, it is exactly like the Great Pyramid of Giza, which, according to the age -old Wisdom, has another pyramid, reversed, beneath it.[17] It has been revealed that the Great Pyramid was never intended to be a tomb but was used in the rites of initiation into the higher dimension which is why the tomb in the King's Chamber is empty. When the seer Edgar Cayce was asked the meaning of the empty sarcophagus he replied that it is to show humanity that there will be no more death.

We immediately started casting around for a likely site at the southern point of the diamond as we had been given the most clues as to its location. One of them was the name of a character called Wren in the book Duncton Found, by Michael Horwood. Cassie had recently read the series at Robert's suggestion as he said it was another story that had been 'inspired' and which cast light on Man's lost past. To her relief she quickly found the place in the book where, just as Robert had suggested, the character called 'Wren' mentions 'Buckland'. Looking at a map there was indeed a village of that name and, once again Robert was right for it was twenty miles to the south-west of Oxford. There is also a connection with Tolkien's trilogy for one of the hobbits in the Fellowship came from Buckland in The Shire[18].

Looking in the vicinity of Leeds for the northernmost point we spotted a town called Calverley on the outskirts of Bradford, which immediately made us think of Calvary where Jesus was crucified outside the walled City of Jerusalem. We felt this had to be the place. Quickly putting it to the test, we drew a north/south line and found that it ran through the village of Buckland! We then looked for a likely place near the Wash and felt fairly stunned when we found a village called Walpole Cross Keys – we had recently had a lot of synchronicities to do with 'Cross Keys'. There are two other villages nearby, Walpole St. Peter and Walpole St. Andrew. St. Peter is, of course, the keeper of the keys of the Kingdom of Heaven, and St. Andrew is always depicted holding the cross on which he was crucified. So the words "cross" and "keys" are shown in different ways.

Drawing another line due west the same distance as that between Buckland and Calverley, we came across two places very close to lake Vyrnwy in Wales. But these turned out to be the 'crumbs' Robert had mentioned. One was "Four Crosses" and the other was "Tycrwyn" which we interpreted as "Three Crowns". These both seemed a big clue and we felt that either one of them could be the western point. The "Three Crowns" brought to mind the pagan Queen and the Great Triple Goddess -hence the three crowns and we thought the four crosses alluded to the four points of the diamond.

However, when we mentioned these names to Robert he said that neither was correct. We were taken aback, so sure had we been that either one had to be the site. Obviously, "they" thought this would certainly divert us and, depending on how we measured the distances, we would be sure to pick up on one of those names. We were completely stumped as there was no other possible place in the vicinity. Eventually Robert gave us the name Cadair Idris. On looking it up on the map we discovered it was the name given to a large mountainous area on the western coast of Wales and considerably due West of the "crumbs". What surprised and baffled us was that it was much further to the west than we had been looking which meant that the diamond was not equal-sided as we had assumed.

Now, we only needed to find the energy site on the Western side. At first we were rather daunted at having to locate it in the large expanse of territory called Cadair Idris. Then we realised that it would be easier than we thought. The place of power was very likely to be a hill fort or, a former hill fort on which a castle had later been built. Sure enough this was the case and, better still, there is only one such place in the whole area! It is called Castell y Bere and we were in no doubt that this was the western tip of the diamond. We had found all four points of the Fibonacci diamond. There was now nothing to prevent us from opening the opposing sets of gates.

It was only some years later that we solved the mystery of the strangely shaped diamond. We came across an identical diamond based on something called the Fibonacci spiral whose numerical sequence directly relates to the natural world. In the physical world there has to be a pattern which reflects a definite 'beginning' and 'ending' based on the physical cycle of 'birth' and 'death'. The perfect diamond shape is created by the numerical sequence of The Golden Mean based on Infinity. At the fourth dimension there is no decay and death and therefore no need of the life cycle of birth, decay and death. The lopsided diamond was made up of two mirroring Fibonacci spirals with the uppermost spiral described as 'female' and the one below as 'male'. In other words, it was bringing together the Opposites. So that was the significance for creating the lopsided diamond! Cassie then remembered the diamond stamp on her crystal. Examining the crystal again more closely, she could now see, quite clearly, that one of the points was longer. Who would have thought that there could be such accuracy on a battered, yellowed piece of crystal! Somehow we felt humbled. It also showed the need for closer attention to detail which might have meant we would not have been led astray.

As for the Cross Keys, if you take the letter 'K' for 'Key' and make a mirror or shadow image, all is revealed, for a diamond is created, set within a gateway or entrance! The pair of keys represents two halves of the whole. It is the recurrent theme of opposites uniting so as to be able to enter the Kingdom of Heaven/Higher Dimension.

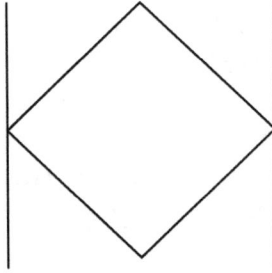

Chapter 44

Opening the Pairs of Opposing Gates

It wasn't until Saturday 5 October 2001, that we were able to set off in opposite directions to the east and west tips of the Fibonacci diamond we had mapped out over the country. Cassie stayed with a friend who happened to live in the town of Barmouth on the Welsh coast just north of the Cadair Idris massif. It had been arranged that we would synchronise the opening of the gateways at noon on the Sunday.

The sun was shining as she set out and there was no wind. It was a stunningly beautiful drive across the estuary and into the mountains. As she drew near her destination, the road became ever steeper and more winding. Finally, she rounded a corner and there below lay a beautiful, unspoilt valley. In the middle of the valley was a rocky outcrop where the ruins of an extensive castle could be seen. She knew immediately that this was the site. Even in that wild place there was a small car park for visitors to the historic ruins as the castle was looked after by one of the heritage charities. As Cassie explored the castle she wondered where best to position herself to open the West Gate. She wanted some privacy as she had noticed a pair of visitors coming up behind her. Finally she settled on a small room, open to the elements but with high walls so that she was not easily visible. It was also at the far end of the castle entrance.

At 11.45 she stood facing east and thought of Caroline doing the same on the other side of the country near The Wash. She took the crystal key out of her pocket in readiness. However, with some minutes yet to go till noon, she heard a voice in her head saying "Do it now". But she hesitated. 'Whose voice was it and could it be trusted? were the thoughts which ran through her head. As she hesitated, time seemed to pass very slowly. Then, after what must have only been seconds, she thought she would just go for it, whatever the consequences. She thrust the key into the invisible lock in mid-air.

Immediately, a most bizarre image came into her head. She saw a heavy, solid white marble door and doorframe with the door not quite fully open. Two strong men clothed in long white robes – rather like muscular angels – were using all their strength to open the door fully. They succeeded and she saw energy coming in and turning at right angles to go sweeping through the door. Such had been the consequences of her hesitation. The energy was being pulled in by the law of attraction of the Opposites, like magnets, as the energy swept through the opposing gateway and they would meet and merge at the centre of the diamond.

Later, we realised why Cassie had to open her Gates some minutes before Caroline. We needed to take into account the difference in longitude of our locations and therefore the time difference. The precision of the whole exercise was extraordinary and, again, somehow humbling. It was a sober reminder that the quest was not a game but a serious undertaking that was in deadly earnest. As Gandalf angrily says to Pippin in the Mines of Moria when Pippin threw a stone down one of the wells to see how long it would take to reach the bottom: "Fool of a Took! This is a serious journey, not a hobbit walking-party…"

Caroline's experiences were not nearly so dramatic! Motoring between the two villages of Walpole St. Andrew and Walpole St. Peter, she decided to trust her intuition to tell her when she had arrived at the right spot. Passing a farm (old farm houses are often built on ancient power points) and then a field beyond, she decided to stop and explore. From the middle of the field there was a view of two tall towers which reminded her of the twin towers in The Lord of the Rings, which confirmed that this was the right place. It was not yet noon, the time at which she and Cassie would, simultaneously, unlock the gates in the West and the East, and so she sat on the grass in the sunlight watching the bees flying from flower to flower, gathering nectar. Everything was very peaceful with no sound but the twittering of birds in the nearby trees and the buzzing of the bees. Time seemed to stand still. Suddenly, she realised that it was one minute to noon. Holding her crystal key, she waited a moment and then turned it in the lock and opened the gateway in the East.

A few months later, at the end of December 2001, the opportunity presented itself for the opening of the north and south points of the Fibonacci diamond. We were spending a family Christmas in the north which was within a day's return journey by car to Calverley at the northern tip of the diamond. Caroline was to return south earlier than Cassie which meant that she could be in position at Buckland at the southern point, whilst Cassie could be in the north.

Two days after Christmas Day Cassie set off for Calverley, whilst Caroline drove to Buckland. Cassie had yet to find the exact location and in this she was to be helped by the landscape providing the major clue. We already knew that the place name was connected to 'Calvary' where Jesus was crucified. Following the road signs to Calverley she turned off the main roundabout and found herself driving up a steep hill. Then she remembered that it was on a hill called Mount Golgotha - which means 'the place of the skull' - where Jesus was crucified. There was also a pub at its foot called The Olive Tree, which was another connection to the Holy Land. Cassie felt hopeful that she was drawing near to the energy site which had for so long been controlled by an evil ring of power.

As she drove up the hill there was woodland and a hotel called Elmwood Hotel, which also somehow seemed significant as it brought to mind the tall, immortal Wood Elves in Tolkien's trilogy. At the top of the hill Cassie found herself driving west along the crest of the hill with a large field on the south side and a golf course on the other. To the south were magnificent views across a steep valley to hills beyond. As she could see a built-up area ahead, Cassie had little doubt that it was here, in the open, where she would find the right place. She spotted a rough, stony dirt track bordering the west side of the field and quickly turned into it. Its name was Priesthorpe Road, which struck another chord. The Christian Church was founded on the life and teachings of Jesus Christ. But it was also the Jewish priesthood who engineered Jesus' supposed death at Calvary.

She was able to park the car in the road as it seemed to be used mainly by walkers. By now she had decided the place where she would open the gateway should be in the field where she could look south. As we were on the same longitude, there was no need to take into account any time-difference. With five minutes to go, Cassie scrambled over the gate in full view of the main road and walked towards the centre of the field. There were six horses quietly grazing who, fortunately, ignored her. She drew out the crystal and stated her intention of opening the gate simultaneously with Caroline in the south. As she did so, she was aware of the horses starting to converge on her as they doubtless thought the crystal was a sugar lump! She then plunged the crystal key into seeming mid-air. In reality, at that other dimension - so close to ours - a keyhole in a door had aligned itself with my intentions. By this time the horses were nearly upon her and a number were behaving aggressively to each other. Putting away the crystal, she walked briskly back to the gate.

As she set off for home along the main road, she noticed a large sign in the northeast corner of the field. Written in large letters, were the words Crossfield Farm which confirmed the Calvary theme of the crucifixion. It also confirmed that she had been in exactly the right place.

Having already visited Buckland earlier to find the location, for Caroline it was just a matter of getting there on time. As it happened, the journey took longer than she had expected and she had to walk rather quickly through the field and up the slight incline in order to turn the crystal key in the lock at exactly the right moment, i.e., noon when the sun is at its most powerful, in order to synchronise with Cassie in the north. This she did and, on returning to home, looked forward to hearing Cassie's experience.

Chapter 45

The Ring Dances Over the Hills

In April 2001 Robert spoke to us of the need to cleanse the Ring in a new place, as the Other Side were now familiar with our movements. We immediately thought of Glastonbury where there is a similar Zodiac to that in London, laid out in the landscape surrounding the Tor. Robert said the Ring would be dancing over the hills with the maidens – whatever that meant – around Glastonbury and we would have to try and catch it! We have to admit that we found this idea dismaying. When we saw him at a later date, he said that we might even be able to catch it as it flew - glided? - past us in our own homes. Mistakenly, for some reason, we presumed that it would be in physical form. Nor did we analyse these hints. We were still hung up on the idea of the need to continue cleansing the Ring.

What he was trying to make us understand was that the Ring was sufficiently cleansed to be free from the call of The Dark Lord. It was therefore free to move at will. But we later realised that this was not entirely accurate either. What occurred was that when the Ring was sufficiently purified it attracted beneficent spirits and it seems that it was they who were giving the Ring its flighty qualities! One was a hobbit energy, which is no surprise as it was two hobbits who were the original bearers of the Ring. These guardians wished us to use the power of the Ring for Good which was why they brought the Ring to Cassie's house. So why had Robert told us that we needed to purify The Ring at a new place? We do not have the answer. Perhaps it was to throw the Other Side off balance. An interesting point to mention is that Robert once told us we might be able to purify the energy of the Ring, but we could never completely rid it of the mark of its maker, Sauron. This has to do with the alchemical process used in its making.

Fortunately, at the time we were so perplexed by this new turn of events that we did not take any action on finding new sites before we spoke on the subject again in December 2001. On this occasion we were told that the Ring was 'hopping about' from place to place and he again talked about having to 'catch it'. At the moment, he told us, The Ring was at Gypsy Hill in South London but that on the 17th December it would be in Cassie's house in physical form. On the day, we searched the house high and low but failed to locate the Ring. Robert told us that it had manifested in the house, on the floor, and had followed us from room to room. He told us that we would be given another chance fairly soon, but that this time we would have to call the Ring to us and for that we would need help.

In the meantime, we could recall the three Elven Rings, Narya, Vilya and Nenya, from Ground Zero, the site of the fallen twin towers of the World Trade Centre in New York, where they were helping those who had passed over in such a violent manner. We could use them to spread light, harmony and peace throughout a troubled world. The war in Afghanistan was at its height and the violence in Israel and the Occupied Territories was escalating. This we did, but still felt disappointed that we had failed to find the Ring when it had been so near. However, two days' later, while watching the trailers on a family visit to the opening of the film, The Lord of the Rings, a voice boomed out, "You will have a second chance to save the world". Because of our recent disappointment those words rang out when we heard them and we felt it meant that we would have another opportunity to use the Ring of Power to help the world.

Christmas was now a few days away and it wasn't until the 30th December 2001 that we got in touch with Robert again about finding The Ring. He gave us the information which he, in turn, was given, which was in the form of a riddle: we were to think about the connection between Mary, Queen of Scots, the Minoans and Bowood House. Mary, Queen of Scots, we knew, represented the continuation of the Royal Line of Numenor/David. We looked at various books and discovered that at Mary's death she had given various personal possessions to her ladies-in-waiting. A book in Cassie's possession on historic houses fortunately listed Bowood House which revealed that it was located in north Wiltshire - not far from

Salisbury – and mentioned that there were many fine collections of jewellery and miniatures.

Suddenly we understood. One of the few heirlooms of the House of Isildur of the Numenorean Royal Line was the Ring of Barahir – most definitely an item of jewellery. This precious Ring Tolkien tells us, has its origins in the Blessed Land of the Gods before it was taken to Middle Earth and was, therefore, a Ring of great power. It had passed down the Royal Line from the very beginning of that Line and was the only possible candidate for the heirloom, which Robert mentioned. On their betrothal, Aragorn gave the Ring of Barahir to Arwen. Its design was of twin serpents, whose eyes were emeralds, and whose heads met beneath a crown of golden flowers, which the one snake supported and the other devoured.[19] We also surmised that it is not impossible that such an heirloom had passed to the Minoan Royal House and, eventually, to Mary Queen of Scots herself, ending up at Bowood House. This was the answer to the riddle and it was only a short step to understanding that we could use the Ring of Barahir to lend us its power in order to draw to us the One Ring. Robert confirmed that this was so.

It was certainly difficult to digest the idea that an heirloom of such antiquity could still be present in our world. Robert had told us that the events narrated in The Lord of the Rings had taken place around 60,000 years' ago, since when the Earth had turned on its axis placing the Poles at the Equator. It is a fact that tropical flora have been found beneath the ice in Antarctica. Could it really be possible for an object as small as a ring to survive these changes when all other signs of this ancient civilisation, and most of those that followed it, had been wiped out?

We realised we should think more in terms of the 'spirit' of the object continuing to exist even after the physical object has been lost. When a similar item, such as a sword or ring, is made in a later Age embodying the same idea, then the energy or spirit of the original will be drawn to that object. In the ancient world, and as recently as the time of King Arthur, the idea that a beautifully crafted piece of work might have magical power was still understood, hence the importance in the Arthurian tales attached to King Arthur's sword, Excalibur. Such logic could also be applied to the Ring of Barahir whose fate became inextricably linked with that of the Royal Line.

Chapter 46

Heirloom of the Royal House

A cold day with a watery sun in early January 2002 found us standing as close as possible to Bowood House. Officially, the House was closed for the winter and would not reopen until April. However, we felt we could not wait that long. We felt that if we were within a sufficiently close radius of the House, we might still call on the aid of Ring of Barahir to draw the One Ring to us.

The big house was nowhere to be seen from the gates and there were various notices saying that both the house and grounds were closed to the public for the winter. We had to steel ourselves to walk up the long, winding drive to the big house feeling that we were trespassing and might be seen and questioned at any moment. Robert had warned us that we would be under attack and that we were to be aware of anything untoward and, at one stage, when Caroline had gone ahead, she heard heavy, thumping footsteps of someone running in the shrubbery on her left. Deliberately crossing over to the other side of the road, she let whatever it was know that she had noticed. No one appeared and eventually the footsteps ceased.

Eventually, after about a mile, we saw the house. A flag was flying from the roof and it was at once apparent that the family were at home. This put paid to standing in front of it, which Robert had told us would be the best place. However, there was a stretch of grass to the side with a field of sheep on our right and views of undulating countryside beyond. Here we could still see the house and, standing together, we asked the Ring of Barahir to lend us its power in calling the One Ring. Cassie dowsed that the Ring was present and it popped into our heads that all we needed to do is speak to it and, as with any such object of power, ask it to do our bidding. We asked that at this critical time for the planet it send out its Power for Good into the World to help bring equilibrium wherever it was needed. We also thought to ask it to protect the Ring of Barahir as its whereabouts was now known to the Other Side. Lastly, we gave the Ring our thanks.

Just as we finished saying these words we noticed two sheep, one with a black head and one with a white head, butting each other with equal force. We understood that it was a sign that the forces of Light and Darkness were now, at last, evenly matched. We remembered that some years ago Robert had told us that this was what he hoped to achieve. In the instant the cleansed power of the One Ring went out over the World, that balance between the opposing energies was achieved.

On the return journey home, we noticed the number plates of two cars which were in front of us for long periods. One was YAM, the Y representing the two-in-one of the Godhead, the 'I AM'. The other, WAM, confirmed our idea that the battle between Light and Darkness was now fully enjoined, with equal power.

As we were editing this chapter some years after the events, we had a synchronicity concerning the Minoans which seemed to indicate that, the blood of the Line of Numenor has, indeed, come down through the Minoan Royal Line. One of Cassie's daughters had recently asked her if they still had the video of the film Labyrinth which she remembered from her childhood. She wanted to watch it again. Just as we were writing this very chapter Cassie caught sight of a copy in a charity shop and bought it. The Minoan culture is famous for the story of the Labyrinth and the Minotaur, a bull-headed monster.

Some years after the events in this chapter, Cassie researched the story of Brutus, Prince of Troy. In a book called Prehistoric London: Its Mounds and Circles by E.O. Gordon, the author refers to the belief held by the Trojans that they originally came from the island of Crete which was the home of the Minoans. So, it appears that the thread of the Royal Line runs via the Minoans, through the Trojan Royal Family, and hence to England with the coming of Brutus, Prince of Troy.

We waited for Bowood House to open again in the spring of 2002 as we were curious to see if we could find the likeness of the Ring of Barahir. It was still the school Easter holidays and the car park in the grounds of Bowood House was full of families picnicking beneath the trees in the sunshine. The frost, snow and sleet of the previous week had miraculously changed to temperatures in the seventies and eighties. We decided to have our picnic first and them make our way to the House. Once there, we forced ourselves to go round the house in the right order and not make a dash for the Room which contained the small collections. We admired the large Orangery and the beautiful views of the ornamental gardens and fountains. Finally, we went upstairs to the exhibition rooms, which housed the collections. These had been acquired by various members of the family from around the world, particularly India during the time of The Raj, and were fascinating but we began to feel, as we walked from room to room, that we were not going to recognise the 'Ring of Barahir' in its new guise.

Suddenly, we came across a display of many double, miniature portraits of Kings and Queens, and there, in the centre, was a small, painted miniature of Queen Victoria. What caught our breath was the frame, which was of gold, less than two centimetres in diameter made from two, entwined snakes. Then we noticed that the young Queen, who was crowned, wore a delicate string of emeralds round her neck. We knew this was the piece of jewellery that embodied the spirit of the Ring of Barahir. Here were the two snakes, their emerald eyes now emulated by the emerald necklace. The Queen herself represents the Royal Line. It would suggest that the Ring of Barahir came to be seen as the symbol of the Royal bloodline running through the Feminine and, indeed, in Tolkien's tale we know that it came into the possession of Queen Arwen. The marriage of Aragorn and Arwen saw the coming together of two branches of the royal line so that the royal stock was replenished for the start of a New Age. It was also held that the royal line came down through the female line as it is called 'the Line of Luthien'.

Both Luthien and Arwen were dark-haired and we find this theme echoed in Laurence Gardner's book, Genesis of the Grail Kings. The Sumerian Gods, known as the Annunaki, created a royal line whose qualities were superior to those of ordinary men, which reminds us of Aragorn's superior gifts and longer lifespan compared with that of other men. However, what caught our attention was that the Keeper of the Malkhut - which means Kingship – was Eresh-kigal, the Dark Goddess or Queen of the Underworld. This seemed to connect directly with Luthien, the dark-haired Elven Princess, who founded the Royal Line. It seemed to be a link with that remote past and was proof of the ancient prophecy that the Line of Luthien will never die out.

Chapter 47

The Centre of the Diamond

We had successfully opened the opposite pairs of Gates (if only by a squeak!) at the West/East Gates. The next step was to find the exact centre where the energies converged. After a false start, we knew we had found it: Castle Gresley. The clue was in the word 'Gresley' for 'gris' is French for 'grey' which represents the blending of the opposites of black and white, and 'ley' reveals the site to be on an energy line. Curiously, 'Gresley' is also a Milton family name.[20]

That the place name contains the word 'castle' is highly significant. Some years ago Caroline read Carl Jung's Memories, Dreams, Reflections. Through mandala drawings and dreams, Jung comes to the realisation that the goal of psychic development is the Self, and that everything points to the centre, which he calls the golden castle. As with all quests - and it was the same for Frodo and company - the journey is also an inner one. Caroline then experienced a series of extraordinary synchronicities spread over the next seven days, all connected with castles. She even ended up in a castle of sorts - a meditation class in the tower of St. James's church, a stone's throw from London's heart, the statue of Eros in Piccadilly Circus. A rather telling point is that she never went there again.

Castle Gresley was the place where we could anchor the fourth dimension - but how? Robert had told us to be careful about approaching it, as we could go up in flames! Whether or not he meant this literally we are not absolutely certain, but, since being toast didn't sound a bundle of fun, we decided to treat the place with great caution and not go there until we knew more about it. Then it came to us - we would be able to anchor the fourth dimension on Earth by channelling and grounding it through our bodies, but we would only be able to do this when we had raised our own vibrations. This centre of enormous power would then no longer be a danger to us.

Caroline immediately contacted Robert to find out if we had found the answer, and he replied that we had.

Later, we learnt that this is where the Ark of the Covenant comes in, for the purpose of the Ark is to protect the pure energy of the higher dimension from being profaned. There is a dramatic scene in Steven Spielberg's film The Raiders of the Lost Ark where we see the Ark in action. The Nazis dare to open the Ark and are killed by the force they release. Originally, the Ark of the Covenant was placed in The Holy of Holies in the Temple of Solomon in Jerusalem. There, it was screened from view and only the Priest might enter the sacred space. In a telephone conversation with Robert he said that, as well as bringing down the Light of the fourth dimension, we had to bring something up from below to balance it. This was, of course, the Darkness. If we were able to do this we would also be balancing all the other opposites at the same time. As we were going to be bringing in something new we asked him what was the leitmotif of the new Aquarian Age and he asked us to think about this. Meditating on the resolution of the opposites we came up with the words, SYNTHESIS and HARMONY to which Robert agreed, just as the word LOVE had been right for the Piscean Age.

So as to be in harmony with the universe, we decided we would anchor the new energy at the Spring Equinox 2002, when the 24-hour day is evenly balanced between light and dark. It was exactly a year after our first attempt at Buckfast Abbey in Devon. It then occurred to us that the most appropriate time of day would therefore be before the sun rises, when there is a blending of night and day. We also remembered to ensure the site was cleansed and protected.

At last, the eve of the Spring Equinox arrived. We set off early for the Midlands so that we could find the exact site in preparation before going to our B&B for the night. The energy site turned out to be an ancient motte and bailey in the form of a small, very steep and rather muddy mound at the back of a small housing estate. The location was curious as there was open countryside all about but, at the same time, you were aware that just beyond were large conurbations in almost all directions – to the North was the town of Derby; to the East,

Loughborough and Leicester; in the South were Birmingham and Coventry and Lichfield and Birmingham spread around to the West. Such a location seemed highly symbolic reminding us that the poet William Blake had set the New Jerusalem in Britain's industrial heartland.

The next morning we rose at 4.30 am and were at the site in the grey light of pre-dawn. It was a still, clear day. When undertaking something of importance humans feel the need for ritual as it helps create a peaceful and receptive mood. We chose to walk a spiral path to the top sounding the 'Om' as we went which we knew would also raise our own energies. When preparing for this moment it had seemed to us that we would be treading the spiral path back to our Beginning, when the energies were higher. At the invisible Gates we remembered to ask permission of the Ark to enter. All was still as we stepped into the centre of this ancient place of power. We then called upon the Darkness to rise up and take its rightful place and for Light and Dark to synthesise and create Harmony.

We stayed on the mount for some time enjoying the views and watching the sunrise and human activity replace the still quiet.

Chapter 48

The Silver Ring

In the Autumn of 2001 Cassie woke up one morning thinking about the One Ring and with the certainty that the 'writing' on her silver version was not just a random squiggle but actually had a meaning. She was excited and wondered why the idea had not occurred to her before. We were shortly to pay a visit to Wales to see Robert and Cassie put the idea to him. He replied that this was indeed the case and that the writing on her Ring demonstrated the coming together of the Opposites. He said, rather sadly, that she had not brought this into her own life. At the time she was divorced and still single.

We examined the sinuous line around the Ring which stands proud from the band. The line began with a gentle curve and then formed two loops, side by side, flowing into a long gentle curve and ending with two blobs one above the other, rather like two full stops. Then another sentence began, so to speak, with a gently curving line which flowed into two loops curved around each other to resemble the Chinese symbol of the Opposites, the Yin and Yang. Again, the line tapered off in the same fashion, this time ending with one large full stop. An idea came to us. We held the Ring so that we were looking at the two large loops side by side and then turned the Ring so that we were looking exactly at its opposite side. Our idea was confirmed: on the opposite side the two loops became the Yin and Yang symbol, that is, the Two became One. Next, we repeated the experiment with the two full stops and, as we had hoped, the two smaller blobs became one large one on exactly the opposite side of the ring. Was the silversmith who made the Ring for Cassie aware of the significance of the wavy line he made across the plain silver band? If not, he was guided by some higher purpose.

The writing reflected a theme which has continuously cropped up in our Quest which is that 'the Opposites are One' and that in order to raise our vibrations there is a need for the divided energy to unite once again. The inner quest also requires us to face our divided nature, or Shadow Self, which is not an easy task as the subconscious mind holds the most sensitive areas of our psyche where we conceal all that we most fear and hate in ourselves and because the problems are too painful to confront. Nevertheless, in recent years many people have felt compelled to undertake just such a process – perhaps in preparation for the opportunity to enter a Golden Age to which so much recent literature points.

We feel that the writing on the Ring represents the purpose of the new Ring we are creating by repeatedly cleansing the Master Ring in the life-giving elements of this world. Perhaps ultimately it will play a part in helping to raise the planetary vibrations so that all who live here can rise also and thereby experience a quite different relationship with the Source and the world about us. When we do raise ourselves once again, perhaps the Elves or Young Gods, as Robert called them, will return to Middle Earth and teach us how to live with a greater connectedness with the true reality, for they were meant to be Humanity's guides but the Dark Lord worked hard to alienate the two Races and in this he succeeded only too well.

Early on the Quest we mentioned that Robert told Cassie she could ask the Ring to help her but she had refrained from doing so thinking it would draw the attention of the Enemy. Shortly afterwards, a neighbour told her that her Ring was tingling with energy. She has never quite been able to make sense of this so she sent an email to Robert some years later. In reply he said that each level or dimension has its own set of rings. At the beginning of the Quest we were interacting with the Story that was closest to us here on earth and, as Robert put it; "at a level when things could manifest for you". The writing on the Ring alters with how the wearer is responding to her/his present circumstances – happy, sad etc., and the Ring amplifies what you are feeling. Thankfully, he said, with the work our group are doing we are thinning down the number of rings.

Chapter 49

The Story Re-enacted in a Day

The intensity of the days when we met at a series of monthly meetings in 1999 in the Wye Valley, were over. Robert was now holding four weekend workshops a year at the same location. One such was to take place on Sunday, 30 June 2002. However, we had decided not to attend and rang to let Robert know. Caroline made the phone call and was taken aback by his uncharacteristically strong reaction. He told her that if we did not go he would leave us all. Caroline told Cassie that she could not bear to see Robert upset so we decided we would show up after all. We were soon to understand why it was necessary for all members of the Fellowship, and more, to be present that day and why Robert had been upset.

As usual, Robert talked on a variety of subjects which were relevant to the people there that day. He touched upon the need to eat seasonally as many illnesses and imbalances stem from not doing so. Those who suffer from Seasonal Affective Disorder (SAD) – and we all suffer from it to a degree – should wear yellow clothing. He recommended that we have a bowl of gemstones and the one you pick out will be the one you need. Humans were never meant to be stuck in houses. We moved around but we have lost this ability. Also, as many people know, electrical waves from DECT phones for example, are harmful to our energies. On his journey to the Wye Valley that morning the idea that came to him for the day was that we need to be selfish: only then can we help other people.

There was a large gathering that day but it wasn't until Robert dropped a hint at the morning break that we started to be aware of what else was happening. He showed Cassie a small tin, like an old-fashioned tobacco tin. Ingeniously, a number of the key themes of Tolkien's Story of The Lord of the Rings were captured in tiny pictures on the lid. In the centre was a tree encircled by a fiery gold ring. Robert pointed to something quite new, a twelve-pointed star, which he called the

Double Star of David. He then let slip that there were four rings present at the meeting. That was the big clue for it meant that all four ring bearers were present in the room. These were the Robert/Gandalf, Laura/Elrond, Tups/Galadriel and the fourth ring had to be the Master Ring forged by the Dark Lord worn by Cassie/the Ring Bearer.

Suddenly all became clear. A full cast of characters in the Story of The Lord of the Rings was gathered in the one room to re-enact the events of the saga in one single day. She thought of the tall, dark-haired man dressed all in black who just happened to be sitting right behind her and who kept looking at her. It came into her head that this man was Boromir, one of those chosen to make up the Fellowship, and the son of the ruling Steward of the Kingdom of Gondor. He fitted the description for he was exceptionally tall, dark-haired and wore black which was the colour of the Royal House and therefore worn by the Stewards. The reason why he appeared drawn to Cassie/Frodo was because Boromir was instantly ensnared by the power of the One Ring when he first he set eyes upon it at the Council of Elrond in the Elven kingdom of Rivendell.

In Ring Quest I, we discussed how the events of the Great War of the Ring have become trapped at successive levels and how, at the end of every Age, the replay button is pressed once again. However, in our explanation we felt we had not grasped a full understanding of such a complex subject. We also suggested that there was already scientific proof of multi-dimensions which Laurence Gardner mentions in his book Genesis of the Grail Kings but that such knowledge is being withheld from us. As we edit this part of the Quest, some few years after the actual events, Robert happens to have written a piece that has improved our understanding on this very subject:

> Every Age or time still exists on some level or another and the people in Ring Quest are clearing up the debris of many thousands of lifetimes for our earth. Energy once created by strong thoughts creates in reality what the thought wants and can manifest itself in our everyday reality. If there is life

after death and some people die yet retain some form of consciousness and their beliefs are fixed and religious, then they may create a dimension or time slot of their own, and each age creates these time slots, dimensions, etc. A lot of the great philosophers all say the same thing: if a thought is held long and hard enough it may move from purely a thought into reality and actually manifest into a physical reality.

Just as Shakespeare's plays are frequently performed in the costume of different historical periods, such as the First World War, in just the same way Tolkien's drama has been played for real. The energies and people remain the same but the props and costumes change. So it was with our play that day. In this ingenious way, with the wizard Gandalf/Robert helping to orchestrate events, we were linking with unfolding events of the Story in one of those time slots. By earthing those energies we were erasing that time slot.

Chapter 50

Excalibur

In an earlier chapter we compared King Arthur's sword Excalibur with Aragorn's sword, Anduril. Both were magical so that none might withstand the blazing light of the blade when roused in battle. In the original tale the blade was broken at the end of a long war when the Dark Lord is killed and his spirit hides. The blade of the renowned sword remained broken for many ages awaiting its time. That time comes with the arrival of Frodo at the Elven sanctuary of Rivendell, bearing the Ring of Doom. The Elves forge the blade anew for Aragorn, heir of the Royal Line. Once again, the Spirit of the Sword can dwell in the blade. The power of the sun, moon and stars are magically captured in the blade so that it is very bright and the 'light of the sun shone redly in it, and the light of the moon shone cold, and its edge was hard and keen'.[21]

It all began with a series of synchronicities, or coincidences. On Sunday evening, 18th August, 2002 Cassie's daughters returned from holiday. The next day, her daughters decided to watch The Lord of the Rings. As Cassie went about her business in the house, she found herself catching snatches of the film which just happened to coincide with scenes showing Narsil, the Sword-that-was-Broken, where Boromir, man of Gondor, stands gazing at the shards of the famous sword. In another scene she saw Aragorn raising the newly forged sword, renamed Anduril, 'Flame of the West'.

The following day her daughters watched a film on television that just happened to be 'Merlin' which is about the sword Excalibur being given to the rightful King. Once again, she walked into the room at the moment the young Arthur draws Excalibur from the stone and is claimed King. As if this were not enough, the next day, Cassie and daughters took a long-planned trip to the village of Street in Somerset which lies close to the town of Glastonbury. It was to Glastonbury Tor, or the island of Avalon as it was then called, that King Arthur was conveyed by boat when he was dying. The synchronicities were being piled one on top of another.

The very next day, Cassie bought the local newspaper in which there was an article about a Bronze Age crown. Uncharacteristically, she also bought a copy of the local magazine, Wiltshire Life, and was stunned to find that it carried an article entitled "E is for the Story of Excalibur". It suggested that the sword might have come from Wiltshire. Many lakes have been put forward as being the one where the Lady gave the sword to King Arthur. These are Dozmary Pool on Bodmin Moor, Pomparles Bridge near Glastonbury and Loe Pool in South Cornwall. The article suggests, however, that evidence points to a lake location in Wiltshire.

> When convinced he is about to die after being wounded, ... Arthur asks Sir Bedivere to return Excalibur to the lake from where it came. After three bouts of procrastination, his charge delivers Arthur's wish only to find on his return that the King has been taken from his deathbed via Stonehenge to be buried at Glastonbury. Would it be too tenuous a link to suggest that the mysterious lake is that of Wilsford Cum Lake in the Woodford Valley?

We were stunned by the suggestion because Caroline lives in the same valley not a mile away! Given Caroline's role as Aragorn, we realised this was no mere coincidence, particularly in view of all the recent synchronicities. They seemed to be pointing to the fact that Aragorn's sword and King Arthur's are one and the same. Considering the extraordinary proximity of the lake to the stone circle of Stonehenge – three kilometres as the crow flies - it is surprising that the lake at Wilsford Cum Lake has not been included before in the list of possible lake locations for the Excalibur.

As luck would have it we had an appointment with Robert in two week's time, Sunday, 7th September 2002, where we hoped to learn more. Perhaps we should have cudgelled our brains a bit more as to what needed to be done but we regret to say we did not. At the meeting Robert agreed that the lake in the valley was the one into which Arthur's famous sword had been thrown. He then shooed away Merlin and Nimue[22], who he could see had appeared, saying he did not want them around. They were after power and mention of the Sword had drawn them.

He told us we needed the Sword to keep the balance of power we had recently achieved at Bowood House in January when we used the power of the One Ring for good. However, due to the corruption and many evils at the physical level, we obviously needed to work hard to maintain that equilibrium. He went on to say that we should take the Sword to Stonehenge and put it to the North, South, East and West and then we should lay the sword on the stones. We were somewhat bemused by these instructions. It brought to mind the story of how King Arthur acquired Excalibur by drawing it out of the stone. We realised the reason for laying the sword on one of the stones in the sanctuary of Stonehenge, was one of protection in just the same way a stone had protected Arthur's sword. He said he would say no more for he had already said more than he should. Rather ominously, he told us to be quick about it.

Sometime later, we realised why there was a sense of urgency to our retrieval of the Sword. As the article mentioned suggests, there is some dispute as to the actual lake into which Excalibur was returned. However, when Robert confirmed our supposition, this was no longer the case. The secret was 'out' which meant that those people in physical bodies working for the Other Side would quickly learn of it and move to acquire the Sword for themselves. Fortunately, we did not waste too much time and six days later we made our move.

Chapter 51

Excalibur Retrieved

The following Friday, 13th September 2002, on a sunny afternoon, we descended on the village of Wilsford cum Lake, parked the car and looked around for a suitable spot, as close to the house as possible. We finally settled on a small grove of trees where we would be partially protected from the road. The original Sword must have rusted and disintegrated but, clearly, the spirit of the Sword was still there. We knew, therefore, we must call the sword to us in its perfect state at the etheric level. To do this we needed to get as close as possible to the lake which was in the grounds of a large country house belonging to a pop singer, as well known for his work to save the world's tropical forests, as for his songs.

Using fitting words for such a bold and fearless spirit, we called the Sword to us and then, with our inner vision, waited until we knew the Sword was with us. It came eagerly to our summons as it was keen to be wielded again. With our visual imagination we saw ourselves handling a sword, knowing that the etheric one would fit in with our movements. Caroline then sat at the back of the car, carefully holding it point upwards, as Cassie drove straight to Stonehenge, which was about two miles away. We continued driving to the north end of the Valley whereupon you turn left onto the busy A303, which is one of the main routes to the South West. Almost immediately, at the crest of a hill one looks down on the dramatic scene of the megalithic Stone Circle in its magnificent setting of undulating down land and fields dotted with the round barrows of Bronze age chieftains.

Having parked the car a little way down the rough track bordering the site we mentally projected ourselves to within the Stone Circle, holding the Sword. We knew that once within the circle of the Stones, we would be protected. Holding the Sword point up we sent out its energy to fight for Truth and Justice to the North, South, West and East. Carefully laying it down, we left the Sword lying on the Stone knowing that we could call upon it whenever its power was needed in the world to combat terror and injustice.

Once again the same pattern had been repeated. The Sword had lain hidden at the bottom of the lake at the etheric level – and therefore safe – until its time came again. In Tolkien's saga, we learn that the broken Blade was protected through many lifetimes of Men as it was carefully passed from father to son in an unbroken line. Latterly, it had been kept safely at Rivendell. Thus it was protected from falling into the wrong hands. Likewise, in the Legend of King Arthur, only the rightful heir might draw the Blade from the Stone into which it had been set, so safeguarding it for the rightful owner, the King.

An interesting point to note is that, in its long history, Stonehenge has been both a temple to the moon as well as the sun. Aragorn's sword, Narsil, also combined the power of the sun and moon in its blade and therefore it is more than likely, so too did King Arthur's sword, Excalibur. Thus, the Temple of Stonehenge is a fitting sanctuary for the Sword of Kings.

Some years later we discovered a rough road in Wilsford cum Lake, which is opposite the big country house in whose grounds the lake is to be found. The rough road is also only some twenty yards from the grove of trees where we stood to summon the Sword. It runs along the valley floor, past Springbottom Farm, a racing yard, until it climbs onto Normanton Down. In November of 2007, we walked its length for the first time, passing horses in fields on either side. Quite suddenly the grass changed to a pale, shaggy green as we ascended Normanton Down. Sheep now replaced horses in the large field on one side. From there we looked down on Stonehenge and saw that the road, now a bridleway, leads directly to the Stone Circle. There was little doubt in our minds at that moment that this was the route King Arthur's bier took to Stonehenge.

Two curious synchronicities later and we realised we were being made to rethink the traditional view of kingship. Three days after we retrieved Excalibur from the bottom of the lake Cassie happened to watch an episode in the television series called The Scarlet Pimpernel was written by Baroness Orczy. It is set during the French Revolution in France in which the King and his family and thousands of noblemen were beheaded by that infamous implement of death called 'Madame Guillotine'. In this particular episode a sentence uttered jumped out: "One day there won't be any kings".

A second synchronicity swiftly followed. It came in an episode in the American TV sitcom, Friends, in which Chandler wears a golden paper crown. Although now a married man, Chandler feels he missed out by not having a Bachelor Party so he decides to hold one. However, there is no spirit in the event: the opportunity is gone and in the past. We realised that we were being shown that the old form of kingship - where a King sits on a throne wearing a golden crown - is over, or in the past. Certainly, this time round, the renewal of the Sword of Kings has been unorthodox – an invisible sword at another dimension retrieved and wielded by two women, albeit, one of them in the role of Aragorn, King of the Numenorians.

Through all ages, the tokens of kingship have also been a metaphor for the spiritual elevation of men and women. The crown represents the golden halo, or corona of light, and the Sword is a symbol for the opening of the higher energy centres, or chakras, of the human body. These are the three jewels on the handle of the sword. A higher state of consciousness is achieved when the top three chakras, are opened. The message seems to be that when we have raised our consciousness to a higher level we will have won a crown and mantle for ourselves, and the Kingship of old will no longer be necessary.

But as with so much else, this wonderful symbol has been parodied. The Sword is also the symbol of the Christian Cross. So once again we are faced with the inexorable truth that you cannot have Good without Evil.

Chapter 52

A Second Fibonacci Diamond

A year after visiting Castle Gresley we learned from Robert that, yet again, we had failed to secure the Fourth dimension on Earth. The energy had simply floated away. Imagine our dismay after all the effort we had put into it. We thought we had been at pains to anchor the energy through our bodies but it turns out that this was not enough and that we should have thought to anchor it firmly deep in the earth and for this we should have thought to ask for help.

He continued: we were to call on Iridium in the skies and Euridice below. The latter was a Goddess of the Underworld and she would be able to anchor the energy deep in the earth. In Greek mythology Euridice was the beloved of Orpheus, always shown holding a lyre with which he enchants both men and the wild beasts. Euridice dies prematurely from a snakebite and Orpheus enters the Underworld to plead that she be restored to him. This he is granted on condition he does not look behind him as he returns to the surface. However, he cannot resist turning round to look at his beloved whose footsteps he hears behind him. At that moment she slips back into the Underworld and is lost to him forever.

But who or what was Iridium? Our best source of information proved to be a book by Laurence Gardner called Genesis of the Grail Kings. Iridium is a bright silver metal belonging to the plutonium group of metals. It was known to the ancient Sumerian Master Craftsmen or Alchemists and was used, along with gold, to create a substance which reversed the ageing process and gave long life.[23] In other words a person's vibrations might be raised in this manner. Iridium is a rare metal on this planet but not so in outer space nor deep within the earth. Meteorites containing the metal have hit the planet in the past and the metal has sunk to deep layers within the earth's crust.

We realised that the name Euridice is similar to 'iridium'. In an email Robert divulged that Iridium was once a God-like being, who transformed things and energies – just like the alchemists. He also remarked that in those days a God was neither sex, a God is a God, and that male and female belong later on: 'humanness crept in to create the duality of the sexes.' At last we understood. This particular metal, using the language of the alchemist, has the power to be transformed from a 'base metal into gold', in other words, it is the Philosopher's Stone. Like gold, Iridium is able to switch between the dimensions. The God in the heavens, from whom we were asking for help, represents the metal in its higher state, where there are no opposites. But deep within the earth, where we still have duality, we were using the properties of Iridium in its baser, metallic state. Hence we were asking Euridice, a female deity, and one half of the male/female duality, to help anchor the energy on earth.

The question on our lips was, why could Robert not have given us this vital piece of information sooner? We can only conclude, once again, that he is only permitted to help/interfere up to a point. One of his constant refrains to all of us is to trust ourselves more, to which he always adds that he trusts every one of us. He had therefore trusted we would work this out for ourselves.

On 17 August 2003 a chance walk along The Ridgeway to the south of Avebury stone circle gave us the idea for making another, and very much smaller, Fibonacci diamond. As we set off, walking in a northerly direction, our attention was drawn to a large copse of trees. We thought we could dimly make out round barrows within the clump of trees and decided to investigate. Sure enough, we soon saw the distinct shapes of three round barrows in a row. On the middle round barrow we were struck by there being only two trees on the top, growing slightly apart, which created the semblance of an entrance.

We were not prepared for what we found on the summit of the third and most southerly barrow. Someone had created a shrine to the Goddess. Three evenly spaced trees were on the crown creating a triangle. Within the triangle a five-pointed star had been laid out made out of small white stones with three points touching the tree trunks. The three trees stood for the Triple Goddess of old and the five-pointed star is associated with the Goddess Venus because that planet traces a five-petalled flower in the heavens during its eight-year orbit of the sun. On one of the trees someone had engraved a heart in which were the letters 'YAS' on one line and, immediately below, the letters 'CAS'. Rearranging them gave a startlingly close rendering of 'Cassie', i.e. CASSAY. A small sheaf of wheat was leaning against one of the other trees and there was a posy of flowers in the centre of the star. We stood gazing in wonder at the enchanting scene. An occasional gentle breeze moved the branches of the trees through which we could glimpse fields and rolling green hills beyond.

It begged the question, had someone deliberately set this up for us to discover given the name on the tree trunk? If so, it had the desired effect for it occurred to us that if the round barrow on the other side were masculine, the doorway at the centre was where the opposites came together and where the energy of the fourth dimension might be drawn down through the opening. We would use this centre as our guide to create a much smaller Fibonacci diamond.

Looking at a map we used a length of knitting wool to follow the lines running due north, south, east and west of the central barrow. The line running due east ran through Marlborough College, which is a boys' public school. We knew that in the grounds there is an ancient mound or 'tot' of the same kind as the one at Totnes, Windsor Castle and the White Tower of London. Such mounds were connected with kingship, as discussed earlier, and were also sites of power. We were confident we had found the eastern tip of the diamond.

We could now use the distance between the round barrow and the ancient mound to find the points north and south. To the north the line ended close to a place called Elm Cross, which we realised exactly reflected the themes found at Calverley ie the Elmwood Hotel and Crossfield Farm. The distance to the south ended on the very top of a low hill, called Woodborough Hill in the Vale of Pewsey. This gentle landscape can be compared with the Shire and the low hill is like the one at Buckland on the southern tip of the large diamond.

All we had left to discover was the western point, which we knew was going to be further away. Looking along the line extending due west, we saw the word moat and knew we had found the elongated western tip. In Alfred Watkins book, The Ley Hunter's Manual, he describes round moats as water sighting points on energy lines, as they are visible from a great distance, especially when they catch the light. The name of the adjacent farm Blackleaze Farm - as in 'Black-leys' - confirmed this; it is common for farms to be placed on or close to energy lines to ensure abundant crops. Furthermore, moats are associated with castles and it was a ruined castle which had formed the western tip of the earlier Fibonacci diamond.

We wished to move fast so, on a hot, sunny afternoon three days later, we made our separate ways to the western and eastern tips of the Fibonacci diamond. As before, Cassie was in the west and Caroline in the east. A few days after we took our positions to the north and south respectively and, at the agreed time, simultaneously opened the opposing gates, thus drawing down a higher energy to the dense physical plane. Now, all we needed to do was to anchor it at the centre at the autumn equinox, less than a month away.

This time there would be no mistake. On the day of the autumn equinox, sounding the 'Om', we walked a spiral path to the top of the round barrow where stood the two trees forming the gateway. We asked the Ark of the Covenant if we might enter and we stepped into the space between the trees. We called up the darkness and united all the opposites but, this time, we asked the God Iridium in the heavens to send the energy of the Fourth Dimension through our bodies and we asked the Goddess Euridice below to anchor it deep within the Earth. We then turned to the four points of the compass and sent the energy winging across the surrounding hills and fields and, thence, around the world. As we walked away, we saw a flock of birds flying in the distance, which suddenly changed direction and, flying over our heads, flew over the copse which we had just left. As Robert put it, "it was a reaction" to the change in the energy.

Chapter 53

The Opposing Gates Open on Middle Earth

It was one of those moments when Robert took us completely by surprise. He asked us when the Gates opened in The Lord of the Rings that let in the energy for the forthcoming Age. In that moment we understood that he was suggesting that at the end of every planetary cycle of approximately 2,200 years in our time, a new energy is introduced which gives shape to the new era. Because our reality is one of separation and duality, opposing Gateways need to be opened simultaneously as the energy has to divide in order enter our reality or domain. As to the answer to his question, we had no idea. We racked our brains trying to work it out, without success, and the question remained unanswered for many years.

In September 2007, whilst sorting out the material for Ring Quest II Robert's original question came back to us. Fortunately, Cassie had been re-reading Tolkien's trilogy and had a better grasp of the sequence of events. In a flash, she realised she knew the answer. How could she not have thought of it before? The gateway in the East opens when the two hobbits, Frodo and Samwise, escape through the Gates of the Tower of Cirith Ungol[24] in the land of the Enemy. Simultaneously, in the West, the massive Gates of the White City of Minas Tirith are burst asunder by the Captain of Sauron's army, one of the Living Dead and Leader of the Nine Ringwraiths.

The hobbits break the magic spell of the evil Stone Watchers on either side of the Gate by using the power of the Star of Earandil captured within the crystal phial given to Frodo by the Lady Galadriel 'to be a light in dark places': they were certainly in a very dark place at that moment. Scarcely have the hobbits made their escape than the Watchers let out a piercing cry and the Gate collapses under the strain. At the same time, across the Great River in the West, a huge battering ram has been pounding the Gates of the White City. Then, the Chief of the Nazgul stands up in his stirrups and, uttering a black spell in a terrifying voice, the massive steel Gates burst apart. This is the moment when the energy of the New Age of Man entered the physical world of Middle Earth. It was of a lower vibration than that which went before, for we are told that the Elves would fade and much would pass away.

The power of Good was used to break out of the Gates of its Enemy, and the power of Evil was used to break in to the stronghold of its Enemy. Discussing this in an email with Robert, he points out that in both instances the same energy is used, exactly the same, but welded by different hands. He asked us to think about this as it may provide a way of shortcutting the sagas repeating themselves.

Chapter 54

The Ring Comes Home

It was three years since we had last interacted with the One Ring. On that occasion, in January 2002, in the grounds of Bowood House, we used the energy of the Ring to create a balance between the opposing forces of Good and Evil. Little did we know that at the workshop in the Wye Valley, held on Sunday 28 February 2005 three years later, we were to fulfil the main aim of the Quest: this was to unmake the Ring so that the sagas might cease being endlessly repeated through Time.

The workshop was already underway when we arrived. It was a large gathering with a number of new faces. At one point Robert mentioned that the words "the Ring has come home" came to him as he was driving to the meeting. Naturally, as Ringbearer, Cassie wondered what those words meant. It was not until the lunch break when Cassie and Jean happened to be talking to Robert outside that Cassie remembered his words and decided to tackle him on the subject. He replied that we had the opportunity to do something very important. This did not answer the question and only served further to arouse her curiosity. She was forced to start musing out loud in the hope of finding the answer to the riddle. Logically, she suggested, talking aloud, this could only mean that the Ring was at Mount Doom (at another dimension of course) where it was forged so that the volcano could, in a manner of speaking, be called The Ring's 'home'. Robert then said something that really startled them both. He repeated that we could do something very important but that we only had a small window of opportunity - until 2.10pm to be precise - which was only 20 minutes away. What was this thing of such importance?

Back indoors and munching sandwiches, Robert came in and did likewise. Cassie again asked him what was meant by the phrase "the Ring has come home". He asked us what we should do with the Ring. Some months earlier we had discussed this very subject and come to the conclusion that the ideal would be to take the energy out of the Ring and into ourselves as we stood in a circle holding hands, thereby making a living Ring. In this way the Ring would be rendered harmless so that it would not matter if it ever fall into the hands of the Enemy. Between us we suggested to Robert that all of us at the workshop that day should form a Circle and do just that – ask for the purified energy of the One Ring to enter those present.

Feeling confused by Robert's cryptic remarks, we did not at that time fully appreciate that we were in tune with that part of the Story - at that other dimension - where Frodo and Sam have reached Mount Doom at the very heart of Sauron's Kingdom. Unbeknownst to them so had one other – Gollum. Robert now took the part of Gollum and asked Cassie if she would give him the Ring. Without thinking, she gave it to him. He proceeded to turn into the wheedling, cringing creature that was Gollum. When he called it his 'Precious' Cassie became alarmed and asked for the return of the Ring. Unsurprisingly, he would not give it back and Cassie actually went up and prised it from his grasp! Robert remarked that he had not thought she would be so strong, which was entirely in character with the Story. We are told that the only thing which could arouse any strength in Frodo at the bitter end of the journey when both hobbits are weak from hunger was if someone tried to take the Ring from him. Earlier, when Sam innocently offers to carry the Ring, which has become such a weight for Frodo, a 'wild light' comes into Frodo's eyes which quickly dies and Frodo explains that he is "almost in its power now. I could not give it up, and if you tried to take it I should go mad." Robert wondered if her finger was tasty!

Most people had trickled back into the room and we quickly informed them what we were about to do and that we needed to form a circle. Again, Robert pressed upon us the need for speed as time was running out. The need for speed was because we needed to intervene and change the story before Gollum, once again, topples into the fiery chasm still holding Frodo's finger bearing the Ring. Hastily, suitable words were written and then we were only waiting for the last person with just four minutes to go. The moment had come: we were all present. The situation was explained to everyone. Finally, we stated that the One Ring had returned home and we asked for its energy to enter the living Ring made up of many links. At that moment many of us felt the energy enter us. Cassie also felt as if a great energy was leaving her which made her feel so emotional she burst into tears.

In Tolkien's book he writes that while these momentous events were taking place, the world and its peoples held their breath, awaiting the stroke of Doom. When the Black Tower collapses, due to the violent upheavals of the earth, the evil spirit of Sauron finally loses its grip on the physical world and becomes a vast black cloud that reaches so high it is seen as far away as the White City. Tolkien describes that the earth and its creatures uniformly gave out a great sigh as the evil departed and felt their spirits lighten. Rain began to fall washing away the defilement.

What next took place after the unmaking of the Ring can best be seen in the context of the healing that follows in the aftermath of the recent battles outside Minas Tirith and at the Gates of the Dead Lands. Aragorn, the King-in-Waiting, proved to be a knowledgeable and tireless healer. In particular, he used a small and little-known flower called 'Kingsfoil', which was the only herb that would cure those wounded by the Black Breath of the Nazgul/Black Riders. We all felt that a flower from the forsythia, which was growing just outside the room, should be brought in to the room and placed on the floor in the centre of the room. A feeling of peace stole through the room, and beyond.

Chapter 55

Unfinished Business

Due to personal circumstances in Cassie's life there was to be a long period before we took up the Quest again. In October 2004, just over a year after anchoring the higher energy at the round barrow near Silbury Hill and Avebury stone circle, Robert had to resort to saying that we had 'unfinished business' and that Caroline had yet to pass through the Paths of the Dead. He told us that we needed to go to the White Horse at Uffington on the Berkshire Downs. Accordingly, we made a date for a Saturday in October but we were forced to cancel the date and it was not until 7 May 2005 that we were able to make the trip.

It was some weeks before our journey to The White Horse that Cassie had a curious experience one night. As she lay in bed she was aware of being fully awake and experiencing a living, green energy made up of prisms or triangles. The energy was so powerful she was only just able to bear it. Afterwards, reflecting on the experience, she realised that it had to be the energy of the Green Stone, which Arwen gave to Aragorn and which was set in a brooch in the form of an eagle. Thinking about Robert mentioning the Paths of the Dead, we realised that Aragorn had worn the brooch as a fastening for his cloak. The Green Stone must have been of great, if not vital, assistance to Aragorn and his companions enabling them to navigate successfully the fearsome Paths of the Dead. We felt the experience was a hint that we were to call upon the energy of the Green Stone before embarking upon this harrowing journey. When Cassie mentioned her experience in an email to Robert he replied that it was a fluid energy that others could use for good or ill and that she should use it wisely.

The Paths of the Dead were so-called because they ran through the kingdom of a long-dead people who still haunted the area. Long ago, they had sworn an oath to Isildur, King of the Northern Kingdom, to come to his aid in the War against Sauron. However, when the call came, they did not heed it for they were secretly worshipping Sauron. Isildur laid a curse upon them at the Erech Stone, calling them 'oathbreakers', and condemning them to remain on Middle Earth, even after death, until they fulfilled their oath. The Path was much feared as anyone who dared enter did not re-emerge. There was a palpable feeling of evil at the entrance of the tunnel because those people had practised the Black Arts when they worshipped the Dark Lord.

Desperate to come to the aid of Minas Tirith in time, Aragorn was forced to take the Paths of the Dead as they were a short-cut. For Aragorn and his small band to come out the other side was no mean feat. It is possible it could not have been accomplished without the protection of the living energy of the Green Stone. This would have helped to keep fear at bay as well as the Black Magic in which the tunnel was steeped. As Isildur's heir, Aragorn knew he had the right to call upon the Oathbreakers to fulfil their oath and so be free. Half-way through the journey, therefore, where the path opened out into a large space, Aragorn summoned the Dead to the Erech Stone. Doubtless, this action also helped the companions to pass unhindered.

It was a on a bright May morning when, at last, we set off for the White Horse at Uffington. We thought we knew the purpose of our journey but were to find out that we were wrong. In retrospect, we realise that our destination was merely given as a guide and was simply meant to get us to drive in the general direction in the hope that we would pick up on the clues along the way. Fortunately, being alerted to the possibility of taking the Paths of the Dead we were, indeed, able successfully to do this and, finally, accomplish that part of the Quest. It was a vital part of the story to experience for, as already mentioned in an earlier chapter, the pivotal battle on the Pellenor Fields at the feet of Minas Tirith would have been lost without Aragorn's timely arrival at the head of a large fleet with a fighting force.

As we made our way towards the White Horse, we took a 'wrong' turning and ended up at a crossroads where we didn't recognise any of the village names on the signpost. We had the feeling of being in a remote, strange place, high on the Berkshire

Downs, with the ancient track called The Ridgeway running close by. There was a pub on the corner, named 'The Shepherd's Rest' and, as we were now quite thirsty and hungry and feeling in need of a rest, we decided to go in and have lunch as well as to ask the way to the White Horse.

While we were waiting to be served, we began to notice that we were surrounded by strange-looking people with what can only be described as rough, uncouth features and manners and, when Caroline visited the bathroom, she was shocked when someone suddenly thumped on the door. On coming out, she said to the surly woman who was waiting outside and who tried to sidle past her, "You don't do that", to which the woman muttered something indecipherable in a guttural, foreign accent.

Suddenly Caroline understood. These were the Oathbreakers who were gathering and waiting for the summons. We are told that when Isildur cursed them, they cut themselves off from the world, which would explain the strange language which would have become stuck in a time warp. Their numbers would have dwindled until they simply died out. More than likely this process would have resulted in some intermarriage that would also account for the exaggerated features of a few of the people in the pub. Many years ago, at the outset of the Quest, Robert had mentioned the Paths of the Dead and said that Caroline would make many friends when she went through them. Now we understood why. The Oathbreakers longed to fulfil their oath and be free and would be grateful to Caroline/Aragorn for helping to bring this about. It explains why one of their number had banged on the loo door to draw Caroline's attention to their plight. And the name of the pub, The Shepherds Rest, was telling us that the Oathbreakers wanted to 'rest', at last, by being, as ghosts, laid to 'rest'.

As we were lost, we also decided to consult the more detailed Ordinance Survey map which we had fortunately brought with us. We soon noticed that along the route we now had to take to reach the White Horse we would be passing through a village called Kingstone Winslow. The thought came to us: couldn't the Erech Stone legitimately be called the King's Stone? After all, it had been set there by Isildur, King of the

North Kingdom, when the remnant of his people returned to Middle Earth after the sinking of their island? We realised the journey to the village of Kingstone Winslow would constitute the journey through the Paths of the Dead.

After lunch, as we returned to the car, Caroline summoned the Dead to meet her at the Erech Stone. She also called upon the power and protection of the Green Stone as we entered upon the Paths of the Dead.

As we reached the village we nearly missed our destination - a war memorial in the form of a granite cross - and where, to our astonishment, embedded in the upright of the cross, was a beautiful metal sword – Aragorn's sword, Anduril! We immediately stopped, realising that this was the Erech Stone where Aragorn stands, unfurls his banner and speaks to the Oathbreakers.

There were the most incredible signs surrounding the memorial. It stood on a triangle of grass beside a tall tree and the first name at the bottom of the cross was 'Flight Sergeant Bishop', killed in the Second World War, and the last name was a Corporal Higgs killed in the Falklands war. At the foot of the memorial was a red poppy left there on Armistice Day the previous November, thus bringing together the three wars of the 20th century. The tree of course symbolised the Royal Line but to the side of the memorial was a cottage called 'The Crossed Trees', another name for the crucifix where so many Sacred Kings, among whom was numbered Jesus, perished (although, of course, some people believe that Jesus did not, in fact, die.) By the tree on a wall was a plaque on which was written the fact that the village was mentioned in the Doomsday Book. And just behind the cross was a signpost to Shrivenham and a cottage called 'The Elms'. This had to be the place where Aragorn gives the Oathbreakers a chance to 'shrive' or cleanse themselves of their sin so that they can be free.

It is worth noting that it was also the third time we had seen the Elm tree mentioned at important sites. It had figured at the north points of both the Fibonacci diamonds. Our conclusion is that the tree is symbolic of the Elves who loved the natural world - perhaps the Elm was a tree particularly beloved. Perhaps it is showing that Elven blood runs through the Royal Line and that both Elves and Men have waged war against the Dark Lord and his allies through the Ages. The cross tells us how the Royal Line – as symbolised by the King Stone and the single tree – has been particularly persecuted.

Parking the car, Caroline, in her role of Aragorn, stood before the cross and asked the Oathbreakers why they had come, to which we knew that their King replies that they have come to fulfil their oath and be set free. Aragorn then answers that all the land must be rid of the armies of the Enemy and then he will hold their oath fulfilled. He tells them to follow him on the long and arduous journey to the port on the great river.

We continued on to the White Horse, our initial destination. However, we knew that we had already fulfilled our purpose. We did, in fact, accomplish another task that day, which comes into the next chapter.

Naturally, we had been aware – who could not be – that the next day, 8th May, was Victory in Europe Day - VE Day - the day the defeat of Hitler and his allies was celebrated throughout the West. We had not made a connection between this and our visit to the White Horse because we had not known how it would turn out. However, the fact that VE Day was the very next day after we went through the Paths of the Dead suddenly made the celebrations take on an extraordinarily significant meaning. Given the scale and importance of VE Day, we feel the celebrations also represented the downfall of Sauron himself and the end of the War of the Ring. The inference is that Hitler can be compared with the Dark Lord.

Some years back, on the day the Fellowship met at Avebury, we experienced the battle of the Pellenor Fields. But there had never been a celebration. This must have been because not all the pieces that made the defeat of the Dark Lord possible had been put together. The missing part had been the journey through the Paths of the Dead. However, it now appeared that all the important events that lead up to that victorious day had at last been re-enacted. It seems that our intention to go through the tunnel had drawn those events to us. We picked up on the clues as they overlapped with our dimension. Then, by synchronising with the journey as it took place at another level, we earthed and cleared those energies.

There was one final twist to the day on the Berkshire Downs. We just happened to read that the very day we took the Paths of the Dead was also the one day in the moon's cycle called 'the dark day of the moon'. It lasts for twenty-four hours and then the moon starts its forward motion again and becomes visible. We were stunned by the timing because, for Aragorn and his companions, that day had indeed been very dark.

Chapter 56

Bishopstone , Idstone and Kingstone Winslow

The commemoration in 2005 of the victory celebrations at the ending of the Second World War fifty years ago was confirmation that we had completed the greater part of the Quest. At last, after six years, the repetitious cycle we had been locked into would cease. The Dark Lord had been defeated and the known world liberated. We could now move on to the next phase of the Story. This was the return and coronation of the King which had been foretold in Bilbo's poem: 'The crownless again shall be king.' The marriage of the King Elessar (Aragorn) to Arwen Evenstar follows on swiftly after. However, we had worked out that at some point in Man's history things had gone wrong and the King's coronation had not taken place in all its original glory. To accomplish this part of the Quest we had to correct those events which had brought about a deviation from the original pattern.

One deviation was that the power of true kingship had become divided. A power-hungry priesthood had slowly but surely usurped many of the functions of kingship. In Europe, during the last two thousand years, the growing power of the Christian Church enabled the Pope to strive for supremacy at the expense of the power of the King. Looking at history, we can see the strife that has arisen because of this state of affairs.[25] In our times, the source of this pattern can be found in the concept of the Twin Pillars of Ancient Egypt. The left-hand pillar stood for 'strength' and was named Boaz,[26] whilst the right-hand pillar known as Jachin, stood for the spiritual power of the High Priest.[27] Therefore the Pillars represented the role of the Leader on the one hand, and that of the Wise Man and healer on the other. This has also led to a separation in the spiritual and material life of man; yet we are a mixture of the two, being spirit in a physical body.

We realised that for the King to have the full power to lead and care for his people, these two aspects needed to be reunited in the one man.[28] Both Aragorn and Jesus combined the two aspects of kingship. When Aragorn is crowned outside the shattered Gates of Minas Tirith he is described as having '…strength and healing…' in his hand. The healer in the House of Healing in the White City comments on this, marvelling that the hand that wields the sword is the same hand that heals. Aragorn brought back three people from the brink of death, such was his healing power. Even then, so long ago, the nature of true kingship had been forgotten. After all it had been over a thousand years since a king had sat upon the stone throne. As we know, Jesus was a healer, but he also said he came with a sword.[29]

A friend commented "what about Henry VIII?" It is true that through the breaking away from the control of the Pope in Rome King Henry became both a spiritual and temporal ruler but his attempt at true leadership was marred by syphilis affecting his brain. He also appears to have the mark of a former sacred king in his habit of beheading his queens. It could be argued Henry's desire to combine the roles of both spiritual and military leader reveals a past memory of such leadership before it became perverted by the Cult of the Sacred King where the king became an object of worship.

It was interesting to discover that these self-same Pillars are used in the rituals of modern-day Freemasonry.

So when we consulted the Ordinance Survey map in the pub, The Shepherds' Rest, on the Berkshire Downs, we noticed three villages neatly in a row – Bishopstone, Idstone and Kingstone Winslow. We understood that this was an opportunity to unite the two aspects of kingship - clearly demonstrated by the villages, Bishopstone and Kingstone – at the point between the two, Idstone. 'Id' in Latin means 'I'. We marvelled at the extraordinarily convenient set-up on the physical plane which would facilitate this being done. The 'Win' in 'Winslow' seemed to be a good omen and to foretell the ultimate victory of the king in the long battle between the two powers.

There is a place in the village of Idstone where three roads meet and it was here that we re-united the two aspects of kingship. We then drove on to the war memorial – or Erech

Stone - at Kingstone where Aragorn spoke to the ghostly army. Here we received proof that the two roles should be present in the one person for, carved on the King's stone was a soldier whose surname was 'Bishop'. As Robert has told us, change can only be effected here at the dense physical level. It will then change the pattern throughout all the levels. In turn, the transformed energy will then interact with us here on earth and so help bring about change.

Chapter 57

11 Kensington Place

In February 2005, before we took the Paths of the Dead, we met up with the other members of the Fellowship at a meeting in the Wye Valley. At some point during the day Robert mentioned a place in London where we and two other members of our group, Tups and Jenny, needed to go. There was much work to be done there and the location was very precise: 11 Kensington Place. We were bemused by such a strange destination. As to what we were to do there, Robert had already asked Jenny to do some historical research on William Blake, as well as various other matters such as the Twin Pillars and the Feminine/Goddess aspect.   While Jenny and Tups were working on their lines of research, Robert gave us further information that all the clues were to be found in the address.

Caroline now decided to compose a lexigram from the actual letters in the address. For the number '11' she substituted the spelt-out word 'ELEVEN'. For those who do not know what a lexigram is, it is like a verse of poetry with each word using only the letters in the phrase. Occasionally, if a word is missing one letter, it is permissible to put in that letter in brackets. Small words such as 'the', 'a', 'is', etc., even if they are not in the text, can be written in lower case. Getting to work, Caroline came up with the following: (see overleaf).

It was only after she had written it down, that she saw that the verse was in the shape of a chalice or loving cup where Man and Woman are 'AT ONE'. (See overleaf)

ELEVEN KENSINGTON PLACE

This is the PLACE of the KINGSTONE
The PLACE of the PENTACLE
The SONG of the KING and
The SONG of VEN(U)S
INTONE A NOTE
A TONE
AT ONE
ELEVATION

In the light of our new understanding as to the full nature of the Quest, we were able to understand the significance of the number 11, for we now realised that the Story has been altered for the worse through the passage of time and that this has had to be taken into account. What went wrong needed to be corrected. Only by so doing could the happy ending in The Lord of the Rings, be attained. With Cassie's research into the largely forgotten Cult of the Sacrifice of the King, we at last understood that this period of history had to be included. One of the main problem areas was the relationship between the King and the Queen and, therefore, that of man and woman, for their relationship is the blueprint. The Cult had created a gulf between the sexes because of their mutual fear and hatred resulting from the twisted nature of the Cult. At the subconscious level, that hatred can still persist today in those, who in a former life were intimately caught up in the grisly cycle of the death and rebirth of the King. It therefore became clear that the number 'ELEVEN' is made up of the feminine FIVE-POINTED Star of Venus and the masculine SIX-POINTED Star of David, which is the Star of the Royal Line. And this was a major clue: we realised it was at this site we might have the opportunity to bring together the opposites of Masculine and Feminine in balance, love and harmony. However, there was something we needed to do first before this was possible.

We were grateful to Jenny who passed on to us some of her research in which she mentioned the Rosicruceans ('rosecross').

Their symbol is a cross within a five-petalled dog rose. The name, Rosicrucean and its symbol represent the combined energies of the Feminine and the Masculine – the **Rose** is the Feminine but it dawned on us that the **Cross** represents the Masculine energy crucified upon the Cross. The Feminine number **five** is, of course, shown in the five- petalled Rose - one of the lines in the lexigram of the address is 'PETALS OF VENUS'. But the number represented by the Cross is **four**. If a simple diagonal line were to be drawn across the centre of the cross, it would be transformed into the **Six** pointed Star, which then makes the desired, combined number of '11'. In a powerful, symbolic way the Love Goddess, Venus, would no longer be sacrificing the Masculine upon the Cross.

Funnily enough, the only date on which all four of us were free was 19 June, which is mid-summer. We realised this date was highly significant because the sun would then be at its zenith. At some time in our history the sun had become associated with kingship and mid-summer represented the King at his most glorious and powerful. In former times, it was, therefore, a day to celebrate Kingship. Later, the ideas were deliberately perverted, so that the King came to be tortured and sacrificed on mid-summer's day. It was also the day on which the King Elessar, i.e. Aragorn, wedded Arwen Evenstar. Now, therefore, we can understand why their marriage can only take place when the negative energy of kingly sacrifice is cleared.

Leading up to that date, we were given other pointers. In the first week of June we attended a performance of sacred dance by a troupe of Tibetan monks staged by the Salisbury Arts Festival. It took place at Wardour Castle in Wiltshire, south-west of Salisbury. We discovered that it is the only six-sided castle in the country. Part of the musical ensemble consisted of two extremely long horns, which make a very deep and powerful note or 'TONE'. We remember observing that it sounded like the 'Om' and realised that such a loud tone would clear any negativity there might be in the neighbourhood. At the time, however, so immersed were we in the event, we did not connect this with our visit to London. We had to be given another hint before we realised the significance of the horns and the six-sided castle.

Another curious event occurred when a friend of Cassie's came for a vist in early June and brought her a large brooch in the shape of a five-petalled flower made of clear, pink plastic with a green centre. In the circumstances, Cassie was stunned by this piece of synchronicity. She was also struck by the flower's green centre as it made her think of the Green Stone. Perhaps we were to call upon the Stone's revitalising and balancing power? Green is the colour of balance, being mid-way in the colour spectrum. This would be a vital factor in bringing together the opposites of Feminine and Masculine so that they can be 'AT ONE'. But first, they must be brought into balance and harmony, with equal power.

Sunday (sun day), 19 June, 2005 dawned sunny and extremely hot. We were travelling by car and, on the outskirts of London, we saw a small black boy dressed as a king with a long, silk, embroidered cloak and a high, golden crown. He was walking along an avenue of trees holding the hand of a parent. It struck us as a very odd scene for a Sunday morning. Immediately we understood that the image echoed the return of the line of the Numenorean Kings who were dark-haired, grey-eyed and clad in black and whose progenitor was Luthien, the dark-haired Elven Princess. Next, in a flash and then it was gone, we saw the words 'Big Horn' on a vehicle. At last we made the connection with the Tibetan horns: they needed to be sounded at 11 Kensington Place to help dispel the negativity.

We were dropped off in the Bayswater Road, giving us a short walk into Kensington Gardens to The Orangery (sun symbol) where we were to meet Tups and Jenny at noon. By now, the heat was searingly hot and, as the four of us set off for 11 Kensington Place, it felt like the hottest day we had experienced all summer.

Kensington Place turned out to be a quiet residential road up a small hill. We walked past a young silver birch tree with a very white bark which made us think of Nimloth, the White Tree of the Royal Line, and then we were there, standing in front of an innocuous, terraced house. However, it differed from the others in an important way. Whereas the houses on either side all had two windows top and bottom, at Number 11 these had been replaced with one large window top and bottom. We felt this feature symbolised the union of the two opposites, Masculine and Feminine. Jenny noted that the door was green which represented a wooded place.

We then all proceeded to tune in and carry out the transformation of the energies. Calling upon the balancing and living energy of the Green Stone to help us and sounding the note of the Big Horn in our minds' eyes and ears, Cassie and Caroline turned the Cross of the Crucifixion into the Royal Star of David. We then 'INTONED the NOTE' by reciting aloud the lexigram and asked for the Masculine and Feminine energies to come together in balance and harmony - to be 'AT ONE'. We all supported one another in our different endeavours.[30]

When we had finished, the atmosphere was so charged and life-enhancing, we felt loathe to leave the quiet street. Finally, Caroline noticed a woman in one of the houses on the other side of the road looking at us out of her window, and we knew it was time to go.

Chapter 58

The Mid-summer Marriage

After our visit to 11 Kensington Place, the four of us repaired to the car park where Tups had parked her car and, since she and Jenny had one last place to visit, the Eleanor Cross just outside Charing Cross Station before heading home, they asked us if we would like a lift anywhere. As it happened, we were interested to see the renovations which had just been completed at St Paul's Cathedral not far from the station and so asked to be dropped off there.

In our journey across London from west to east, we passed through Trafalgar Square which was full of people of all nationalities who appeared to be having some sort of joyful celebration. We gazed in wonder at the incredible height of the column - or pillar - that is the memorial to Admiral Nelson. Surely this represented, and was confirmation of, the bringing together of the Two Pillars of Kingship and Priesthood, which we had enacted in the village of Idstone on the Berkshire Downs. It seemed to us that the figure of Admiral Nelson, so high above the ground, symbolised the nobility of the 'Sea Kings' of the Royal Line from whom Aragorn was descended.[31] Later, we perceived that the rejoicing crowd reflected the celebrations at the Coronation of Aragorn as the King Elessar / Elfstone.

We then drove up the Strand and Fleet Street towards Ludgate Hill and Cassie and Caroline found themselves saying, "Can you see St. Paul's yet?" And then, with great delight, "there it is," just as if something special were about to happen. Tups and Jenny dropped us off and, as we entered, we were delighted to see the magnificent makeover of the interior, but surprised to find a crush of people who were listening to an organ recital of triumphal music. Managing to make our way to the front of the crowd we, too, listened spellbound as the music suddenly increased in grandeur and volume. For some reason that was unclear, the nave had been cordoned off, and we could go no further. As we stood there, we both suddenly realised that we had, once again, stepped into the Story and were witnessing the mid-summer marriage of Aragorn and Arwen, for it was midsummer's day. By entering the Story we were grounding it at the physical level. It would have been difficult to find a more fitting place for the royal wedding. Exceptionally, The Prince of Wales and Lady Diana Spencer had chosen to be married in St Paul's Cathedral and not Westminster Abbey, as was the custom for royal weddings. In addition, and perhaps significantly, their wedding had been televised and transmitted around the world, and viewed by millions.

It was a wonderful moment, for it told us that we had successfully healed the breach between the King and the Queen so that their marriage could take place. The King had forgiven the Queen and had ceased punishing her for what she did to him. At long last, they could come together in love and harmony, just as they did, long ago, in Tolkien's Story. The original template, as given in The Lord of the Rings, had been restored. It was time to leave and, as we stepped out into the sunlight, the great bells of the Cathedral began to peal: the royal couple was being greeted by the world, 'and together they (the King Elessar and Arwen Evenstar) went up into the High City, and all the stars flowered in the sky.... and the tale of their long waiting and labours was come to fulfilment.'

As we descended the steps into the square in front of the Cathedral, Caroline drew Cassie's attention to a tall man in a dark suit with a red shirt – strange attire for such a hot day. He stood completely still amidst the milling crowd, looking directly at us and smiling. Who was he? Somehow we knew he was part of the Story. We soon realised that he had to be one of the Oathbreakers whom Caroline/Aragorn had recently released. The black and red colours of his suit and shirt were the colours of Sauron, the Dark Lord, whose device was a red eye upon a black ground. Those colours, therefore, suggested to us the one-time affiliation of that people to the Dark Lord. However, the smile reminded us that Robert had said how grateful they would be to Caroline for setting them free. This was their way of thanking her - he had even come dressed for an important occasion such as a wedding in a smart suit! For a while we stood with the crowd, listening to the pealing bells and then, just as we turned away, the bells gave two loud peals and stopped.

The afternoon was drawing on and we decided to walk towards a tube station in the direction of Trafalgar Square. By now we were rather tired and thirsty and decided to stop off at a cafe. As we were leaving, something rather strange happened: the youth who had served us looked up and gave Cassie a most remarkable smile, remarkable in that it was an expression of pure joy.

We continued along the Strand pausing to enjoy a wonderful sight in the vast courtyard of Somerset House. In the centre were jets of water springing up from the paving slabs and, being a hot day, the place was full of families playing and cooling off in the fountains. Again, we realised we had stepped into the Story, for it immediately brought to mind the transformation of the stone City of Minas Tirith upon the restoration of the King and Queen. Before the War of the Ring, the City is described as having too many empty houses and courtyards and too few children. But after the King's return, the City was made even more beautiful with trees and fountains and the houses were filled with the sound of children's laughter. We were witnessing those very scenes. We remembered how Caroline/Aragorn had been barred from walking along the river path in the Woodford Valley by a woman and two men who represented the Cult of the Sacrifice of the King. With the return of the King and, following his marriage, the people were now able to bathe in the Waters of Life, their spiritual birthright restored.

Cassie had another curious experience with a young man, this time on the tube. No seats were available so she stood, strap-hanging, in front of a young Asian man who looked up at her, immediately sprang to his feet as if stung and offered her his seat. Feeling somewhat embarrassed, she felt obliged to accept graciously but felt particularly uncomfortable when she realised that he had been sitting next to his girlfriend. What had made him do this when it was obvious that she was neither old nor infirm? Again, at dinner in a Chinese restaurant, the young Chinese waiter, a tall, elegant young man, became tremendously happy when he was at our table and was particularly charming to Cassie and they chatted and laughed together. It was interesting that the three young men were from three different cultures. We took it as proof that the terrible Cult of sacrifice of the male had indeed been worldwide, as Cassie had discovered during the course of her research. It later dawned on us that, for a brief period, and in gratitude for our having atoned for her, there was something of the Goddess in Cassie's aura. It was to this energy that the young men were responding. It was clearly showing us that Sacred Kings, all of whom were young men, had lost their fear of the Queen/Goddess and that her true, loving nature has been liberated from the perverted image created by the pagan Cults.

Reflecting on the day, we realised that with the victory on the battlefield going to the West, as indicated by VE Day on 8th May, and with the restoration of the power of the King by the uniting of the Twin Pillars, the Story could flow to its happy conclusion.

Upon our return, there was an email from Robert who had given us further information as to what we needed to do in London. This was in response to Cassie's of the day before but she had not thought to check her emails before setting off. He mentioned that in London we would find ourselves at a crossroads and there would be a road we could incorporate so making a six-pointed star. The Green Stone would pass us by several times, once on the hat of woman on a bus and once on a ship. We remembered passing a pirate ship in the children's playground in Kensington Gardens, which had been built in memory of Princess Diana. In other words, the energy of the Green Stone has to find a suitable object at the physical level, just like the Ring of Barahir. The Stone would be with us briefly, but we were not to hinder its progress as it needed to return to Scotland.

Cassie believed she remembered the crossroads and the road to make the six-pointed star. As there is no linear time, she simply visualised herself at the centre of the crossroads and drew the third road into the pattern, so changing the cross into the Royal Star. It is interesting how important it is to ground all our work in our physical surroundings.

Chapter 59

The Dead Land

It is in the light of The Lord of the Rings being trapped at many layers - each one created after another repetition at the physical level - that Cassie was finally able to make sense of a particular experience in her role as Frodo. Three times she made the pitiless trek across the arid plain of Mordor to Mountain Doom, with each one becoming an increasingly physical experience. Perhaps it was more a case of it being the three occasions she happened to notice: others may have escaped her notice entirely.

The first was so subliminal that it would have gone unnoticed if Robert had not made a passing reference. The energy of the final stage of Frodo and Samwise's journey was drawn to Cassie when, with a sense of urgency, she was single-mindedly writing an earlier book. This echoed the same feeling of urgency and total focus with which Frodo and Samwise made the gruelling trek to the volcano. That was in the summer of 2001.

The next experience was much more real and occurred on 25th November 2006. Cassie had spent the evening at Caroline's in the Woodford Valley but when it came time to leave, the device that operates the electronically controlled wooden gates, could not be found, as her father had mistakenly taking it with him. We stood before the solid wooden gates in pitch dark wondering what to do. Cassie was impatient to get home so she found herself scaling the fence despite the slippery wooden cross bar on which she put all her weight. The next minute she was sitting astride the fence unable to see the extent of the drop on the other side. Gingerly she began letting herself down hoping her feet would touch the ground before she had to let go. Fortunately, they did. As she was performing this the thought went through her head that she was repeating an event in the Story but she could not immediately think which one. Caroline was also thinking the same thing as Cassie heard her voice from the other side of the fence saying, "I am sure you are reliving something in the Story".

It took a little while for Cassie to equate this curious episode with one of Frodo's adventures on the journey into the Dead Lands or Mordor. Finally she felt sure she had found the one. A strikingly similar event occurs when Frodo and Samwise have managed to escape the evil Tower of Cirith Ungol which guards the pass over the Mountains of Shadow into the Land of Mordor. They are fleeing the Tower and the alarm has been sounded. Just as they reach a bridge over a chasm they hear two search parties on the road, one behind and one in front. There is only one course of action open to them: it is to jump off the bridge 'but it was too dark for them to guess the depth of the fall'. This was exactly what Cassie experienced when climbing over the gate in the Woodford Valley. Fortunately for the hobbits the drop was no more than a dozen feet and, although they landed on thorn bushes, it was better then landing on rocks.

However, this was not the end of the experience. Turning on the television when she reached home, she found herself watching a man dragging himself across a glacier with a broken leg. As she watched, she realised this mountaineer's desperate attempt to reach camp before his friends departed, mirrored Frodo and Samwise's equally desperate effort to reach the volcano in time. All three were short of food and suffering from dehydration. Two moments in particular, exactly reflected the hobbit's journey. The terrain changes from ice to jumbled rocks and the mountaineer prepares for the last haul by jettisoning all extraneous gear and strapping his leg to keep it straight as he has to drag himself over the rocks. Frodo and Sam do precisely the same for the final stage, discarding their orc gear and Samwise's beloved pots and pans. The other moment was when the man mercifully finds a trickle of water amongst the rocks just as Samwise does. The mountaineer was in physical and mental agony as were the hobbits, particularly Frodo, who was having to resist the evil will of Sauron now beating down on him ever more strongly as they drew closer to the Black Tower with Sauron's Eye placed at the very top. And, like the mountaineer, at the very end Frodo begins to crawl through extreme exhaustion. This courageous man miraculously wins through – as do Frodo and Sam. (The documentary of this true story is called Touching the Void).

Cassie was left in no doubt, following on as it did on the heels of the gate incident, that by watching this courageous man's terrible ordeal, she was indirectly experiencing his journey. She had, therefore, channelled, earthed and cleared those energies from that other dimension.

In the third experience of Frodo and Sam's dangerous journey through the Dead Land, Cassie actually experienced the trek itself, but in a less severe form for she took the part of Sam. Again, as before, it was set up most carefully, lending strength to the conclusion we came to that this was something which had to be experienced, just as we had undergone the journey through the Mines of Moria. Without this last gruelling and most dangerous stretch of their journey, the One Ring would not have fallen into the volcanic fires with Gollum, thus causing the instantaneous collapse of Sauron's vast army at the moment the Army of the West was about to be overwhelmed.

In June 2007 a part-time job exactly fitting Cassie's requirements fell into her lap. It all started with a bizarre incident over the weekend of September 8/9 2007. Her office colleague dyed her hair but it went horribly wrong and she emerged a frightening jet-black! In her attempt to lighten it, she then went from one extreme to the other for, it went completely white. She tried yet another colour which made her hair turn pink and, finally, she returned to her original colour. It was such an extraordinary story and Cassie could not help noticing that the colours she went through – black, white and then pink - were strikingly reminiscent of the colours of the pagan Goddess as mentioned earlier. These were white for the maiden phase in spring, red for the Mother/Love Goddess in summer and black for the Wise Woman in winter. As the Other Side frequently used elements from that evil cult to attempt to intimidate her – such as leaving a dead toad neatly laid in the gutter in front of her house or, on another occasion, three artificial puddles of sick on the pavement outside her gate, or a battered bag of milk drops with a picture of a red and white cow that was left in her shopping basket as she went round the food aisles of Marks &

Spencer. The meaning behind these was as a reminder of the cruel pagan Queen. The Queen ruled in the name of the Triple Goddess, one of whose sacred animals was the Red Cow. She therefore took it as a warning.

The following day, with her senses now on full alert, whilst eating lunch in the office, it dawned on her that over the past month her lunch had become increasingly frugal. She only wished to eat herbal oat-cakes, nuts, dried apricots and apples and she realised that her diet compared with that of Frodo and Sam's as they infiltrated enemy country. The oatcakes could be likened to the magically sustaining Lembas biscuits of the Elves. In normal circumstances Cassie ate a much more substantial packed lunch. Next, she realised that the events of the past couple of weeks could be viewed in a new light.

She had not long returned from the Christian Green Belt Festival held every year at Cheltenham Race Course at the end of August over the Bank Holiday weekend. She had partly gone to help her sister-in-law look after a member of the party who was blind. A very enjoyable time was had but, now, one incident in particular stood out. It being a large Festival, naturally Cassie and her blind companion had done a lot of trekking around the huge encampment. On one occasion towards the end of the afternoon and in hot sunshine, they became lost and trudged on for what seemed like forever. Cassie remembers feeling weary and her feet hurting before they finally found the campsite. On returning home, she discovered she had broken her little toe as well as sustaining sunburn to her right eyelid – which struck her as very strange as she had never before had sunburn in such a place.

Everything now slotted into place. She realised that her patient companion had been in the role of Frodo, whilst she had been fulfilling that of Samwise on the final and most dangerous part of the 'hopeless' journey. Increasingly, Samwise had to guide Frodo who was by now almost completely 'blinded' by the increasing power of the Enemy's Ring hung around his neck on a chain. That power was getting stronger the closer they drew to Mount Doom in whose fires The Ring was forged. Frodo tells Sam:

No taste of food, no feel of water, no sound of wind, no memory of tree or grass or flower, no image of moon or star are left to me. I am naked in the dark, Sam, and there is no veil between me and the wheel of fire. I begin to see it even with my waking eyes, and all else fades.

Later, Cassie realised the sunburn to her right eyelid was a consequence of the increased fiery power of the Ring whose Master is The Eye. She felt grateful that the endless trekking over the weekend of the Festival had been shared with her blind friend, just as Samwise and Frodo had each other for company and even, for a while, shared the burden of The Ring, the part of Samwise being taken by Caroline and, towards the end, by Cassie while Caroline became the Ringbearer.

In the weeks that followed Cassie experienced shooting pains at the base of the fourth finger of the left hand. Finally, on 15 September, three weeks after trekking in the heat at the Greenbelt Festival, as she and her daughter were loading up the car for the start of a new year at university, the Red Arrows flew directly overhead in a 'V' formation with a great roar. The experience seemed to Cassie to reflect the arrival of the great eagles at the battle in the Dead Lands. It was Gandalf who called out in a loud voice "The Eagles are coming!" They flew down in 'long swift lines... speeding on a gathering wind' in the nick of time. At that moment, far away in Sauron's Kingdom, Frodo was engaged in a fierce struggle with Gollum on the edge of the volcano for possession of the One Ring.

Chapter 60

Ring Cycle

After writing this chapter in July 2008 we passed it to Robert for comments. These we now include in brackets.

The increasing severity of the three journeys across the Dead Land experienced by Cassie set us thinking as to the nature of the multidimensional world we live in. We recalled that Robert told us the original Story first took place 60,000 years ago. If an Age or cycle is approximately 3,000 years, this means the Story has been repeated twenty times. Suddenly we understood. Each new re-enactment pushes the other 'time slots' further away. (Time – ages within ages – create lessons. Time to end duality. Clearing ages, time slots – reducing the amount consciousness impinges on space.) It would follow that the energies from the layers furthest away would have the weakest impact on us here at the dense physical level. It now seemed logical to us that if Robert has been orchestrating which layers are cleared - which we now see is a distinct possibility - he would choose to clear the outer 'time capsules' first so as to mitigate, as much as possible, the severity of having to interact with the Story closest to us, and therefore with the strongest energies. (Not Robert but part of something that has always been and chosen this Robert to work through, yet at same time wholly Robert).

Musing further on the reason for the story of The Lord of the Rings being repeatedly recycled, the following occurred to us. At the beginning of every new cycle, when the Forces of Evil have traditionally been defeated, the new era gets underway with the restoration of peace and order and goodwill. However, as a whole, people's conditioning is, in reality, scarcely different from before so, gradually, old patterns will begin to re-emerge. This is why the story keeps repeating itself: because humanity does not change. Robert has set out to change this by forming a new Fellowship. (Change the levels of consciousness and begin an end to the 4 races plus.) One way of changing the old patterns would be to change the enormous power of the Master Ring, thereby reducing the power of the Dark Lord since we know that he put much of his own power into the Ring. The transmuted energy could then be used to help bring balance and calm to the world so that war is avoided this time around.

There is another factor to be considered. As those old patterns begin to repeat themselves at the physical level, they are given added power, through the Law of Attraction, from all those invisible layers around the planet. In other words those energies will be drawn to similar patterns being repeated on the physical domain. This is what Robert meant when he told us that the One Ring is exerting an evil influence in the world today. All the One Rings trapped in all those layers of time are focussing their energy through the One Ring closest to our world. (This is it, if not sorted, then move on to another planet. One Ring. This year, 2008, Duality and Quadality should begin to reduce. R showed how the 2 and 8 merge to form two rings, just as do the two '00s'. Then they can be merged from '4' rings to '2' rings and thence to just The One. R called it the Modality of Time. The aim is to create just the ONE time, ie no past and no future, only the Present or the NOW at which point we will have WON.)

It is in this context that the job which fell into Cassie's lap was one which would attract the energy of Frodo and Sam's journey through Mordor. The final stage of their quest coincided with Sauron launching war on the West. The job in question was working part-time for one of the political party Associations which are constantly in a state of war as they ceaselessly seek to do down the other political parties so as to emerge the victor. She was deliberately put in this warlike situation so as to attract those energies. The sequence of events that unfolds in the original tale leads inexorably to the destruction of the One Ring in the fiery 'Cracks of Doom'. Even the breaking of her little toe, we realise, can be compared to Frodo's Ring finger being bitten off by Gollum just before he falls into the molten lava while still holding Frodo's finger. The violence of the deed was re-enacted but in such a way that she did not actually lose either toe or finger.

Imagine our consternation when Robert's comment on the above was "Lesson gets harder unless you learn!" He went on to say that it is all to do with the world of energy and its very simple rules – ie if you do nothing then there is no change. Little did we realise that our attention was being drawn to a part of the Story which we might change – as we had done before in transforming the energy of Kingly sacrifice. We were at a loss as to what was meant by his remark. For one thing, by this date we had completed the Quest, (or so we thought) by reaching the ending in The Lord of the Rings. Consequently, we were not able to take the necessary action. This came shortly afterwards - and only at the very last opportunity.

Chapter 61

Repeating Patterns

Whilst watching a documentary on the love story of the Princess Elizabeth (our present Queen) and Philip Battenburg, a Prince of Greece and Denmark who was also an officer in the British Navy, the idea came that there were striking parallels to be found in their love story and the one between Arwen and Aragorn. In the original blueprint, the match meets with the disapproval of Arwen's father (her mother having left Middle Earth long ago). Aragorn was not of the same race as the immortal Arwen, but human and therefore mortal. However, he was of the Line of Luthien and therefore connected by blood to Arwen who was also descended from that stock. Before winning her hand, Aragorn had to be found worthy in the eyes of her father and there ensues a long period of waiting during which Aragorn's love for Arwen never falters. The wedding takes place at the end of a war in a city still bearing the scars of battle.

When the Princess Elizabeth fell for the dashing naval officer the match met, not with the disapproval of her parents, but they felt she was too young and that there should be a cooling off period when the two would not meet, although they could correspond. Like Aragorn, he was an outsider, being foreign but just as Aragorn was distantly related to Arwen, so was Prince Philip related to the Princess Elizabeth through Queen Victoria. In the event their love for each other proved steadfast and their marriage took place, again at the end of a war in a city battered by bombing. Just as in the original, the wedding lifted the spirits of a people long oppressed by war, giving them hope for the future.

Chapter 62

Pilgrimage to Salisbury

It had been some time since we had met up with Robert, so we had arranged an appointment for 17 January 2006 in Robert's hometown on the coast in South Wales. As we sped along the dual carriageway it occurred to us that we were, once again, in the Story, i.e., that we were travelling to the Grey Havens on the coast of Middle Earth from where all the Ring bearers – Gandalf, Elrond, Galadriel, Bilbo and Frodo - took ship for the island of the Elves – an island which was taken from mortal circles many centuries ago. On our way, we remembered seeing the curious sight of a man mounted on a white horse standing in the middle of a footbridge spanning the motorway watching the cars. Then, as we entered the town, we became hopelessly lost but, after many wrong turns which took us right down to the docks, we eventually found Robert's new premises, arriving only a little late.

He agreed that we had just made the journey where the four Ring bearers leave Middle Earth and, just as Gandalf had been waiting for them beside the ship, he was there when we arrived. The man on the white horse had scrambled our brains to try and prevent us from reaching our destination, which was why we missed our usual turn-off. We had reached the end of the story. Robert described it as having spiralled the story up through all the levels but, now, we needed to spiral it back down and pin it in the earth. We also needed to pin down the Cult of the Sacred King once and for all. Robert spoke with a sense of urgency and asked us to make reservations in a hotel in Salisbury for the Nine as soon as possible. The earliest date was over the weekend of 4th/5th February 2006 and it so happened that there were nine of us who could make it. It was a bitterly cold weekend. Below are extracts from notes of the weekend's events and Robert's teachings.

We all met in the conservatory of the guesthouse which, appropriately, was reached by a spiral staircase. Robert said the weekend was to do with the rings. He told us we needed to find four rings to north, south, east and west of the compass. Old Sarum, an Iron Age fort to the north of Salisbury, was one of the Rings. Robert told us that the druids had a university close to Old Sarum and that they possessed rings of power, which were not material rings, but rings of consciousness. They sought psychics whom they could train to develop rings of consciousness. Which ties in with the concept behind the rings of power. Since all teaching was originally oral, no written records exist but the information is still available to those who seek it.

The three elf kings, Gandalf, Galadriel and Elrond, tie in with the Cathars, which means 'the pure' and Montsegur, where so many died. Like many books, the battle ebbs and flows, good versus bad, the few controlling the many. Robert said that most of us present could liken what we are doing with The Lord of the Rings, repeating acts of what happens to the Ring and its companions. Caroline handed us information on the Belinus Line, an energy line running the length of the country. Her map showed us that the line crosses the Michael and Mary line at Winchester, which lies just to the east of Salisbury. The Michael/Mary line runs diagonally in a West/East direction from Cornwall to the East coast. Beneath Winchester Cathedral there are two temples dedicated respectively to Bel, the Celtic/Roman sun god, and the sun god of the Greeks, Apollo. The Pilgrim's Way to Santiago de Compostela in Spain starts at Penallt Old Church in Monmouthshire and inside the church is a memorial to the pilgrims. The route passes through Winchester and on to the south coast. Pilgrims from Salisbury set out from the St Ann's Gate of Salisbury Cathedral along Clarendon Way to join the pilgrimage at Winchester. The ancient route goes directly past the former royal palace, which now lies in ruins. The Lord of the Rings links to the pilgrim routes.

Robert continued that, for us to understand the weekend, each one of us would have to make several shifts in consciousness. We needed to take a huge step forward. A lot had changed recently and the four rings would reset the Seal of Solomon. Five rivers flow through the city and each of us needed to tune into our intuitive self and listen to what it tells us. We would not progress from the thinking or emotional part of ourselves. We had to be in different vibrations in order to do things quickly, working at all levels. The nine of us corresponded with the Nine Walkers and we should try to be wholly present, existing in a real living meditation, living in the moment, the Now. A change in consciousness would allow us to connect and become interactive with the world we live in – not in Robert's world, or anyone else's – ours. It is not reliant on understanding – it just happens and another ring of consciousness opens.

After visiting the Cathedral, we set off for Old Sarum where we cleared a lot of negative energy, which entails harmonising and balancing the energies. As we did so, a micro light aeroplane circled above us repeating in the air the clearing work we were doing on the ground. After lunch at an inn in the nearby Woodford Valley, we drove north up the valley and Jan suddenly said she wanted to stop and walk down to the riverbank just before we reached the bridge. A shot was heard and a fish jumped clear of the water. This was a link to Ted Sandyman's mill in the Shire. Two swans swam towards us and one came on land and waddled up to Caroline who said she was sorry she had nothing to give it. Darren, the only male in our group apart from Robert, said that the swans understood what was happening and were very happy. This linked with the Fellowship's stay as the guests of Galadriel in the Golden Wood of Lothlorien. From boats shaped like swans, the travellers were sent on their way with gifts of great worth. Cassie threw her ring – the One Ring – into the river. It was quite a moment as it spun and sparkled in the air before falling into the water. Once again the One Ring was lost in a river, just as before, when it slid off Isildur's finger into the river Gladden. Robert said it would not now matter if Gollum found it. We took this to mean that this was because the Ring had been divested of its power.

We crossed over the bridge and continued on our way to Figsbury Ring, an Iron-Age hill fort, which lies to the east of Salisbury and was clearly one of the four rings. The name means a fertile place. Parking the cars, we climbed to the top of the bank from where we had a magnificent view of the surrounding countryside, a patchwork of fields and woods, spread out beneath us. As we walked the perimeter, we came across three posts with broken wires standing in a line and Robert said they represented the three crosses of Golgotha and something needed releasing. This was done but we omitted to do something else of great importance, which was to have horrible consequences for Caroline in her role as Aragorn. Someone commented that the crucifixion was a myth and that Jesus had survived and had a family. We walked on and came across some trees, whereupon, Darren climbed into a hollow tree and put out his hand. Robert immediately cried out, "No, no, stop him"! Darren had suddenly taken on the role of Saruman whose symbol was a white hand and who had cut down a great swathe of the forest of Fangorn to fuel his war. Jenny threw her coat on the ground, which announced the arrival of Gandalf who played a vital part in Saruman's defeat. All was well and Robert said that a lot of The Lord of the Rings was taking place here.

Shortly afterwards, there was an awkward scene. Jenny, who had dressed all in red that morning, thus taking on the role of the Queen/Goddess, the colours of the triple goddess being white for the maid, red for the queen mother and black for the priestess or crone. Later she explained that she 'knew' she had to wear red that day. She now turned to Laura - and not to Caroline - and told her she was Aragorn. We had been told that, at different times, we would all play different roles, so Caroline presumed it was some fresh turn in the Story. Robert then commented that Laura was Aragorn for the moment and must look for his sword. We thought no more of it and returned to the guesthouse.

It was time for tea and, the conservatory being occupied, we convened in Tracy's bedroom as it was the largest room with a double bed. Hints as to the 'Old' King's fate immediately became apparent. Cassie pointed out some objects to Robert when he came into the room but he looked at the casket on the windowsill and said, "I don't like the look of that; it's for putting heads in." The room was painted green, ominously reminiscent of a sacred grove where human sacrifice once took place. On the wall above the bed-head was an Indian woodcarving of the Indian God Vishnu and his consort, Lakshmi, and above them was a grand mock canopy. In other words, this was a bed fit for a royal couple. Robert Graves reveals in his book, The White Goddess, that one of the ways in which the King met his ritual death was in the marriage bed, having been bound to the four corners of the bed. His head was preserved and, indeed, often placed in a casket.

Caroline sat down at the end of the bed and Darren came and sat next to her. After a few minutes he got up but something made her grab hold of the back of his jacket and try to pull him back, which both then found amusing. Caroline herself was puzzled as to why she so wished him to stay there. It was, of course, because she wanted to be protected from the Queen/Goddess and the terrible fate which awaited her. Robert then asked her to read out some verses from the I Ching, which she had copied from a stone slab in the city. As she began to read, she was suddenly overcome by an inexplicable and overpowering fear, which she was helpless to withstand. In normal circumstances, if something so untoward had happened, she would have asked someone else to read her notes and made some excuse to leave the room, but she was as if frozen, bound hand and foot which, as a Sacred King she would literally have been, and she was forced to carry on to the bitter end. Afterwards, Tracy said that while Caroline was reading, there were shifting layers in front of her face.

The following day, Sunday, Caroline, who was recovering from 'flu, did not join the rest of the group and Cassie, unaware at the time of what had taken place in the guest-house, happened to ask Robert whether or not the marriage of the King and Queen was going to take place over the weekend. At the time, Robert's reply was confusing. He said that too many people wanted to be king and that we should get rid of kings. Certainly, one of the terrible legacies of the Cult is that, subconsciously, reincarnated sacred kings perceive that they should be king, thus we have such tragic stories as Shakespeare's play Macbeth. The ambitious Macbeth and his wife murder King Duncan under their own roof so that Macbeth ca become king. Perhaps this is why Jesus was tortured and put to death and why, until humanity is cleansed of the corruption of this Cult, he cannot openly come amongst us again.

All this was confirmed in an article by Gary Linekar in a Sunday paper called "Sol's torment". The Sacred King was identified with the sun and 'Sol' means sun. It is clear to us that one of the channels through which the energy of the Sacred King Cult - trapped at other dimensions - has been manifesting in our time, if not shaping, is through the Cult of Celebrity, which also includes footballers such as Sol or David Beckham. The energy moves around from one victim to the next. (See Appendix IX Fashion Victim, Pop Idol.)

A final confirmation of Caroline's ordeal in the bedroom at the Guest House, was the obituary in the papers the following week announcing the death of Prince Carol of Romania, heir to the former deposed King of Romania. Caroline is the feminine form of Carol.

Chapter 63

A Black Carriage

The visit ended in the early afternoon on the Sunday in the centre of town by the rapids, a fitting juncture in The Lord of the Rings where the Fellowship disperses. Largely thanks to Robert's cryptic comments, we finally worked out what had really taken place in the guesthouse bedroom. Caroline, as King, had been ritually sacrificed, whilst all those assembled had unwittingly looked on at this grim spectator sport. How had this come about when we had changed events first time around and experienced the happy marriage between King and Queen? Going back over the weekend it became clear that the moment to have changed the pattern was when we were all gathered at the three crosses of the Crucifixion on Figsbury Ring. It was here we should have repeated what was done at 11 Kensington Place. This was to take Jesus down from the cross and turn the cross into the six-pointed Star of David.

We felt it was not too late to make the correction so, nearly two weeks later, on Friday 17 February 2006, Cassie again made the journey to Figsbury Ring on her own: Caroline was unable to go as she was still recovering from flu and it was a cold day. The morning atmosphere was so very different to the Group's last visit late in the afternoon on a heavily overcast day. It was one of those invigorating blustery days where there are plenty of white clouds scudding across a blue sky – and the sun was shining, which Cassie took as a good omen. The Ring is high and exposed giving the feeling of being on top of the world. She made her way to the crosses on the far side of the Iron Age circle and, standing in front of them, called on the energy of the group and of the Green Stone to help neutralise the negative energy of the cult. She then placed a stone at the foot of each cross, at which moment, the sun came out. Suddenly, overcome with joy she did a dance first in one direction and then in the opposite, which had the effect of blending the energies of the Opposites. Picking up a stick she drew a circle and a cross within, lastly placing the stick so as to make the six-pointed Star.

On the drive back to Caroline's house in the Woodford Valley she passed signs representing both the King and the Goddess: a white horse signifying the goddess and a notice saying: Honey for Sale. The bee, of course, is also sacred to the Goddess. Further on, she saw a stunning sight - a long hedge of winter-flowering, yellow forsythia in full bloom. What more fitting reminder of the Sun King! It was also a certain sign that the King had been healed for, on an earlier occasion in the Wye Valley, a flower from the same shrub stood in for the healing wildflower known as kingsfoil.

But there was still outstanding business to be done before the marriage of King and Queen could take place. We needed to join the sundered aspects of kingship – military and spiritual - as we had done at the village of Idstone, which lies between the villages of Bishopstone and Kingston Winslow. A place was to hand in the town of Salisbury itself at St Thomas à Beckett church. In fact, we had already visited the church over the weekend of the group visit but, once again, we had not picked up the clues. St. Thomas a Beckett had been Chancellor of the Exchequer and a close friend of King Henry II who, thinking to place an ally in such a powerful position, had made him Archbishop of Canterbury. However, the demands of the paramount spiritual leader in the land set the Archbishop on a path opposed to the wishes of the King. The story is well known. Personal knights of the King, after his famous outburst, "Who will rid me of this turbulent priest", took it upon themselves to murder the Archbishop in front of the altar in Canterbury Cathedral without the knowledge of the King who then performed a public penance in the Cathedral. What more symbolic place to unite these two roles than at the church named after this Archbishop?

The following day, therefore, we made our way to the church and to the Lady Chapel where we proceeded to speak the appropriate words. Scarcely had we begun when the organ suddenly burst into loud joyful music. We then became aware that the church was filled with flowers in readiness for a wedding and realised that we were experiencing the echoes of the wedding of Aragorn and Arwen taking place at another level of existence. We stood for a while happily listening to the organist as he practised the triumphal music, just such music as would have accompanied Aragorn and Arwen as they walked together down the aisle, man and wife.

The royal line was renewed through this union and signs of this were evident everywhere. On the south wall of the nave there was a truly enormous coat of arms, which stood out, partly because of its size and partly because there was a preponderance of bright gold in what looked like the Royal Coat of Arms but slightly different. Instead of the lion and the unicorn, there was a lion and a dragon. Reading the inscription underneath, we learnt that it was the coat of arms of Queen Elizabeth I, the dragon being the Tudor dragon. We knew, of course, that it symbolised the Pendragon line of King Uther/Arthur and that this line was ancient. Another famous female progenitor was also in evidence. The organ was a gift from Queen Victoria who is sometimes called 'the Grandmother of Europe', from whom most of the European Royal Houses descend. The royal line was clearly being shown as descending through the female line. As we left the church, a man dressed in black held open the swing doors for Caroline and smiled at her and. Then, as we walked through the town, two more men, also dressed in black, unaccountably seemed to acknowledge her with a smile as they passed by. Black, of course, was the uniform of Aragorn and the Royal House of Numenor. There was further confirmation that we had successfully changed the story. On returning home, what should Cassie find lying in the middle of the table but a small pair of white lovebirds facing each other so that their beaks were touching. Her daughter had just returned home from university and left the lovebirds on the table.

Curiously enough, there was a popular TV series being shown on the life of Queen Elizabeth, one of several series in quick succession at around that time and, close to where Cassie lives, are the Queen Elizabeth Public Gardens. There was yet another twist in this tale. The very next day Cassie and her daughters were invited to Sunday lunch with friends where it transpired the husband could trace his descent back to Mary

Boleyn, elder sister of the beautiful dark Queen, Ann Boleyn, mother of Queen Elizabeth !

A few days' later, Caroline was to have further confirmation that we had changed the story. She was just paying the bill in a shop when a carriage drawn by two black horses drew up outside and a footman, dressed in black with silver braiding, stepped down and stood waiting on the pavement. The girl at the till then said, "Your carriage awaits you". After she had paid the bill, the girl again said, "Your carriage is still waiting for you". Aragorn and Arwen had, indeed, celebrated their mid-summer wedding at Minas Tirith.

Chapter 64

The Corruption of the Shire

The members of the Fellowship lingered on in the White City after the high point of the marriage of the King and the wedding feast. At last, they had the time to listen to each other's adventures during the Quest. Finally, the time came when they became eager to return home which resulted in the natural breaking-up of the Fellowship. If we wished to proceed to the next phase of the Story, we, too, had to end the Fellowship. This we did, but not until the following year at the end of August 2006, and we were not prepared for the extraordinary events that were to follow.

Two months later, on 28 October 2006, Cassie/Frodo had an experience which exactly mirrored events towards the end of the Story when the hobbits are at last homeward bound. She bumped into a young man who was a friend of her daughter's. Immediately, she had the impression he had grown taller and thinner since last she saw him, and commented as much. He agreed, saying he had just had a growth spurt. During the hobbits' return journey to the Shire, members of the Fellowship noticed that Merry and Pippin have both grown uncommonly tall for hobbits of their age. Musing on this, they realised that it must be due to their drinking Treebeard's magical Ent brew. Whilst in the Elf valley of Rivendell, Bilbo also comments on their height and warns them that if they do not stop growing, hats and clothes will become expensive! This young man also resembled a hobbit in other ways in that he possessed a happy nature and was very fond of his family.

We were reminded how Robert had told us that England is the Shire and that we would be living the experiences in The Lord of the Rings. Beyond doubt, Cassie/Frodo was in that part of the tale when the four returning hobbits – Frodo, Samwise, Merry and Pippin – set about rousing the people of the Shire to rid themselves of outsiders who are systematically ruining the country. The Shire is in a sorry state. Ugly brick buildings with scant comfort have been built, pubs closed, a curfew imposed, and beer and food are in short supply. Worse still, the seeds of corruption have been sown, for some hobbits have changed for the worse. The majority, of course, hate the oppressive yolk and others are cowed, but some are enjoying their little bit of power as 'shiriffs', whose numbers have been vastly increased. Frodo and friends learn that the Mayor, whose chief function hitherto was to attend celebrations and weddings, has been imprisoned. The hobbits have been hedged in by a proliferation of 'Rules', things they can and cannot do which are being imposed upon them by a small band of thugs who are not averse to the use of force. The thugs appear to be half orc and half man with squinty eyes and evil natures. They quickly suppress any opposition and, as a result, many hobbits have been jailed, something virtually unheard of in former, happier days, and some have even been killed. Finally, they discover that someone, rather sinisterly known as 'The Boss', is the source of oppression and he is based at Frodo's former home, Bag End no less!

We were now on the look out for events in our daily lives which might reflect those in the Story and remembered an incident a month earlier, when we took a walk in the Woodford Valley just to the north of Salisbury. Three of us were caught trespassing – in other words, breaking 'Rules'! Thinking it no longer applied, we had chosen to ignore a battered sign saying 'Private Property' pinned high on a tree trunk. Scarcely had we entered the woodland when we heard a warm country voice behind us asking us to stop and come back. He was a real countryman - woolly hat, a brown wrinkled face, in which was set two bright blue eyes looking anxiously at us. He just happened to work for the landowner, and just happened to be driving past at that very moment. What bad luck! He was apologetic and helpful, saying there was a bridleway close by. One of us started to protest but was shut up by the other two. Retracing our steps, we did as we were asked. The incident somewhat echoes the reception of the four hobbits on reaching the river boundary of the Shire at night. Where there had once been none, now there stood spiked gates at either end of the bridge which were locked. The hobbits who emerged seemed frightened and told them to read the sign saying 'No admittance between sundown and sunrise'. The tired travellers retorted that they could not possibly read the words in the dark! Our 'No Admittance' sign had similarly been overlooked by us, partly because it was high up on a tree on a small, faded piece of wood, and partly because of the shade of the woodland! Merry and Pippin simply scaled the gate and quickly dealt with the Chief's Big Man, whom they sternly ordered to leave the Shire.

On 2 November 2006 there was an article in The Daily Telegraph on surveillance. It described how we in Britain were the most spied-upon country in the world. The very first night Frodo and friends spend in the Shire, news of their arrival has reached Bag End, forty miles away, by the following morning. Saruman had set up a spy network, reminiscent of George Orwell's Big Brother as well as the evil culture of betrayal of your nearest and dearest fostered in the communist satellite countries of the Soviet Union and China. Also topical was the subject of ID cards, which every citizen would be required to carry with them. This would create the need for a database for the storage of personal details.

In August 2006 Cassie began working for a chartered surveyor who specialised in 'Commercial Development', which involves the selling of land for the construction of housing or industrial units. It placed Cassie at the very heart of the goings-on in the Shire at the end of the Story. Of course, in real life such houses are not built indiscriminately - as was the case in the Shire - but are subject to the planning process. Nevertheless, there is a comparison to be drawn.

On 5 November, the sentencing to death of the former Iraqi President, Saddam Hussein, by hanging for crimes against his own people, made front-page news. We realised that Saddam Hussein was another Saruman, for it was none other than he who was the Chief who had appropriated Bag End and was the root cause of all the problems in the Shire. Comparing their names, we worked out that the letters in 'Saruman', bar the letter 'r', are to be found in 'Saddam Hussein'. Like Saruman, Saddam Hussein had invaded another man's country and, like Saruman, it is rumoured he conducted gruesome experiments in genetic engineering. Saruman created a superior form of orc called the 'fighting Uruk-hai' by his experiments in the interbreeding of orc and man.

The cleansing of the Shire is achieved when the four friends successfully arouse the people and call them to arms. A great battle is fought at Bywater in which Saruman's thugs are defeated. The army then proceeds to Bag End where, to the amazement of Frodo and friends, they discover that The Boss is none other than the traitor Saruman. Frodo orders him to leave the country and he is about to go when, goaded once too often by his master, he is unexpectedly killed by his own lackey, Wormtongue. It represents the final stroke in the War against Sauron, at Bilbo's old home, Bag End. It was whilst we were experiencing this part of the story that on 30 December 2006, Saddam Hussein also met his death.

Chapter 65

The Shire in the Surrey Hills

A friend of Cassie's had told her about a Franciscan Friary (which comprised both men and women) and which welcomed visitors who were free to stroll about the grounds, join the friars and nuns in the chapel and have a glimpse of monastic life and she suggested that we should visit it on Saturday 5 November 2006. Caroline was slightly sceptical that this would be a nice day out but, luckily, went along with the idea. We had quite a long journey to get there but we finally arrived to find the place completely deserted. The Friary was surrounded by a certain area of rough lawn encircled by rather gloomy trees, but there was not a soul to be seen – no jolly families picnicking at the table and benches provided, even though the weather was unseasonably warm. No friars or nuns in sandals and habits with rope belts walking across the lawn – nothing. For a moment we thought we heard chanting coming from the chapel only to find the door was locked. We even ventured inside through an open back door but, finding no one around, retreated mystified. By now we couldn't wait to get away. The whole place reeked of decay and seemed to us symptomatic of the slow death of institutional religion.

Cassie then came up with another idea: we would visit the Harry Edward Healing Centre, which was just five miles further along the road. As we drove into the village we saw, to our astonishment, bouncing and floating along the road in front of us, two balloons, one pink the other yellow, tied together with pink ribbon. We were much intrigued by this as we had each recently seen a hot air balloon in the sky and here they were again on a smaller scale. It was only later that we realised that they represented the Sun God and the Love Goddess, the King and the Queen, coming together in balance and harmony. Just managing to avoid running over them, we missed a turning, which would have taken us to the Healing Centre, and found ourselves back on the main road. We turned around and re-entered the village and, once again, found the balloons bouncing gently along in front of us. This time, we took the right turning and found ourselves in the centre of the village, which widened out into a beautiful space. At one end was an old Inn called The White Horse', at the other end a small medieval church. In the middle was a grassy triangle on which stood a young oak tree and, further up another street, there was a hotel called 'The Prince of Wales'. The weather was perfect - the sun shone brightly in a cloudless sky and the air was fresh and sparkling. It was an idyllic scene with the lime white Elizabethan houses with their black beams and hanging flower baskets and we felt as if we were in Heaven! However, we were still very much in our bodies and, having discovered that 'The White Horse' served tea and coffee, we decided to go in before continuing our journey.

By now it was 2.30 pm and we found the maze of Tudor rooms inside still full of happy family groups enjoying their Sunday lunch. It was obviously extremely popular and the only free tables were outside. As we sat in the sunshine watching people coming and going – happy families with children, grandparents, young couples holding hands - Caroline found herself saying: this is where we are meant to be – with people. And it was then that we realised we were in the Shire, a Shire that had recovered from the devastation wreaked on it by Saruman and which had returned to its peaceful, happy way of life. At any moment we expected to see Merry, Pippin, and Samwise joining us as they sauntered towards The White Horse, enjoying the fruits of their victory over Saruman (and the backbreaking work undertaken to raise the Shire from its ruined state) and bent on sustenance and a pipe of best South Farthing tobacco. Looking more closely at our surroundings, we realised that the Inn sign, which showed a white horse pawing the air, also represented the inn at Bree called 'The Prancing Pony'. This was where Aragorn near the beginning of their epic journey rescued the four hobbits. The young oak tree in front of us was at the same stage of growth as the newly planted trees might have been in the Shire. Saruman, in a deliberate act of desecration, had chopped down most of the trees in Hobbiton where Frodo and Samwise lived. The oak tree, of course, represents the masculine energy, whilst the sign of the white horse just behind where we sat, being sacred to the Goddess, symbolised the feminine. This was the secret of this beautiful and happy village: the opposites are here in balance and harmony in the physical surroundings.

It was quite a large village and we decided to wander around for a while and do some exploring. Down a lane we came across a stream with three white farmyard ducks on the opposite bank and children fishing from the bridge. Sitting on a bench overlooking the water was a young family, husband, wife and small child. The man was wearing a white sweater and, as we walked by, he turned and gave us a beautiful smile and we smiled back. We were fairly faintly surprised, as he had turned round to do this. We walked on a little further and then, on our way back, the man again turned round and smiled at us. Later, we thought he must have been from elsewhere and was recognising us in our roles in The Lord of the Rings. And it wasn't only the village that reminded us of the Shire. The surrounding countryside, known as the Surrey Hills, had the same peaceful, pretty villages, pastures, streams and wooded hills. All thought of visiting the Healing Centre had now gone. It was obvious that to get us to this place the Friary and the Centre had been merely a ruse. And here comes its name – the village was called Shere! The penny didn't drop until we were on the journey home!

We eventually ended up at the beautiful little church of St. James, which stands close to the Pilgrims' Way, an ancient road between Winchester and St. Thomas à Beckett's tomb at Canterbury Cathedral. The church has its own tale to tell. In 1258, Bishop de Lusignan of Winchester and fifty men broke the law by trying to take out of England valuables kept at Shere. Local men, one of whom was killed, tried to stop him at the 'Battle of Shere' and, although the people of Shere sued him for compensation through the courts, the Bishop gained pardons for all his men. The brave stand taken by the men and women of the village is reminiscent of the hobbits and their courageous defeat of Saruman and his minions – the scouring of the Shire - although in this case, sadly, they did not win. But this time around we had got the story right. By successfully anchoring the overthrow of the tyrant Saruman and seeing the people's goods and freedoms restored, we had got the story right. As Robert later put it, the Shire was now safe. Four weeks later, on Sunday 3rd December, the words 'PEOPLE POWER' were written across the front page of The Sunday Times in large letters.

Chapter 66

A Journey North

You might, with reason, suppose that our quest had ended. Certainly we thought so; but we were mistaken. Quite unexpectedly, over Christmas of 2006 we found ourselves interacting with events from another level which go back to before the Fellowship of the Ring. Tolkien wrote them down in his well-known children's book, The Hobbit. Gandalf is instrumental in galvanising a group of people to set out on a seemingly hopeless quest. A grumpy band of dwarves, one hobbit with help from Gandalf, plan to kill a dragon, which long ago destroyed the dwarf kingdom under the Lonely Mountain. For many years now the dragon Smaug had slumbered on the heaped treasure belonging to the dwarves who had never given up hope of reclaiming their own one day.

Many years later Gandalf tells the Fellowship that if Smaug had not been killed the Dark Lord would have been able to bend his thought upon the dragon to fly across the Misty Mountains and destroy Rivendell with his scorching flames. Amongst many other evils, this would have resulted in their being no Queen on the throne of Gondor, for Arwen Evenstar would have perished. In short, this prequel is an integral part of the saga. The Hobbit also gives an account of how the lost Master Ring was found by the unlikeliest of people – a hobbit, and Bilbo Baggins at that – which precipitates the grand drama of the War of the Ring.

We had made the long journey north to Wakefield in Yorkshire to spend Christmas with family. Taking a walk one evening we found ourselves standing on the ruins of Radley Castle on top of a hill looking across a large lake in the distance. The sun was setting amid white clouds and the lake was shining. All of a sudden, a ray of light pierced the clouds in a most dramatic fashion. As it so happens Cassie had not long ago re-read The Hobbit and later she marvelled at how accurately the moment echoed one in that very book. It occurs when the hobbit and dwarves are on the side of the Lonely Mountain with the dragon asleep deep inside and with the Long Lake in the distance. They have found the secret door but it cannot be opened. As the sun is setting, a single ray of light shines directly on the door and a flake of stone falls off revealing the keyhole.

It was only after several other uncannily accurate recreations of other parts of that journey that we realised we were once again interacting with events taking place at another dimension. (As we have mentioned before, it is not always easy to spot the clues when our thoughts are focussed on our everyday lives). Or, put another way, those energies were shaping events at the dense physical level around us because we had agreed to be part of this endeavour. (For the moment, Cassie appeared to have slipped into the character of Bilbo).

One example of this adventure being played out was when Cassie found herself visiting the Mining Museum for England, housed in a disused mine on the edge of Wakefield. They even keep four pit ponies, one of which was the last pony to have worked in a mine. As Cassie looked at the row of small ponies in their stalls she was reminded of how the hobbit and dwarves rode on ponies during much of their journey. Then the penny dropped: dwarves are renowned for their mining skills!

Chapter 67

Welding the Ring

The last we had heard mention of the One Ring was in November 2006 when, on a pilgrimage to Weston-Super-Mare with Robert, the energy of the Ring went into four members of the Fellowship. Apparently, four is the number to guard so as to ensure that the power does not fall into the wrong hands. Robert also gave an extraordinary revelation: "So many but so few stand within the ring – the one Ring is yet to be activated – yes it has been found many times and put safe....' He went on to say that it had never yet been welded. This statement made us think how the energy of the Meonia Stone, in the book, The Green Stone had also been guarded through aeons but was finally welded in the 1980's by a group of Nine. For safety in Egyptian times, the energy of the Meonia Stone was split between <u>nine</u> people, who, subsequently, made the journey to England. There, to keep the power safe, 'the nine lights' were distributed amongst nine energy centres throughout England and Wales. The book relates how there has always been a group of Nine throughout Time. The authors touch upon such a group existing at the time of the Gunpowder Plot (1604). A similar group appears in the Victorian era and, in the 1980's, an ever-changing group of Nine comes together, once again and 'the nine lights' are re-united in the One Stone - which is comparable to the cleansed Master Ring – and is used to defeat the Dark Lord in that particular story. However, natural law at the third dimension dictates that when one Dark Lord is defeated, another automatically takes his place, because our world is still one of duality.

At the beginning of April 2008 events took a curious turn. It began innocently enough on a sunny evening when the two of us decided to go for a walk, taking in the Cathedral Close and part of the town. Walking through the centre of town on the way back, Cassie spied a two-penny coin on the ground. It was sticking up in an odd way, which made her stoop down and pick it up. A few minutes later as we were walking by the River Avon in the Queen Elizabeth Gardens watching a beautiful sunset from across the water meadows, we suddenly noticed two youths, at some distance from one another, throwing what we took to be a ball backwards and forwards. We could also hear a curious high-pitched whining noise and wondered where it was coming from. We then realised that it was being emitted from the object, which the two young men were throwing to each other. Looking more closely, we could see that it resembled a bomb with a guiding tail. In fact, it exactly resembled a missile! We were stunned. We had never before seen such a thing and realised it represented the polarisation of humanity. How first one side attacks and then the other side retaliates in unceasing conflict.

Somehow, we didn't know why, but the two events – coin and missile – seemed significant, so we sent an email to Robert to which, as ever, he sent a cryptic reply:

Well, you found a ring yet to be, flat and not yet made into a ring - coin has two sides - a rim and lots of writing, needs to be worked out. The kids playing war is near.

At the time, this is how we interpreted Robert's reply. The Ring yet to be is the One Ring because there is 'lots of writing', just as there was on Sauron's Ring, which had the words:

One Ring to rule them all, One Ring to find them,
One Ring to bring them all and in the darkness bind them.

It is flat as it has yet to be pumped up with the energy of the One Ring. This will happen when the Nine weld it. The fact that the coin incident occurred immediately prior to seeing the boys playing at war was telling us that we can use the One Ring to prevent this happening. From what Robert said in his email, time is short as war is near.

It was perhaps not by chance that we were due to attend a workshop of Robert's in the Wye Valley on Saturday, 5th April, only three days after finding the 'ring yet to be'. However, it was not until the following morning that Cassie awoke with the

241

realisation that the Nine were meant to have welded the One Ring at the workshop. She was horrified as she now recalled that Robert had talked about us acting together as a group and giving each other support. He also told Cassie she had unfinished tasks and he seemed worried and anxious when we took our leave of him. Yet we had all failed to spark over the need to weld the Ring that day even though many at the meeting had been apprised of events in advance of the Saturday meeting. Once again, it appears that Robert is not able to tell us outright what to do, he can only hint.

First, Cassie telephoned Caroline and told her that, if needs be, we would have to make the long journey to the Wye Valley again - as Robert's talks are always held over both the Saturday and the Sunday. Then she telephoned Laura to say that we had omitted to weld the Ring yesterday and to tell Robert that we were willing to drive over. The answer came back that we should do this. Fortunately, something intervened which was to save our making the journey. That same morning Cassie, while doing a balancing exercise, suddenly saw, in her mind's eye, a shining gold ring came tumbling towards her through space and landing in the palm of her hand. It was a plain gold band and, at once, she recognised that it was the One Ring. She put it in her pocket and as she did so Gollum's words went through her head, "What has it got in its pocketses?" Messages flew back and forth again, the upshot being that Robert said it was unnecessary for us to drive down, as the Ring was safe. We put it in a white envelope with the energy of a grey stone for protection.

On the Monday we received an email from Robert in which he gave a big clue. The sentence which struck us the most was that 'nine could weld the ring if and when they reach the same vibrations - but it seems not to be.' So why had the One Ring come to Cassie on the Sunday morning? Gradually, the pieces came together. A long time ago Robert told us that the two of us were a joint energy. The two-penny coin has two sides – on one side is the bust of a young Queen Elizabeth II and on the other are the feathers of the Prince of Wales, that is, a pair of opposites – feminine and masculine. As a joint energy, weren't we also a pair of opposites? This is what the two-penny coin was telling us. We could become one energy and therefore weld the Ring because, as Gandalf reminded Saruman, only <u>one</u> person can weld the Master Ring. Robert's hope had been that The Nine could become One and so weld the Ring. We were the fall-back position.

After that realisation we quickly worked out what to do. Time was short and we planned to weld the Ring as soon as possible, which would be Thursday 10 April at 6.00 a.m. when night gives way to day and the two are blended. The place was to be at the confluence of the rivers Avon and Nadder, by the willow tree in Queen Elizabeth Gardens. We told Robert of our plans and he said he would be there with us.

At 5.30 am, in the early morning light, we made our way to the appointed place, only a short walk from Cassie's home. The Morning Star of Venus was still visible in the sky and the air was full of bird song. A mist rose from the river and from across the water meadows. The night before, the words of the old song, 'D'ye ken John Peel at the break of day' had come into Caroline's head and we felt John Peel represented Blake's Albion. Arriving at the meeting of the two rivers, we stood beneath the willow tree and sounded the 'Om' before Cassie tipped the ring into Caroline's cupped hand and then placed her own on top creating, we only realised later, a circle. Feeling calm in the stillness and beauty of the setting, we spoke the words we had prepared for the welding of the One White Ring and, at the same moment, the great bell of the Cathedral chimed the hour. Afterwards, we recited together Siegfried Sassoon's poem, "Everyone Sang", which he had written after Armistice Day - and we had averted war by welding the One Ring. The first two lines of the poem had come into Caroline's mind the previous Friday, just before the meeting in the Barn. It continued to haunt her over the weekend. In fact, so much so that by Monday, not remembering how the poem continued, she looked it up on the internet and then printed it and sent a copy to Robert. With hindsight, it was obviously prescience of what was to take place.

Everyone suddenly burst out singing;
And I was filled with such delight

For a while, we stood breathing in the still and gentle air before making our way back through the gardens.

Chapter 68

The Dove and the Albatross

The following morning we received an email from Robert confirming that we had been successful and that the 'dove and albatross were free for the moment'. Only then did we recall an experience we had as long ago as February. We now realise that we were being alerted to the imminence of war. Here is an account written for the Fellowship on 15 April 2008.

It happened not long after the meeting in January when Robert pointed out that the outline of an albatross could be made out on the cover of Ring Quest. It was 10 February and three of us had gone for a late afternoon walk in the Woodford Valley to the north of Salisbury when, looking at the sky, we noticed that some clouds had formed into the vast wingspan of an albatross. There was an eerie quality to the afternoon as there was not a breath of wind. Smoke from chimneys just hung in the air - something we had never seen before. We also noticed that the sky had turned a ghastly, bloody red and realised that, in this supposedly unpolluted part of the world where there is no industry, the air was criss-crossed with vapour trails from nearby Boscombe Down, the RAF station, and that it was these that had turned red from the rays of the setting sun. Cassie remembered a prophecy of the Native American Indians which says that humanity would be given warnings that it was destroying the planet but that it would be too late if the whole sky turned red. We now understood how that terrible prophecy might be fulfilled – when the air is completely polluted.

We knew that something important was being communicated to us and felt that it was connected to Coleridge's poem 'The Rhyme of the Ancient Mariner'" in which the mariner kills the albatross. Caroline came up with the quote "A painted ship upon a painted ocean" and we realised that this was a description of a dead world.

Caroline sent the following email to Robert on 13 February 2008:

We've been having more thoughts about the albatross Cassie and I saw in the sky and which has also appeared on the cover of our book. The line in Coleridge's poem, 'A painted ship upon a painted ocean' which comes after the mariner has killed the albatross, the wind has died and he alone survives, suggests that everything else has died too. In other words, the world itself is dead. This must be a warning of what will happen unless humankind takes immediate and effective action - unless it is already too late to save this beautiful planet at the dense third dimensional level.

This was Robert's reply:

The world is not yet dead but HANGS in the balance of cosmic consciousness - it is our thoughts and feelings that hold this fragile connection to our living breathing world - this is why clearing and helping 'learn to Be' - needs to be speeded up.

Walking through the park days before welding the Ring Cassie had seen, for a second time, the same young men playing at war with the same toy missile but now they were throwing it to each other across a small river flowing through the Gardens. It was telling us that a missile attack over water was possible. This could only mean one thing: the USA would be attacked from across the water. So when, after we had welded the Ring, Robert mentioned that the Albatross was 'free for the moment', we knew that it was nuclear war that had been averted, hence the albatross on the cover of Ring Quest. The reference to the dove being free was showing us that, for the moment, conventional war had been averted for the dove is the traditional symbol of peace.

On 2 April at the local theatre there had been a one-day play called The Rime of the Ancient Mariner but unfortunately we were unable to go. Then followed another synchronicity. The day after we welded the Ring, Cassie saw the new play at the Salisbury Playhouse - Touched by Stephen Lowe. The lives of a family of women from Nottingham is shown during the 100 day period between VE Day and VJ Day. The first celebration is for the end of conventional war but the second celebrates the end of the nuclear attack on Japan. We realised that the day on which the Ring was welded was **10** April, i.e. One to weld the Ring. Across the stage in Touched, written up on a banner in large letters, was the number **100** (for the number of days between VE Day and VJ Day) which echoes how the Ring was used to prevent the two types of warfare as symbolised by the dove and the albatross. The circle suggests the world so the two circles represent the world being subjected to two different types of warfare.

Chapter 69

The Crossroads

In 1998, at the beginning of this quest, Robert told us all that we had a unique opportunity to change The Lord of the Rings. Our aim was to put a stop to the endless recycling into which mankind was locked. So far, we have changed one relatively minor incident in the journey, as well as doing away with a cruel chapter, which, later in time, came to supplant parts of the original story. The minor event was Cassie/Frodo asking Aragorn to go south on the journey from The Shire to Rivendell, thereby avoiding the encounter with five of the dreaded Nazgul on the hill called Weathertop. This way Cassie/Frodo avoided a repetition of that particularly frightening episode where the Nazgul stabbed her in the shoulder. The other change came about with the discovery of the forgotten period in our history where the King was regularly sacrificed for the so-called benefit of the community. This meant that Tolkien's original story was no longer stuck. The sequence of events could flow once again so that the crowning of the Aragorn, the King and his marriage to Arwen, together with the liberation of the Shire, could once again take place, as they had not done for many ages. Little did we realise there was one other crucial way in which we might change events. However, we were to work this out only just in time before the opportunity was lost forever.

A day or two before Cassie's trip to Cheltenham for the Greenbelt 2008 Festival, Robert sent her the following email:

.... a quick rerun clears the Paths - take the dead to the stone of Erech and set them free - a path between two waters awaits a lonely boat ride.

On the return journey to Salisbury on Tuesday 26th August Cassie decided to take the A417, which was a straight road and which she noticed sliced off a large loop from her original journey. After a little while, she found herself driving between two lakes, just as Robert had described. She then realised that the shortcut she had just taken exactly reflected the short-cut Aragorn and company had also taken in their anxiety to reach their destination before it was too late. But where was she to find the Erech Stone? She thought she knew but events turned out quite differently. Arriving at the market town of Marlborough, she stopped off for a take-away coffee and croissant and, as she looked at the girl serving her, she realised she represented that strange race which had died out but were still tied to the earth because of the unfulfilled oath. Her face was unusually pale and her eyes were very large and heavily rimmed in black. It was by now a familiar feeling of things being more than they appeared on the surface. Of course the girl behind the counter was unaware that she was being influenced by these other energies and she would not have understood or even noticed why she felt more than usually friendly towards a particular customer. In Tolkien's book, it is not clear that this forlorn people felt tremendous gratitude towards Aragorn for being instrumental in their release. But I too was unaware of the cause of her unusual helpfulness and warmth. Nor had it sunk in that, temporarily, I appeared to be cast in the role of Aragorn.

Cassie then decided to look for a pleasant spot in which to take her break and, driving out of the town, she caught sight of an enticing view: a sloping field at the end of a track. She hoped there might be a view from the field of the ancient mound, which had formed the eastern point of the second Fibonacci diamond we created some years ago. As she entered the field she could not believe her eyes. There, at the top of the field, was a standing stone: the Erech Stone. As it happened, she was carrying a red, blue and white rug, which are the colours of the British national flag, and which she realised she could use as a substitute for the great flag Aragorn unfurled at the Erech stone. This revealed to the ghostly host gathered round that he was indeed the heir of Isildur to whom they had sworn their oath. He therefore had the right to bid them fulfil that oath and, by so doing, set themselves free.

However, on returning home we wondered why this repetition had taken place when we thought the quest was over.

We put the question to Robert who replied that "ref the stone of erech and the continual journey - until one has learnt the actual task given to one - it keeps repeating...". This was a blow and a horrifying prospect. The episode smacked of repetitions Cassie experienced of Frodo and Samwise's journey across Mordor, with each re-enactment becoming more physical and harder. The same thing was now happening with this second re-enactment of Aragorn's journey through the haunted tunnel. Once again, the journey was less symbolic and more physical – the short-cut, rug/flag, provisions in the form of coffee and croissant and, lastly, the trek to the top of the field.

What had caused this part of the journey to repeat yet again? Then it came to us. The thing to do would have been to cancel Isildur's Oath and give the ghostly Oathbreakers unconditional freedom. However, in order to do that we would have to prevent war taking place altogether for, as long as the world hovers on the brink of full-scale war, Aragorn is doomed to pass through the haunted tunnel – as his timely arrival at the head of a large fleet bristling with troops changes the course of the Battle of the Pellenor Fields; and Frodo is doomed to make the journey to Mordor because, when the One Ring falls into the chasm of the volcano, Sauron is instantly defeated. Only in this way can victory be assured for the free peoples of the West. It now appeared beyond doubt that one of the tasks set us was to avert the War of the Ring.

Thinking things through as to how we might achieve this, the answer came. War is all about opposing forces – East and West, Good and Evil. At a very early stage in the quest, Robert had asked us to think of Good and Evil as one or, put another way, the same energy used by a different hand. If those opposing energies, which were still rushing towards each other in open conflict, were united, then war could not take place. We remembered the point at which the energy for the new Age in The Lord of the Rings – a divided energy - entered simultaneously at the two Gateways, one in the West and one in the East. Might it not be possible to create a single Gateway mid-way between the two? We thought of all the landmarks between the Gates of the Tower of Cirith Ungol on the heights of the Mountains of Shadow in the East, and the Gates of the

City of Minas Tirith in the West. The ruined City of Osgiliath came to mind, and so did the Crossroads. The latter was a major crossing point where the great North/South road was crossed by the East/West road which, anciently, linked the former capital City of Gondor to the Tower of the Moon, now in the hands of the Enemy.

As soon as we thought of the Crossroads we knew we had found the right place. We could draw a diamond within the circle of immense trees which surrounded the ancient crossing point. The centre of a crossroads is a place of neutrality and equipoise, the still moment before the irrevocable step is taken. So it had been for Frodo. As soon as Gollum, Samwise and Frodo set off on the East Road, the Ring around Frodo's neck began to weigh heavily and become a burden once again. It was at this still point we could unite North and South, East and West. There the One Gateway could be opened which would unite the energies, just as we had done on top of the round barrow near Avebury when anchoring the energy of the Fourth Dimension. And the timing? It should be done when Frodo, Samwise and Gollum reach the crossroads on their journey into Mordor, which is shortly before total War is launched on the West.

Lastly, it dawned on us that, at that particular moment, Good and Evil are both equally present. On the one hand we have Frodo and Sam and on the other, Gollum. There was also a statue of a seated King, which had been defaced by orcs:

> Its head was gone, and in its place was set in mockery a round rough-hewn stone, rudely painted by savage hands in the likeness of a grinning face with one large red eye in the midst of its forehead.

The ancient statue had been turned into both the King of the West and the Dark Lord/The Eye - Good and Evil. This, indeed, was the place where we might perceive those energies as one and the same.

An email was sent to Robert with the above suggestion and he replied that 'you cannot go back to change it – we will try at the stone tomorrow.' As luck would have it there was a long-scheduled meeting in the Wye Valley the very next day and Robert said he felt sure there was a standing stone nearby which could be used.

Never had it occurred to us that we were to change Tolkien's original drama on such a grand scale, which is why it took us such a long time to work it out. But at this point we were none too certain that we weren't too late.

Whilst writing the above, the last part of Robert's email kept niggling us. Where did the 'lonely boat ride' fit into the picture? Finally we understood this clue, though its purpose was now over. If the single Gateway were created at the Crossroads at that particular juncture in the story and Aragorn liberated the Dead from their Oath unconditionally, Aragorn's journey up the Great River to Minas Tirith by boat would, indeed, have been 'lonely'. War had dissolved and there was now no need to brave the Paths of the Dead and ride to the rescue of Minas Tirith.

So why was there still the need for Aragorn to risk the haunted tunnel which is implicit in Robert's clue? The only answer we can find is the compassion Aragorn would feel for these beleaguered ghosts. As Isildur's heir, only he was able to release them from their Oath. With the protection of the Green Stone he would have gone through the tunnel on his own, not wishing to inflict such a terrifying ordeal on his companions. Finally, with no need to muster an army, he takes ship for Minas Tirith, alone, whilst that City awaits the arrival of their king.

Chapter 70

The 11th Hour

The following day, Saturday 6th September, we made the journey from Salisbury to the Wye Valley. We were hoping that, somehow, we would be able to step into the Story and change it so that World War would be done away with at all those dimensions which affect us here at the dense physical level. We did not know how this was to be done. As Robert wrote, we could not change the past and Cassie had missed the opportunity at the Standing Stone near Marlborough. We could now see that all the clues needed to make that momentous change to The Lord of the Rings were present at that window of opportunity when Cassie was consciously interacting with the Story. The proximity of the Erech Stone to the Ancient Mound, which formed the eastern tip of the Fibonacci Diamond we had made in 2003, was meant to prompt her to think of creating a single Gateway, thus uniting the energies of the opposing armies. Fortunately, Robert intimated we might have another opportunity.

At the meeting, in the course of the morning, we discussed the ethics of healing a person who was in a coma. However much loved ones might wish to draw the soul back into the body, it all depended on the freewill of the person. What was allowed was to place your presence in the person's essence to remind them of their earthly ties. Robert commented that not many healers know this and, as a parting shot, he remarked, 'and nor do Ring Bearers'. Cassie then understood that this was the way to re-enter the Story at the point where Frodo, Samwise and Gollum reach the Crossroads. She could place her presence in Frodo's essence. She would then be able to create the One Gateway which would unite the opposites, thus recreating the One energy. In this way would War be nullified and the Dark Lord and the King become one and the same.

The meeting took a mid-morning break during which Cassie discovered, well hidden from view, a large Standing

Stone. It formed part of a stone wall, which supported the topmost terrace, but it was partially buried and covered by a fern. It was clear that the Stone could serve as both the Erech Stone and the stone statue of the King at the Crossroads. Indeed, you could say that both were King Stones, as it was King Isildur who had set down the Erech Stone which came out of the wreckage of Numenor. Fittingly, the Erech Stone was black, in contrast to the stone statue of the King.

Early in the afternoon Robert suggested that it would be a good time to make the changes. The day had turned still and sunny as ten of us gathered around the Stone. Then, speaking aloud, Cassie released the Dead unconditionally from their Oath. Robert drew our attention to a light wind which blew up from the southwest and we all knew that the ghosts had departed. Cassie then created the single Gateway through which the One energy entered so that the vibrations of the planet were raised instead of falling. In that moment War was no longer possible. Again, a small wind blew but this time from the opposite direction – as Robert pointed out. Before the proceedings Robert had put a small spiral seashell on the grass in front of the Stone. He now picked it up and passed it to Cassie suggesting she place it on top of the Stone. Clearly, it symbolised the upward spiral of the energies. He also pointed to a graceful trailing plant on the wall that was growing towards the Stone. The significance of this escaped us at the time but, later, we remembered. As the hobbits and Gollum stand at the Crossroads, the light of the setting sun escaping the dark pall sent out over the world by Sauron, catches the fallen head of the King and Frodo cries out to Sam that the king has got a crown again:

> ...about the high stern forehead there was a coronal of silver and gold. A trailing plant with flowers like small white stars had bound itself across the brows ...and in the crevices of his stony hair yellow stonecrop gleamed.

Again, the white and yellow flowers suggest the coming together of the Opposites – of Moon and Sun, Feminine and

Masculine, as if foreseeing some point in the future when this will be fulfilled. An old glass coffee jar happened to be lying on top of the high wall which Robert handed to Cassie. It was full of 2" long steel nails. As she looked wonderingly at the jar and its contents, she understood they symbolised the weapons of war, contained and rendered harmless. It was a moving moment for, somehow, it represented the culmination of all our endeavours over the years. Cheerfully, Robert said we could now dispense with Frodo and Samwise and Gollum. Having cleared away War, we could move seamlessly to the coronation of the King and subsequent marriage of the King and Queen and, to symbolise the changed narrative, Robert and Cassie, who were standing on the grassy knoll near the Standing Stone, stood side by side and we all shared a wonderful moment of rejoicing.

Shortly after writing the above, Cassie turned on the radio and, in a wonderful piece of synchronicity, music written for the Coronation of King William and Queen Mary was being played. It seems that in the changed Story, in place of just the Coronation of the King, the crowning of both King and Queen takes place. With the energy changed to one of synthesis, the Queen can now step out of the shadows. The need for a strong arm at the helm has gone as the energy of conflict is no more.

On the same day, 6 October '08, as writing the above, there was an unusual headline in bold letters on the front page of the Daily Mail's Lifestyle Section. It read 'THE KING & QUEEN OF STYLE'! On 8 October, on the front page of the local paper was a photograph taken in Salisbury Cathedral of the Archbishop of Canterbury with the Dean of Salisbury, a woman, at his side. The occasion was the re-dedication of the Cathedral on its 750th anniversary. In the foreground is the new font (specially commissioned for the occasion and installed on 24 September – ie at the Autumn Equinox) with its large expanse of smooth water showing the reflections of the Dean and Archbishop. In the background, between them, is a single pillar and a flower display shaped like a pyramid. The Dean is dressed in Madonna blue and the Archbishop is in black robes. Here are the King and Queen, side by side, in perfect balance and harmony with each other and with their shadow selves - as shown by their reflections in the still water. He wears the black of the Royal House and the pillar is the White Tree, symbol of the Royal Line, which goes back into the mists of time. The occasion is showing us that a new and different beginning has been made in The Lord of the Rings for the energies have spiralled upwards, instead of sinking, and this is being conveyed to us through the pyramid-shaped flowers. The picture also clearly demonstrates the spiritual nature of the true roles of the King and Queen.

The Archbishop also consecrated the new font and baptised two babies during the special anniversary service. Two couples holding their babies flank the 'King and Queen' and their reflections are also to be seen in the waters of the font. The occasion chimes with the happy ending in the Story where we are told how Minas Tirith once again became filled with the happy sounds of children playing.

The new blueprint is now in place for us to go back the way we came but to a higher turn of the spiral - just as Robert foretold all those years ago.

Chapter 71

Completion

At the beginning of the Quest we discovered that humanity had reached the lowest vibration possible and we were in a 'make or break' situation; we have to retrace our steps in order to raise our vibrations to what they once were. To that end, Robert set many of us off on a quest to clear the energies of the past, which have built up around the planet over eons. Our aid was the famous book, The Lord of the Rings, and the quest coincided with the release of three films of the book from 2001 to 2003.

Only when the opportunity to change the story was nearly closed to us did we make a vital change in the drama: we united the energies of Good and Evil by creating a single gateway. It occurred to us that this new opening could now align with the gateway we anchored at the physical level some years back. And indeed, the effect of this new, powerful atunement soon became apparent in the world around us. We began to notice an emphasis on the 'Dark' side. Immediately after the collapse of the Investment Bank, Lehman Brothers, on 15 September 2008, we read in the Sunday Times a week later of a rescue plan put forward by the US Treasury Secretary which involved the creation of a 'Bad Bank' where all the, hitherto, hidden toxic securities could be placed. It was as if the Dark was coming into the open so that Light and Dark might come into balance first before merging and becoming one energy. In Tolkien's sagas, that energy was still present on Middle Earth, but only in the Golden Wood of Lothlorien.

In the same Sunday paper there were several articles showing the Dark revealing itself. One article was on the evidence for dark matter in outer space, which has recently been discovered by the European space probe named Pamela. The front page of one of the supplements showed the top of the devil's head reading a newspaper and, turning the page, there was an article on the world's fifty most well known villains. On

257

television that week, there was a programme called 'The Dark Side of Fame'. Most stunning of all was the picture on the front page of Culture Magazine. A man seated in a dark leather chair, dressed all in white, is looking nonchalantly at his nails: even the wine glass in his hand is white. Significantly, however, his shoes are black. The image reminded us of the statue at the crossroads in The Lord of the Rings of the seated King and is telling us that the Dark Lord and the King have become one. The fitting caption, in large lettering, reads: 'SITTING ON TOP OF THE WORLD'.

The very next day, Monday 22 September, Cassie walked into a shop and received a shock when a huge poster of the leering face of Dracula, complete with bloodshot eyes and fangs, greeted her. The shop in question was Poundland where all items for sale cost just one pound. This was the most amazing confirmation that the repeating story of the battle between Light and Dark is no more, for they are now one. We found yet further proof in an article at the time called 'Briton shows his dark side in Paris'. The avant garde British designer, Gareth Pugh, recently made his debut at the Paris Fashion Show with a range of clothes entirely in black and white. The models came on as if from the "dark side of the moon", in articulated, armour-like designs, which were white at the front and black at the back.' Only later did we realise that these synchronicities took place at the time of the autumn equinox when night and day are equally balanced.

In these times there are many who believe that human beings are going through a process of raising their consciousness and it is in this context that we place Ring Quest. But, as Robert says, "Everything depends upon humanity and its choices." Clearing work is ongoing and, if people find themselves drawn to a particular chapter of history, they might wish to set out on a quest of their own to clear that time slot. If they do, they will find the universal consciousness supporting them and providing clues and synchronicities.

APPENDIX I

Sir Gawain and the Green Knight

In the Arthurian legend, on New Year's Day a very tall and immensely powerful man on horseback enters King Arthur's great feasting hall. What astonishes all the knights and ladies gathered there is that his armour, his clothes and his skin are a vivid shade of green. He bears a huge battleaxe. Addressing the assembly courteously, he says that he just wants to play a New Year pastime. The man of greatest prowess at the Court of King Arthur is to strike one blow against him with his mighty axe on condition that he, the Green Knight, is allowed to reciprocate the blow a year and a day later at a pre-arranged place of the Green Knight's choosing.

There are no immediate volunteers but in the end Sir Gawain takes up the challenge. He raises the Green Knight's mighty axe and cuts off his head with one blow. Blood spouts everywhere. Then, to the amazement of all present, the headless Green Knight stands up, picks up his head, which then begins to speak, reiterating that he expects to meet with Sir Gawain a year and a day hence, at a small chapel in the woods.

The year passes and, reluctantly, Sir Gawain sets off for his meeting with the Green Knight at the Green Chapel. He reaches a castle on Christmas Eve close by the Chapel where he is welcomed by the Lord and Lady and given hospitality. After three days, having resisted the overtures of the Lord's beautiful wife, Sir Gawain sets out to meet the Green Knight.

He finds him whetting the blade of an axe in readiness for the fight. As arranged, the Green Knight moves to behead Gawain, but only strikes him on the third axe-swing, barely cutting his neck. The Green Knight then reveals himself as Sir Gawain's recent host. He spares Sir Gawain's life and explains that he has passed the tests set him.

'The Beheading Game' features widely in Celtic myth and it clearly has its origin in that earlier period of history when the Sacred King was sacrificed at that time of year – the midwinter solstice – and beheaded. The pagan custom has been replaced with the Christian festival of Christmas, celebrating the birth of

Jesus or the 'New' King who took the place of the 'Old' King. However, the memory of that terrifying end lived on for a long time.

The purpose of theatre is often to make us confront our fears and then see the story changed to offer a happy ending. This reassures and helps to re-educate the subconscious mind. So it is with 'The Beheading Game.' The cruel and barbaric practice, reserved solely for men of royal or noble birth, is turned into a 'mere Christmas pastime', at which everyone can laugh light-heartedly. In the original poem, great emphasis is placed on the Beheading Game being fun and frivolous. This way many men's fear was kept under control. Subconsciously, it would have been a huge relief for those of King Arthur's knights who had once been Sacred Kings themselves, to see Sir Gawain return unscathed from his ordeal.

APPENDIX II

The Sun's Journey

The origins of the Cult of Sacrifice of the Sacred King are to be found in sun worship, hence the sacrifice of the King at the summer and winter solstices. The Egyptians believed from the earliest times that 'God is the hidden Being, and no man hath known his form', but the Sun-god Ra was 'the visible emblem and the type and symbol of God who was worshipped in prehistoric times'. He rose every morning, born of his mother, and travelled across the sky in the Atet boat until noon as the sun rose to its zenith. From noon, as the sun declined, Ra continued his celestial voyage in the Sektet boat and was received into the arms of the goddess as the Sun sank below the horizon. Cassie came across a number of beautiful hymns in honour of the Sun-god Raw, taken from the oldest copies of the Book of the Dead, in a book called Egyptian Religion by E.A. Wallis who was one time Keeper of the Egyptian and Assyrian Antiquities in the British Museum. The following composition, part hymn and part prayer, is taken from the Papyrus of Ani from the Book of the Dead:

'A hymn of praise to thee, O thou who risest like unto gold, and who dost flood the world with light on the day of thy birth. Thy mother giveth thee birth, and straightway thou dost give light upon the path of (thy) Disc, O thou great Light who shinest in the heavens. Thou makest the generations of men to flourish through the Nile-flood, and thou dost cause gladness to exist in all lands, and in all cities...thou who art glorious in Majesty in the Sektet boat, and most mighty in the Atet boat! (The Sun's evening and morning boats)...when thou risest in the horizon of heaven, a cry of joy cometh forth to thee from the mouth of all peoples thou beautiful Being, thou dost renew thyself in thy season in the form of the Disk within thy mother Hathor..Hail, god of life, thou lord of love, all men live when thou shinest; thou art crowned king of the gods. The goddess Nut doeth homage unto thee, and the goddess Maat embraceth thee at all times. Thou goest forth each day over heaven and earth, and art made strong each day by thy mother Nut...Ra liveth in Maat the beautiful...Isis and Nephthys salute thee, they sing unto thee songs of joy at thy rising in the boat, they protect thee with their hands.'

When she first read this she was struck by its remarkable similarity in form to the ideas behind the Cult of the Sacred Sun King of the pagan cults. She was especially struck by the way the day was divided in two when the God Ra changed boats after the sun had reached its height at mid-day. This corresponded with the one Sacred King representing the waxing sun and his twin replacing him at mid-summer who embodied the waning sun. The idea that the sun is 'born' from the Goddess at the beginning of the day and received by her at day's end when it sinks below the horizon compares with the idea of the Sacred Sun King also being reborn from the Goddess the day after the winter solstice having been received back into her womb when the sun was sun 'died' at mid-winter.

In the hymn, the protective and nurturing love of the goddesses for Ra is very moving, particularly in the way they protect him with their hands. However, if we imagine a shift in the balance of power in favour of the Feminine, we can begin to understand how the Sun King became subordinate to the all-creative power of the Goddess from whom he had his being. As the personification of the Sun, it becomes a hideously logical step to sacrifice the King in order to benefit from those wonderful life-giving powers which were believed to be stored in his very body.

When the Sun God Ra sank beneath the horizon, it was believed he traversed the underworld before being given birth again from the womb of the Goddess Hathor. One of Ra's titles was Lord of the Underworld. Egyptian texts describe the passage of the sun through the underworld during the night and its dangers are not dissimilar to the horrors of the Christian Hell with 'the river of fire, the pits of fire, the snake and the scorpion' (E.A. Wallis Budge. Egyptian Religion). We find the same Lord of the Underworld in Celtic mythology.

Egyptian sun worship spread to the Mediterranean countries via Crete with whom it traded. Robert Graves tells us in his book, The White Goddess, how bands of Mediterranean peoples were driven out of their own countries by Kings who had overthrown the Queen/Goddess whom they replaced with an all-powerful Father God. Those driven out made their way to Britain taking their religious practices with them. Certainly, we discovered through our clearing work that the greatest numbers of sacrificed Kings were to be found in the south. It is on Britain's southern shores that those fleeing worshippers of the Goddess would have originally landed.

The Sun Warrior

In the course of her research Cassie came across the 'solar hero' and it became clear that his origins are to be found in the former Cult of the Sacrifice of the Sun King. He is a well-known figure in stories from our ancient oral tradition, which we call myth that, as many know, go way back into the mists of time.

The Irish solar hero, Lugh of the Long Arm and the Arthurian Sir Gawain, nephew of King Arthur of Camelot, are just two examples. Their astounding strength is clearly linked with that of the sun in the tales.

When the Irish folk hero, Lugh of the Long Arms and his men   approach the great assembly on the Hill of Usna in the county of Erin, they are described as: 'a stately band of warriors, all mounted on white steeds, coming towards them from the east; and at their head, high in command over all, rode a young champion, tall and comely, with a countenance as bright and glorious as the setting sun.'   On another occasion as Lugh approaches the Formorian enemy, one of them watching Lugh approaching from the West says 'A wonderful thing has come to pass this day; for the sun, it seems to me, has risen in the west'. A druid replies 'The light you see is the brightness of the face...of Lugh of the Long Arms, our deadly enemy'.

In single combat with Sir Lancelot, Sir Gawain is described as having a strength which increased as the sun climbed to its highest point in the sky at noon, and then that super-human strength leaves him as the sun begins its descent: 'Then had Sir Gawain such a grace and gift that an holy man had given to him, that every day in the year, from undern till high noon, his might increased those three hours as much as thrice his strength. And then when it was past noon Sir Gawain had no more but his own might' (Le Morte d'Arthur by Sir Thomas Malory).

By endowing these two heroes with the qualities of the Sacred Sun King, the storytellers of the day were wishing to impress upon their audience the exceptional prowess of the hero and his superiority over other men. Even though the Cult had been ruthlessly suppressed, certain charismatic aspects of it were kept alive, particularly if they enhanced the standing of a champion so that the enemy would fear him. Perhaps in those far off times it was not long in the past that the king had been sacrificed, as the Cult continued to be practised in more remote areas long after its practice had ceased elsewhere. The audience would have understood the allusion to the Sacred King who had been a demi-God, and they would have been in awe of a hero given the attributes of the Sun King.

Another story concerns the Irish Cuchulain, who was Lugh's son. The ruling Queen Maeve sets off for Ulster with her army to capture the famed White-horned Bull of Connaught, which she covets. She carefully chooses a particular time of the year when a spell, laid upon her enemy by an angry goddess many years ago, strikes the warriors of the Red Branch of Ulster: 'That for a certain season each year, as winter was beginning, they would lose all their strength, become as helpless as new-born babes, and fall into a deep sleep.'

This physical weakness that mysteriously overtakes these warriors or heroes alludes to those former days of the pagan Cult when it was believed that the King became 'old', and therefore weak, at the onset of winter. This reflected the growing weakness of the sun which people could feel at that time of year as the weather became cooler. It therefore became 'old' and 'died' at the winter solstice. (Old Celtic Romances by P.W. Joyce).

The Head

Archaeological evidence points to the existence of the Cult of the Sacred King. A third century Celtic sanctuary discovered at Ribemont-sur-Ancre in the north of France, near the Somme, held one of the largest collections skulls and human bones to be found in Gaul. It is 800 metres long and stacked with the skulls and arm and leg bones of 1000 individuals aged between fifteen and twenty years. Their skulls were detached and specially 'treated'. The narrow age range and youth of the victims point to a ritual death. One explanation as to why this cult has been so comprehensively erased from history, is that it stands to reason that when the King finally overthrew the Queen he destroyed all reminders of his terrible past, including gruesome sanctuaries such as the one which survived at Ribemont-sur-Ancre. (The Celts: First Masters of Europe   by Christiane Elurere).

Excavations carried out at Danebury Iron-Age hill fort in Wiltshire by Barry Cunliffe and recorded in his book Danebury, states, 'human skulls were found in eight ritual pits: six were adult males, one was female and one of a child.' The author goes on to suggest that human sacrifice could not be ruled out. On the bronze door kept at the State Historical Museum in Stockholm sacrificial pits are shown filled with bearded, warrior heads and severed hands and arms.

In Celtic mythology there is a direct connection between the Goddess and the severed head. After the slaughter of battle, the heads of the enemy were stuck on what was called the Pole of Macha the Red - the name given to the battle aspect of the Great Queen in Ireland. In the Hindu religion the Goddess of Death and Regeneration, Kali, is shown holding the lotus symbol of regeneration in one hand and wearing a necklace of human skulls.

In many cultures throughout the world, such as that in Indonesia, the people were at one time 'head hunters'. On the island of Borneo, the head was cradled in the laps of women and talked to, as it was believed such behaviour encouraged it to make the crops fertile. Such behaviour makes a direct connection with the fertilising powers of the sun. (The White Goddess, Robert Graves).

The belief in the power of the head of a great champion persisted even after the Cult had died out. The Roman writer, Diodurus Siculus, as he travelled through Celtic Gaul, describes heads being nailed to the victor's house to show off his valour. He records that they might: 'soak the heads of their most

266

illustrious enemies in cedar oil and keep them carefully in a chest and show them off to strangers, each priding himself that for one or other of these heads, either a forebear or his father or he himself, had refused to take a large sum of money'.

A survival from the days of the pagan cult is the custom of rolling a large cheese down a hill on Whit Monday at Cooper's Hill, Birdlip in Gloucestershire. As it gains speed local boys chase after it in order to catch it and claim the prize. Clearly, this practice would originally have taken place at midsummer. The large, round, yellow cheese represents the sun beginning its downward trajectory to the midwinter solstice after having reached its highest point in the sky. We can speculate that at one time it was the King's head which was sent rolling down the hill and the cheese is a substitute. To have been the possessor of the head of the King with its marvellous fertilising and healing properties would have been a prize indeed. Evidently, the people believed so strongly in the beneficial powers of this ritual that they kept alive the practice.

In other parts of Britain, flaming barrels or a flaming sun wheel, are rolled downhill in commemoration of this once most important of pagan, religious festivals. Until recently, on Midsummer Eve the villagers of Leusdon, Devon, would roll a flaming cartwheel down the slopes of nearby Mel Tor. (Mysterious Britain, Janet and Colin Bord).

In her book Lark Rise to Candleford, writing about the lives of poor country people in the 1890's, Flora Thompson describes a particularly cruel game played by the country children which clearly has its origins in that forgotten time. It was called 'Daddy'. A ring was created, with one of the players remaining outside of the ring who proceeded to walk stealthily around the circle to select 'another girl' by striking her on the shoulder. The chosen one broke from the ring and rushed round it closely pursued by the first player whilst the others chanted:

Round a ring to catch a king,
Round a ring to catch a king,
Round a ring to catch a king-

and, when the pursuer caught up with the pursued, she struck her neck with the edge of her hand, and the singers sang:

Down falls Daddy!

'At the stroke on the neck the second player fell flat on the turf, beheaded, and the game continued until all were stretched on the turf.'

It is interesting to see a direct connection between a ring and what has to be a memory of the pagan cult – the beheading of the king/Daddy.

After the ritual sacrifice of the King, his head was often taken to a strategic site where it could detect an enemy from afar. (This fits in with what Robert told us about the King taking an oath to defend the land from enemies.) In the Welsh Hero Tale, King Bran is mortally wounded in a fierce fight against the Irish to avenge their ill-treatment of his sister, Branwen. After the battle he bids his friends to cut off his head and tells them to: 'Take my head and return to Britain. Carry it to London and bury it on the White Mount at Tower Hill with the face towards France. So long as it remains buried there no enemy shall invade Britain from over the sea.' (Hero Tales from the British Isles by Barbara Leonie Picard).

Later, with the advent of Christianity and the desire to do away with the old customs, King Arthur dug up Bran's head at the White Mount at the Tower of London for he declared: 'It was right that the land of Britain should owe its freedom to the courage of its living men, and not to the magical powers of a dead king's head.' (Hero Tales from the British Isles by Barbara Leonie Picard).

For those living on the south coast the greatest danger of attack came from the sea, so they would have set the King's head on a promontory. This is the most likely origin of so many vantage points or headlands, having the word 'head' in their name such as: in Dorset, Durlston Head, St Alban's Head and Beer Head. In Cornwall and Devon we find Gribbin Head, Pencarrow Head, Rame Head, Bolt Head, Scabbacombe Head, and Berry Head.

In 1988 Cassie and her daughters spent a week's holiday with a friend in a rented cottage in Dorset, in the village of Shipton Gorge, not far from the sea. They visited the Dorchester Museum and she was very interested to come across two large, crudely carved stone heads with the description: 'Two supposedly Celtic heads found built into walls at Shipton Gorge.' It occurred to her that these heads had been positioned there to ward off invaders at that weak point in the natural defences of the coastline. As the name says, the village was in a gorge created by a river flowing through it and down to the sea, which had made a break in the cliffs. There was a good sandy beach, which an invading force could have used for landing their boats before working their way inland up the gorge.

A final thought, we have many expressions which include the word 'head' which are very likely to have originated from this Cult, such as 'Keep your head on', 'He has a good head on his shoulders', or 'Heads will roll'. Corporations, businesses, schools, etc., all have the word 'Head' for their leaders, just as the King was the tribe's titular 'head'.

As ever, when Cassie was about to start writing the chapter on the importance of the 'head' of the Sacred King eight years' ago, she experienced a synchronicity. She happened to read The Daily Mail (Thursday, July 8 1999) and Mac's cartoon for the day showed a hospital bed with only the patient's head sitting on the sheet which was very much alive, and looking surprised. A surgeon and nurse were standing by the bedside and the surgeon was thanking this liberal-minded patient for kindly having donated so many parts of his body; so many it appears, that he had only been left with his head.

APPENDIX III

Brutus, Trojan Prince

Many know of the sack of Troy by the Greeks in 1185 B.C not least because of the recent film, simply called Troy, starring Brad Pitt and Angelina Jolie. The well-known hero Aeneas, along with his father and some followers, managed to escape the burning and sacking. His wanderings after the break-up of the Trojan Empire are also well known, such as how he captured the heart of Queen Dido of Carthage, a kingdom in North Africa. He and his followers are also considered to be the founders of the city that would one day be called Rome. Perhaps less well known is that Aeneas' father, Prince Anchises, was a cousin of King Priam of Troy and therefore of the royal blood. Therefore that blood line came to British shores in the person of Aeneas' grandson, Brutus, who came with a large following. He had been unable to find a home in the Mediterranean basin for his people so had finally taken the radical step of sailing north to this island.

Brutus founded London in around 1100 B.C. Its location reminded him of his lost homeland, Troy, which was also built on a tidal estuary. For long it was known as Caer Troia, the New Troy, until the local name of one of the four sacred mounds in London, The Llandin (Parliament Hill), proved more popular. We are not the only ones to be surprised at how this vital link in British history has been so comprehensively kept under wraps. The tenor of E.O. Gordon's book, as well as that of Isabel Hill Elder's book, Celt, Druid and Culdee, is one of deep concern and puzzlement. How did the writings of the old chroniclers and historians come to be dismissed as mere invention and fairytale? They both point out that the old chroniclers of Britain, including Gildas, Nennius and Geoffrey of Monmouth who compiled the legends of King Arthur and his Round Table, were the most learned men of their day, and were held in high regard. They were patronised by the princes of the land and the chronology of Kings and their actions were meticulously written down. As Milton, author of Paradise Lost comments, to paraphrase: 'For the names of successive kings

270

not to have been real persons, nor for them to have at least in some part done what was written they had done, is hard to believe.'

However, put in the context of this book, we should be less puzzled. Ever has the Royal Line been the object of hatred by the Forces of the Left and ever have they striven to wipe it out and destroy all evidence of its existence. What we learnt from E.O. Gordon and Isabel Hill Elder concerning the Royal Line of Brutus and the peoples of these islands in fact turns out to be the opposite of what we had been taught in school. In addition, we find striking comparisons with Tolkien's story.

When the Romans came to the British Isles in AD 43 as children we were taught that the indigenous people were still in a barbaric state. The Romans were greeted by near naked savages coated in a blue paint called woad and brandishing spears. Of course, we have to remember that a great deal of the history that has been taught in British schools has been drawn from Latin sources. They tell us that we owe our civilising influences to Rome. Not so, writes Isabel Hill Elder. Rome owes a great deal to the British. She writes that 'the British, before the arrival of Julius Caesar, were, in all probability, among the most highly educated people on the earth at that time and, as regards scientific research, surpassed both the Greeks and the Romans – a fact testified to by both Greek and Roman writers themselves.'

When Brutus arrived in these islands he did not need to subdue a resistant indigenous people because they were of the same stock. They called themselves the Kymry, or race of Japhet and they were Aryan. Earlier, this People had dispersed far and wide throughout Europe and the near East, including Egypt. E.O. Gordon tells us that Troy was 'regarded as the sacred city of the race of Japhet in the East.'

Instead, Brutus was greeted by his kinsmen, who had come in an earlier migration and were living on Dartmoor. He was taken to the Sacred Mound called Tot Hill from which the present town of Totnes takes its name. There, on the topmost point, called the Gorsedd in Welsh, which means 'Supreme Seat of the Monarch', he was proclaimed Sovereign and King Paramount by the people. E. O. Gordon is at pains to point out that similar artificial Mounds in London -   Tothill in

Westminster and the Mound at The Tower of London - have always been considered Great Seats of Royalty from time immemorial. It was here that British Kings held their courts and their councils. The ancient Royal Palace of Westminster, which was finally destroyed by fire in the time of Henry VIII, was the favourite residence of Edward the Confessor.

After being proclaimed King, E.O. Gordon relates that it is most probable that Brutus would have been taken directly to the centre of administration of the "Mighty Ones" at Avebury where, 'within the supreme Gorsedd, the chosen of the People was "lifted up" by the Elders to a stone seat according to a most ancient custom of the Kymry'. People came to the crowning of the "elected Sovereign Paramount" from all corners of Britain. It took place within the precincts of the mile-wide stone circle of Avebury, a site of high energy, in the presence of a vast number of people.

The symbolism of the ancient practice of the "lifting up", suggests that the King was seen as having a natural spiritual, mental and physical superiority over his fellow men. Tolkien tells us that Aragorn was also a man with superior gifts and a lifespan three times that of other men. On being unanimously hailed King by all the people outside the ruined gates of Minas Tirith, Aragorn, now the King Elessar, rose and we are given the following description: 'Tall as the sea-kings of old, he stood above all that were near; ancient of days he seemed and yet in the flower of manhood; and wisdom sat upon his brow, and strength and healing were in his hands, and a light was about him.' Richard II was the last king to be "lifted" to the throne beneath which was the Stone of Scone, which was kept at the upper end of Westminster Hall until 1833. It is clear that this was no ordinary royal dynasty.

The arrival of Brutus and his followers, bringing with them a High Kingship, can be compared with the arrival of Elendil and his sons on the shores of Middle Earth. Their homeland, the island of Numenor, which means 'Land of the Star' - for it was shaped like a five-pointed star (see Unfinished Tales by J.R.R. Tolkien published posthumously) had been invaded and destroyed. Like Brutus, Elendil was of the blood royal. Once again a new start was being made.

The ancient texts known as the Welsh Triads describe Brutus as one of the 'Three King Revolutionists of Britain,' because he introduced ancient Trojan Law, the recognition of which 'is said to solve all the peculiarities in British Laws and Usages which would otherwise be wholly inexplicable.' These laws set the British apart from their European neighbours because of their unique liberties and high ideals. Every subject was as free as the King. There were no slaves and everyone was entitled to "Common Rights" which were inalienable. E. O. Gordon states that 'Many of these usages are remarkable for their humane and lofty spirit;' For example, the King was subject to the Voice of the People - hence the maxim: "The Country is higher than the King". This is precisely what took place at the crowning of Aragorn: the People were asked whether they wished him to be their King to which the answer was a resounding 'Yes'. The King Elessar had won his spurs during fifty years of toil and hardship.

Another of the high ideals of the Kymric People, which is particularly relevant today with the rise of Muslim fundamentalism, is that women were held in 'exceptional reverence and honour'. This derived from ancient Accadian law in the land of Sumer in what is now Iraq, which makes woman the equal of man. A woman could also inherit the crown as has proven to be the case in Britain. We find the same law applying on the Island of Numenor in Tolkien's trilogy.

Again, a fact that was new to us was that the early Britons were famous for their outstanding physique and athleticism. The Latin chronicler, Strabo, describes British youths as being six inches taller than the tallest man in Rome and powerfully built. The following description given by Isabel Hill Elder could just as well apply to the tall, hardy, grim Rangers of the North, in The Lord of the Rings, who were the remnant of the unmixed Race of Men from Numenor. The Britons 'were patient in pain, toil and suffering, accustomed to fatigue, to bearing hunger, cold and all manner of hardships. Bravery, fidelity to their word, manly independence, love of their national free institutions, and hatred of every pollution and meanness were their noble characteristics.'

The spiritual ideals of the Founding Fathers, enshrined in the American Constitution, can also be compared to the introduction of enlightened laws by Brutus to Britain. So we see that history really does repeat itself through the Ages. As Robert today identifies Minas Tirith as The White House in the United States, perhaps we can see a connection between Numenor, the 'Land of the Star', and the five pointed stars on the American National flag, not to mention the five-sided building known as The Pentagon, Headquarters of the Military Establishment of the USA. Interestingly, one of the four Sacred Mounds in London was called The Penton.

It is interesting to observe that the new impetus in North America did not involve a King. This is because such a person would eventually have attracted the corrupted energy of that institution, so it was best to avoid it altogether. However, deeply embedded in the subconscious of the Western people is a deep desire for just that sort of spiritual leadership. That longing is therefore soon projected on to a family dynasty, which subliminally, fulfils the role of a 'royal family'. Just such a dynasty has been the Kennedy family and we all know how its members appear to have been dogged by ill luck - cursed even.

With Brutus establishing a High Kingship in the White Isles with fair Laws, and the Founding Fathers creating a high minded Constitution for the peoples of the United States of America, we see a link through time with Tolkien's story. For as Legolas the Elf says, there is a prophecy that the Line of Luthien - from which stems the Royal Line of Numenor - will never die. Through repetitions of the cycle of destruction and renewal, that Line is still with us today - although in comparative obscurity - as it was throughout Tolkien's trilogy until the very end of the story.

APPENDIX IV

Clearing Energy Sites

When clearing a site of negativity, the first thing to do is protect yourself. Basically, you need to ground and balance. A thought of protection is good enough or you can visualise a light bubble of protection, or some other image. A minimum of two people is advisable and, preferably, more as you will then be able to work more powerfully and safely together.

It is not only Sacred King sites that need clearing. Reading the local history of an area will perhaps throw up other traumatic incidents such as battles, murders and of course, hauntings. Once the site is known, quickly secure it by encircling it with light or by putting your hand on a map. You do not even need to go to a site. You can imagine yourselves there and that will take you there. Stand, preferably in the centre, in a circle holding hands and keep it simple. Tune in to your intuition. We like to sound the 'Aum', sometimes harmonising and sometimes clashing, on purpose. Robert always says your own words are best. If it is a site where the King was sacrificed, draw in more of the golden light for healing, as sacrifice is a misuse of the feminine energy so balance needs to be restored. You then request the Kings to ask to be released from the oath they swore to their Liege Lord, the preceding King, to defend the Land. You do not have to be a medium to do this: it is sufficient to direct your thought to them. You can call on angels or their loved ones to help guide them. You may also like to ask for help from the nature spirits who, Robert says, have been pushed out by humanity to the outer margins between the worlds.

If clearing a battlefield you can draw in more of the silver light as warfare is a misuse of the masculine energy. At all sites, ask for all trapped sentient beings to be released. Then cleanse the earth and balance the energies.

As for recognising Sacred King sites, this is often made easy as Roman Christianity took over many of the pagan sites of worship. They could not stop people visiting those ancient sites so they appropriated them, and as we know, so many were polluted. You will find that such sites are inevitably on a high point or in marshy land or near water. The ancient origin of the choice of these energy sites is that the masculine energy lines ran through the high points and the feminine ran near water and marshland. You may also find such sites marked by castles, iron-age hill forts, long barrows, stone circles and palaces or grand country houses. They are part of a worldwide energy system set up to try and prevent the earth's energies falling ever lower.

Having made the intention to go and clear a site, look out for the universe responding to you with hints, signs and synchronicities. Afterwards, look out for changes for the better in the area.

While revising the above, we had occasion to ask Robert about clearing sites and we pass on his reply:

'ref to clearing sites – yes it is a continual job.

We clear a site and it is clear:

Someone else knows about the energies of the sites and restarts it again

This happens time and time again because of books, media, people talking and so on

Even the great masters cleared as they went – but it did not, does not last – humans are unaware of the continual dross they make

Until we attain our godlike energies once again, we still have to clear sites'

We remember Robert once saying that there only needs to be a grain of memory left at a cleared site for the negativity to be revived by the reasons given above. One obvious source whereby sites become re-polluted, are groups who re-enact famous battles. Perhaps another is tourists visiting historical sites with the past in mind.

APPENDIX V

Merlin

At some point Robert dropped a hint that the famous wizard, Merlin, might not be the force for good that the legendary tales of King Arthur would have us believe. He had talked about the various 'energies' who were out to grab the One Ring for themselves : Morgan Le Fey, King Arthur's sister; Sauron, The Dark Lord; Saruman, renegade Leader of the White Council in Tolkien's tale of the Ring; and now, to our surprise, Merlin.

Then came a most curious incident. We were at an open meeting being given by Robert in a large room and, being summer, the door was open. Suddenly, a bird flew into the high-ceilinged room. Instantly, Robert stuck his index finger in the air an alert, firm expression on his face, and the bird flew out again. He then told us that the bird was Merlin.

A little later we heard another story, which also flew in the face of the general belief that Merlin was a good wizard. A friend of ours who is psychic had recently paid a visit to Tintagel where he understood that a battle had taken place. He said that the local people were very angry and that the object of their wrath was Merlin whom they proceeded to drive out of the village.

At about the same time, just before the visit to Avebury in early October 1999, we made a trip to Wales. At a Service Station we noticed an unusual collection of jet black figurines and, remarkably, the black material turned out to be coal! We were clearly in an area where coal mining had once been a mainstay of economic life. There was a figure of the wizard Merlin with his staff. But what really drew our attention was Merlin's trademark - the broad-brimmed hat. Saruman also wore a broad-brimmed hat. Perhaps his likeness in jet black was trying to tell us something! It occurred to us that Saruman and Merlin were one and the same person and if Saruman was black and rotten to the core – like the carving – then so too was Merlin.

If this were true, the story of Merlin being run out of Tintagel by the local people becomes comprehensible, even more so, as this is exactly what happens to Saruman in the hobbit country of the Shire. Saruman takes up residence in Frodo's old home in the Shire with the express purpose of corrupting those happy, little people and of destroying their beautiful country. Eventually, his evil thugs are beaten and he is surrounded and ordered to leave by Frodo. It would seem to be a case of history repeating itself.

Such an idea helped us make sense of an experience we had on our return journey from Tintagel. Just in front of our car was a lorry belching out a turgid cloud of thick, black smoke, which is unusual these days with stringent laws in place for the prevention of such pollution. Caroline had quite decided to give the driver a cross look and point to the smoke when she caught sight of the lettering on the driver's door: it said 'Merlin Distributor'. We now strongly began to suspect that Merlin was not the person we had been led to believe.

On the day in Avebury, Cassie was able to find a brief moment in the car park to put the idea to Robert that Saruman and Merlin were the same person. To her astonishment, he burst out that she was too astute and that he couldn't keep anything from her! Then, as he walked away, he said something rather quickly, which she missed but what she did catch was that he was asking her to think of Sauron the <u>Black</u>, Saruman the <u>White</u>, and Gandalf the <u>Grey</u>. As earlier, this demonstrates that because black and white are opposites, they exert a magnetic attraction for each other. Saruman became proud and so fell into Sauron's power. Gandalf, on the other hand, had a healthy respect for Sauron and feared to have a battle of wills. Gandalf the Grey, as a mixture of the opposites, black and white, was balanced, whilst the other two protagonists were not, and could not be, as each lacked its opposite.

Thinking about what Robert was trying to tell us, we realised that the names Sauron and Saruman are similar. All the letters in Sauron's name are contained in the word Saruman, bar the letter 'o'. And the only letter missing in Sauron's name that would spell Saruman, is 'm' (and an extra 'a'). Those two letters make the sound of creation, the 'om'. Perhaps it means that only when there is a synthesis of the opposites – good and evil, man and woman, etc., can the creative note truly be made. Further proof that the Opposites are one and the same is that the word 'live' spelled backwards makes 'evil'. It is only the use to which energy is put which alters it.

On his visit to Salisbury in May 1999, Robert had told us that Merlin has a base at Old Sarum. The full meaning of this now dawned on us: 'Sarum' stands for 'Saruman' who is also Merlin. Even the 'Old' is significant, as Saruman was known as 'Sharku' by the orcs, which means 'Old Man'.

Caroline had had a dangerous encounter with Saruman/Merlin exactly to the south of the Old Sarum hillfort on the energy line that links it with Salisbury Cathedral. She was driving home with a friend from a visit in a neighbouring county when she suddenly had the idea that it would be nice to take an alternative route for a change. However, when she suggested this to her companion who was at the wheel, he said that he would prefer to go the usual way. It was dark and, as they approached the spot in the road immediately below Old Sarum, a car coming from the opposite direction suddenly, and inexplicably, veered across the road and hit their car, luckily, slightly to one side only. The driver was an elderly woman who seemed totally dazed by what had happened. They comforted her as best they could and only let her go on her way after they had ascertained that she felt well enough to drive home. Caroline, of course, knew exactly why they had had the accident: Merlin/Saruman had devised it and it might have proved fatal. The car was quite badly damaged, but not a write-off. The following day, passing the same spot, she saw a parked car with the letters POW on the number plate. When later she recounted this to Robert, he said, 'So you didn't get my message?' She then remembered that she had wanted to take the route, which would have avoided Old Sarum. In other words, she did get the message but, stupidly, ignored it. She did mention that she had remembered to protect the car and Robert replied that, if she hadn't, it would have been a head-on collision. From this she realised that things were really serious and that she must never again ignore the promptings of her intuition, or messages from Robert.

It is sad that the name 'Merlin' is so widely seen and used, whereas you seldom see the name 'Gandalf', the true saviour of Middle-earth. However, in our Quest we have discovered that, so often, the so-called 'truth' of history should not be accepted as gospel and that the real truth has been twisted.

APPENDIX VI

Red Lion Pubs

It was on a trip to Glastonbury in 1994 that we were first alerted to the significance of pub names. We had decided to take the most direct route to the town which took us across country. To our surprise, we discovered that from Daventry, which is to the west of Northampton in what is called 'the heart of England', the A361 took us all the way there. It was as if it were an ancient pilgrim route. Not long after we had set off down the A361 we saw a pub called *The Three Pigeons*. At the time, Cassie was immersed in researching the pagan cults which were centred on the Goddess who was widely worshipped as The Triple Goddess. Pigeons were sacred to her in her role as the Love Goddess, Aphrodite. We wondered, therefore, if the name could in anyway be connected with the old pagan religion.

A few minutes later we drove past another pub called *The Three Horseshoes*. As many people know, the Celtic Goddess of old was widely worshipped as the Mare Goddess, Epona. Our curiosity was fully aroused by now and we kept an eye out for pub names from there on. A little further down the road we came across a hotel called *The White Hart* but what really caught our attention was that the stag on the hanging board wore a golden crown around his neck. The White Hart wears a crown as he was the livery device of Richard II. Cassie had not long learnt from Robert Graves' book, *The White Goddess*, that the stag was one of the animals sacred to the King for it is a noble animal with a regal bearing. In some places the pagan cult of sacrificing the king took the form of a hunt. Robert Graves describes how the king was dressed as a stag and he was then hunted by men and a pack of hounds which, when they caught up with him, tore him to pieces. The crown was clearly identifying the stag with kingship which was yet another link with the pagan cult.

As the idea began to grow, and still on the same A361 route, we drove past a pub whose name was the most exiting piece of evidence for our argument. It was called The Red Horse in the village of Shipton-Under-Wychwood, Oxfordshire . During the ensuing months we kept a special eye out for all pubs with the prefix 'white', 'red' or 'black'. At the time, we were travelling widely clearing sites and the more pubs we saw, the more convinced we became of our hypothesis.

The names of many pubs we drove past reflected the main elements in the pagan cult of the Sacred King/Goddess in a most surprising and accurate way. For one, we noticed that animals sacred to the King, such as the lion, stag/hart, bull or cock (because of its magnificent plumage) were often prefixed by, either 'white', 'red', or 'black'. The most common of these were those called The White Lion, The Red Lion and The Black Lion. But these colours, we mused, were the colours of the Triple Goddess in her three aspects of Maid, Queen/Mother, and Wise Woman, and not typically associated with kingship. Gold is the colour traditionally connected with kingship and the regal lion. So why were the colours of the Goddess being allied to the royal lion of kingship?

The scenario was clear. When the King overthrew the Queen/Goddess he 'usurped' her powers and her titles. As Robert Graves so succinctly puts it:

> Conquering kings their titles take
> From the foes they captive make

By prefixing his own sacred animals with the colours of the Triple Goddess, the King was proclaiming that he had annexed her powers and was the one now in charge.

This theory was backed up by the fact that those colours were also frequently found attached to animals sacred to the Queen/Goddess, in particular, the Mare Goddess Epona, whose memory is preserved in such pubs as *The White Horse*, *The Red Horse* and *The Black Horse*.

We have never again come across another *Red Horse* pub after that original journey to Glastonbury when we were first alerted to the significance of pub names. This in itself is highly relevant to our argument for the King feared the 'Red' aspect of the Goddess the most. When the Queen changed her colour from White to Red, ie Maid in the Springtime, to Queen/mature woman in May at the start of summer, it was a sign to the King of the Waxing Year that the time of his sacrifice was drawing close. It would follow that when the Queen was deposed, any hostelries which reminded the King of his cruel death during the 'Red' aspect of the Queen's yearly cycle, such as *The Red Cow*, or *The Red Horse*, would have either been destroyed or had their names forcibly altered. However, in remoter parts of the countryside, or where the former pagan cult still lingered, the name of *The Red Horse* survived because people are naturally conservative and do not like change and it was not the common people but the royal family who were directly involved in the cruel cult.

We decided to do a random check on pub names in the County of North Yorkshire as listed below:

TheWhite Lion	1	The White Horse	3
The Red Lion	6	The Red Horse	0
The Black Lion	3	The Black Horse	6

The evidence entirely supports the argument. There was not a single pub called *The Red Horse* but there were *three White Horse* and six *Black Horse* pubs. Clearly, there was a greater urgency to destroy all memory of pubs named after the Goddess in her 'Red' aspect.

The battle for supremacy between the King and the Queen is immortalised in the nursery rhyme The Lion and the Unicorn:

> The Lion and the Unicorn were fighting for the crown
> The Lion beat the Unicorn all around the town
> Some gave them white bread and some
> Gave them brown and some gave them plum cake
> And drove them out of town

The Lion represents the King, and the Unicorn is the sacred horse of the Queen/Goddess. There came a time when the power of the Queen waned and the King's began to grow. At the time of this nursery rhyme, it is clear that the King has gained the ascendancy.

As an afterthought, we wondered if there were any more pubs in Oxfordshire called *The Red Horse* so we decided to scan the names of all the pubs in that county on the internet. We received the most astounding confirmation for our argument. There was only one *Red Horse* pub – the one we originally drove past in 1994 - but there were <u>30 </u>*Red Lion* public houses. How this one example survived the brutal suppression of the former cult we will never know. Perhaps the village was remote and access poor. We do remember the building being in a hollow. Perhaps the greater part of the village had been visited by the King's men but they remained unaware of a small extension on the further side of the hill, hidden from view.

A curious insight came when Cassie became puzzled by the number of pubs called, *The Red House.* You might expect one pub to bear that name but so many seemed odd, particularly as they were none of them painted red. One possible explanation was that when the King was establishing his authority, hostellers were ordered to change the names of their establishments if they were in any way connected to his former sacrifice. As we know, it was the Queen in her Red guise who held such terror for Sacred Kings. We therefore suggest that many hostellers simply changed the 'r' for *The Red Horse* to a 'u' so making the new name which did not remind the King of the fearsome past.

Of course the clearest connection to the forgotten cult is found in pubs across the country called, *The King's Head.* And the clearest reminder of the bloody overthrow of the Queen is seen in such pubs as, *The Queen's Head* or *The Nag's Head.* It is in this context we believe we can begin to understand our cruelty to horses in the past. The word, 'nag' suggests the cruelty was meted out more to mares than to stallions. Certainly, the famous mare, Black Beauty, suffered much ill-treatment in the book of that name. There can be little doubt that the reason for many men's hatred of women has its roots in the cult of the Sacrifice of the King. It is curious how we accept without questioning that men should hate women. Have we ever thought to consider what might possibly be the origin of something which is so unnatural?

APPENDIX VII

A Tudor Gentleman

As ever, clearing work was ongoing throughout the Quest and in this episode, it took an unusual turn. Robert had mentioned that there was a Tudor gentleman with a message for us and that he was waiting at the Whispering Gallery in Saint Paul's Cathedral in London.

It was a long time since either of us had visited St. Paul's Cathedral and we, therefore, decided we would combine a visit to the Whispering Gallery with manifesting the Ring for its cleansing in the element of Air, as already described in another chapter. Prior to calling the Ring, we planned to visit the Whispering Gallery in the Dome of the Cathedral and wait to receive a message from the Tudor gentleman. We told Robert of our plans and he warned us that the Other Side would be trying to thwart us and that we should be vigilant.

Feeling slightly apprehensive, we set off on Friday, 14 February 1999, early in the morning, and plodded up the spiral staircase to the Whispering Gallery. What actually happened was rather different from what we were expecting, but perhaps even stranger. We decided we would sit with our eyes closed in the hope that we would be better able to tune in and were sitting thus when we suddenly heard a man's voice saying, 'Do you live in London?' Astonished at such an unusual and rather bold intrusion, we opened our eyes to see a youngish man with some sort of official badge on his lapel standing in front of us. Caroline replied that she did indeed live in London. We chatted for a while and he said that he was a Steward of the Cathedral. He then turned to Cassie and asked her where she came from. When she replied that she lived in Salisbury he became very animated and told us that his family also came from there and that a Tudor ancestor of his, William Wendover, was a well-known merchant and philanthropist. At this Cassie and I exchanged glances and pricked up our ears. It was as if his Tudor ancestor were standing at his shoulder and prompting him to ask these unusually direct questions.

He told us that something very strange had happened. His grandfather had had a dream in which he was told that there was a portrait of his Tudor ancestor behind wooden panelling in a certain house in Salisbury and that, if he went there, he would find it. This his grandfather did. The portrait was indeed there and was subsequently removed to the County Museum. He told us that his family had lived in St. Anne's Street in what had formerly been a Friary but, as with other monastic establishments, it had been suppressed by Henry VIII at the dissolution of the monasteries.

There was obviously a message in all this, which we would have to work out at a later date. For a while longer we talked together with William Wendover's descendent who, quite unwittingly, had passed on to us a message from his ancestor. Then, suddenly feeling that we had to get on, we took our leave.

At the first opportunity, Caroline visited the Museum in Salisbury and found herself gazing at the portrait of a rather grand Tudor merchant who had, indeed, been a great benefactor to the City. She did some further research at the Library and discovered that the friars living at the Friary in St. Anne's Street had refused to leave the Friary when Henry VIII's soldiers arrived to turn them out, and that they had, consequently, all been slaughtered. But they had not left. Tuning in we discovered that they were still 'living' at the Friary, just as they had always done. After he had passed on, William Wendover must have found out that the friars were still at the site and, being a good man, he had wished to get a message through to someone on earth who could help release them.

We, therefore, tuned into these unhappy souls, whom we found kneeling in prayer. They were so addicted to the routine of monastic life that we had great difficulty even to get them to look at us. At last, we had to tell them quite strongly to stop intoning the Office, look up and listen to what we had to say. When, finally, they did raise their heads, they looked at us in terror and immediately fell down again. In the end, we did manage to release them.

APPENDIX VIII

Stonehenge

It began with a series of synchronicities to do with arches. They seemed to be everywhere, from place mats to pictures in newspapers. It occurred to us that they represented a 'Gateway' which immediately spoke to us of creating an entrance between the dimensions. At the same time, and quite independently of one another, we both became interested in lexigrams. This is the practice of making words out of the letters contained within words and using them to reveal the hidden meaning. [32] One in particular caught our attention as we live near Stonehenge, with Caroline living less than a mile away as the crow flies. It was the lexigram for "Druids of Stonehenge". The lexigram reveals that the 'True Note' is hidden in the Stones and, of course, the Stones form three huge arches – arches again, which is what drew our attention to the lexigram. The True Note we took to be the 'Om', the sound of Creation which would help create a connection to the higher energies.

In addition, in a moment of inspiration, we realised that the word 'Earth' turned into 'Heart' by simply moving the letter 'H' from the end of the word to the beginning. The letter 'H' became an arch or 'Gateway' if the cross bar of the 'H' is raised. We checked first with Robert to see if we had got things right but he said that what we would be doing is lowering the barrier as we were bringing the fourth dimensional energy down to earth.

The time of the autumn equinox was approaching and we realised that this would be the time to do it, when the energies are in balance. 'Sunrise' would be the time of day as this is also another word contained in the lexigram. The name 'Horus' is also included in the lexigram and we felt this was also important because it starts with the letter 'H'. Horus is the Divine Child and is represented by the falcon or hawk. The plan was first to lower the barrier of the horizontal line of the 'H' and then to open the gateway.

We no longer recall the origin of the idea but we knew that a key was needed to open the door to allow in the higher vibration. Cassie suddenly remembered the strange crystal she had discovered only a few weeks earlier on a private beach when on holiday in Devon with her daughters. They had stayed in a house on a hillside with stunning views down the River Tamar to Plymouth. Whilst lying on the narrow strip of pebbly beach below the house, Cassie spotted a most unusual stone, unlike any other on the whole of the beach. It was clear but yellowed with age, and was an odd, pyramid-like shape. Strangest of all, it came to a point that was shaped like a diamond and was curiously reminiscent of a seal, or stamp, as it stood proud and was roughened, whereas the rest of the stone was smooth. Later, Robert said that she had been led to it by the nose! We were in no doubt that the diamond shape was a key which could be used to open the gateway but its full significance would only emerge later.

Just before dawn on the day of the equinox September 2000, we stood looking down upon the majestic Stones at a little distance. We sounded the 'Om', lowered the bar of the 'H' and, finally, opened the Gate using the crystal key. Intention – as well as timing - is all. On returning to the Woodford Valley we stepped out of the car just as a 'V' formation of Canada geese flew overhead which we knew was 'V' for victory. Further confirmation of what we had just done came as we sat at the table with a cup of coffee and saw from the window three strangely shaped clouds in the form of columns. The first two were joined at the bottom - the lowered bar of the trilithons - and the third stood alone. Slowly, they changed shape: the left hand one becoming a waterfall - the Waters of Aquarius; the one in the middle appeared as a bird – Horus, the Divine Child; and the third formed into the semblance of a Turtle representing the Great Mother. Later that day we learnt that, just after the power shift which took place when we sounded the Note at dawn and opened the gateway, i.e. 6.45 a.m., there had been an earthquake quite high on the Richter Scale. It was to the north of Stonehenge in Warwickshire and extended as far as Birmingham.

In the following weeks, the universal energy continued to respond to our actions. A week afterwards, Caroline turned on the last few minutes of a television programme called "Meet the Ancestors" and there on the screen were the trilithons at Stonehenge making three arches, with the sun shining through the middle arch. Proof, if proof were needed, that we had done what we had set out to do: opened a gateway. At the closing ceremony of the Olympic Games in Sydney, Australia, on 1st October, everyone had their arms raised in joy in the shape of a V. Five days' later, Caroline was doing a crossword and there were three clues which were uncannily appropriate: A falcon or pastime - answer, hobby; Celtic priest - Druid; and Egyptian god, Judge of the Dead - Osiris. On the 14th, Handel's 'Messiah' was sung all over the world in aid of hospices - an international welcome to the new 'Messiah', Horus the Divine Child.

When we next saw Robert in the Wye Valley on 17th October, he explained that, when we raised the vibrations and made an archway at Stonehenge, we had shifted the gateway to the fourth dimension. This raising of the vibrations allowed 17% of people who were ready to raise their vibrations. If we had done it all at once, people would be frightened. It has to be a gradual incline rather than a steep step. He said that a lot of people, i.e. in Israel and the Occupied Territories, are resisting the change. Hatred finds an outlet in fanatical, religious beliefs. The Dome of the Rock is one of the twenty masculine energy centres around the world and it is there that Ariel Sharon, the right-wing Likud leader, toured the Temple Mount on 28th September, provoking widespread clashes. We were shifting the power to the etheric level, and rebalancing power on different levels. He said that the White Brotherhood and the Black Brotherhood are now sitting down together and are co-existing (Robert has told them to), and they are not under coercion.

Malmesbury and Buckfast Abbeys

When we saw Robert again in October 2000, a month after our visit to Stonehenge, he told us that the gateway had moved away from Stonehenge to two other places and that we must visit them at the winter solstice and spring equinox. He gave us a few clues, such as that the configuration of the three sites formed a triangle, or trine, and that there was an Egyptian centre somewhere along the lines. He said that both places were Catholic monastic foundations, and left the rest to us.

Back home we did some research and decided that Malmesbury Abbey was one of the places of energy and that Buckfast Abbey was the other. In fact, together with Stonehenge, they formed an almost perfect Yod' sometimes known as the 'Finger of God'. In astrological terms this is when two planets are in sextile (60°) aspect to one another and are inconjunct (135°) to a third. The configuration from these aspects forms a long, very narrow triangle similar to a pointing finger and is an indicator of something significant. Buckfast Abbey in Devon was situated at the point of the Yod and of particular importance, it seemed to us, was that the tip was where two energies converged. We therefore realised that we should visit Malmesbury Abbey first, as Buckfast Abbey formed the point of the Yod.

Malmesbury Abbey lies in the north of the county of Wiltshire and, as it was the mid-winter solstice, we did not have to get up too early. We surfaced to a rainy dawn so there was no hope of seeing any signs in the sky, as we had in the summer. Malmesbury itself is a beautiful little town built on a hill leading up to the ruined Abbey with its great, Gothic arches set at the top. It is a Celtic foundation founded in the 7th century which was taken over in the Middle Ages by the Cistercian order of White Monks, as they were known because of their white habits. The rain was falling softly as we arrived. Parking the car, we walked through the gates of the precinct. We stood as far from the public paths as possible where we had a clear view of the arches resembling the great trilithons forming the three arches at Stonehenge. We repeated what we did at Stonehenge– sounding the Om, lowering the cross-bar of the 'H' and then we opened the gateway with the crystal key.

We now had to wait till the Spring Equinox in 2001 when foot and mouth disease was devastating the country and Devon was one of the worst hit areas, but luckily, not in the immediate vicinity of the village of Buckfastleigh close to Buckfast Abbey. We booked into a nearby guesthouse the night before and felt a little awkward at having to explain to our hosts that we would be up very early the following morning and could they let us have a key in order to let ourselves in and out, as we would definitely be back for the cooked breakfast. Caroline endeavoured to make it sound reasonable by saying we wished to see the sun rise over the Abbey. Our hostess seemed to think this was a lovely thing to do.

Once again, as at Stonehenge, we rose to a pale dawn and tiptoed across the sopping grass to the car. The world seemed young and innocent again with only the birds and animals about, safe for a while from humankind.

Our first view of the Abbey was impressive but it was strange to see such a modern building in the likeness of a medieval Cathedral. It stands on the site of a medieval Cistercian monastery which was pulled down after the Dissolution and replaced in 1806 by a Gothic mansion and woollen mill. The Benedictines, or Black monks (so-called because of their black habits) acquired it in 1882 and a handful of monks, with few resources, heroically built a new Gothic abbey.

We made our way towards a view of the West Door and were just wondering where exactly we should stand when a beautiful, little cat, a silver tabby, slim as a wand, came running towards us from behind a tree, mewing wildly as if she were trying to tell us something. The tree itself had a strange shape, the trunk dividing only a few feet from its base into two equal trunks forming a perfect Y. The cat, which matched the silvery light of pre-dawn, then ran to the base of the tree where she proceeded to sit and perform her toilet. We took this as a sign that this was where we should stand and, indeed, it was the perfect place. It exactly faced the West Door at just the right distance for discretion and we realised that its two thick branches leading out of the trunk, echoed the 'Y' of the yod.

There was also a theme of black and white confirming that the merging energies were opposites. The Cistercian monks at Malmesbury Abbey wore white whilst the Benedictine monks now living at Buckfast Abbey wore black habits.

Standing together under the tree we asked for protection. Just as we were about to start, we saw a procession of monks coming from their dormitory to sing Matins in the Abbey. We waited and then to our surprise we heard the monks chanting. We now sounded the 'Om' whilst the monks continued their chanting as the sun rose over the horizon. It was a curious blending of the timeless sound of the 'One True Note' with a chanting that seemed timeless. Another pair of opposites came together at that moment - man and woman joined in in song just like the two halves of the tree under which we stood. We used the crystal key once again to open the gateway, the idea being that the finer vibration would be able to enter the physical domain because we were merging the energy of the opposites at the point of the yod.

Before returning to our guesthouse, we decided to wander round the grounds and, as we did so, we came to a hedge where a blackbird had just alighted. We were so close that we could have leant over and touched him. Suddenly, looking directly at us, he opened his beak and, for what seemed an age, poured forth his song. Eventually, seemingly surprised at what he had done, he hopped over to his mate who had joined him. We knew that we had been thanked.

Suddenly we realised we were tired and wished to be back in bed with breakfast to look forward to. Slowly we made our way back to the car park and, as we came to a wide arch, the tiny tabby came running up to us, mewing, as if we were long-lost friends. She proceeded to accompany us to the car park and, then, a strange thing happened. A car suddenly stopped as it was about to pass us and a man looked out and said, "That's my grandson's cat. She ran away two days' ago and can't have had any food since then." The date was, in fact, the 22nd of March 2000, as we hadn't been able to make the exact date of the equinox on the 21st. We found out later from Robert that the little tabby had been waiting for us since the day of the equinox. The man then went to pick her up, but she appeared very disinclined to return home, and ran away from him. Feeling like a traitor, Caroline coaxed her to let her pick her up and handed her over to the man. Even though he stroked her in a kindly way, she struggled rather pathetically to get down. Whoever had guided the little tabby was ensuring that her fast would soon be broken. We comforted ourselves as we drove away with the fact that she had fulfilled her task and would, doubtless, settle down again after she had been fed.

Back at the guesthouse we returned, rather thankfully, to our beds but oddly, since she was rather tired, Caroline was unable to fall asleep. It seemed to her, as she lay half-dozing, that the two halves of her, Light and Dark, came together and were integrated, and she was to have some sort of confirmation of this later that morning.

After a fortifying breakfast, we returned to the Abbey and, this time, went inside the Abbey. In front of the altar there was a magnificent golden circle, like a golden crown, hanging from the roof and divided into twelve sections containing lanterns. We immediately thought of Jerusalem and the Twelve Tribes and realised that we must cut the chain by which it was hanging so as to bring the New Jerusalem to earth. This we did.

Whilst having a cup of coffee outside enjoying the sunshine, Cassie, keeping very still, quietly said, 'The most enormous, black crow I have ever seen has just sat down behind you'. Caroline turned round to have a look, whereupon this, indeed, truly large crow flew up into the tree above her head, gave a loud squawk and flew off. Crows and ravens have always been taken to represent the dark side of life, harbingers of doom, as in Macbeth, and Caroline took the squawk to mean a 'thank-you' from her Shadow self, or Dark side - call it what you will - which she had accepted that morning.

In the Abbey's Museum we were surprised to see a large reliquary standing on the ground in the form of the Ark of the Covenant. This was interesting, as Robert had said that we would be encountering the Ark at some time in the near future. He said that, contrary to what many people thought, it was at the etheric level and not, therefore, fixed at any one location. There was a photograph showing it being carried in procession by the monks at the completion of the building of the Abbey. Later, that afternoon we passed a shop called "The Ark", and the following Monday, in a radio play, the Ark of the Covenant was mentioned. It was time to leave and, in a final interplay of signs from the Universe to us, we noticed the number plate of a small van parked just in front of us in the car park; the letters were: YOD.

APPENDIX IX

Fashion Victim and Pop Idol

The Sacred King was the first fashion victim. Certain fashions began to catch Cassie's attention, such as those which exposed just one arm or one shoulder. Other clothes had sleeves which deliberately covered the hands. She noticed the huge, puffed up hairdos or eyes ringed with black make-up, all of which began seriously to arouse her suspicions. A moment of insight came one day when she was looking at a page of cut-off trousers. She suddenly realised that the original reason for the shortened trouser leg was gradually to reveal the sacred leg of the King. The reasoning behind this would have had something to do with the gradual build-up of sun energy as the sun's strength increased towards midsummer. Logically, the big cover-up of the King would have occurred when the sun was at its height and people feared they might be harmed by the sun power emanating from his body. So just before midsummer, he would have been made to wear dark glasses, lightened long hair mimicking the sun's rays, a maxi coat and gloves to conceal the sacred hands or hand. He would also have worn thigh-high boots. As the sun's strength began to wane after the midsummer sacrifice, the body of the new King would have gradually been revealed– the trouser legs became ever shorter culminating in what we call hot-pants, the boot became a knee-high boot, then calf-high and finally ended up as an ankle boot. The maxi coat would have gradually become ever shorter until it had become a cropped jacket with short sleeves such as we have seen in extreme fashions. It is this practice which might account for the sexual thrill in glimpsing an ankle or leg etc.

At each new phase of concealment or cover-up, he was made to parade along a raised platform so that the community might gasp in awe and wonder at the sight of this semi-divine being. Of course, when the Queen/Goddess was overthrown, it was she who became the fashion victim and it was she who was made to parade in front of everyone in clothes which variously revealed or concealed. Perhaps, originally, the Cat Walk was called the Cock Walk, Stag Walk or Lion Walk as these are animals sacred to the King, whilst the cat is sacred to the Goddess.

It soon became apparent that it was the King who first wore make-up. To enhance the wonder of his sun eyes, the lashes would have been extended or darkened to make it look as if the eyes were ringed by the rays of the sun. Colours round the eyes were worn to accord with the seasons, such as perhaps green for the greening of the world at springtime, red for the summer months and black at the death of the sun at midwinter. In order to protect the people from the power coming from the shining 'sun' face of the king, he would have had a paste (foundation) applied to prevent any rays (shine) escaping which might harm lesser mortals. In some cults, the King was made to wear a mask and in China, he wore a short beaded curtain which hung just in front of his eyes. So too, would the nails on the Sacred Hand of the King, been enhanced because they were a part of the sacred hand. In some parts of the world the fingernails of the King were not permitted to be cut.

The well-known children's fairytale, The Emperor's New Clothes, took on a new significance. The Emperor or King is wholly preoccupied with his appearance. As a consequence, his vanity allows him to be duped by two con-men into wearing no clothes at all! As many people know, fairytales hark back to our remote history. The idea came that in the pagan cult it is highly likely that there was one day in the year when the Sacred King did indeed parade through the streets or on the 'Stag Walk' totally naked so that all might gasp in awe and wonder at the sight of his naked body which held the power of the sun itself with its life-giving and healing properties. We see the King's revenge on the Queen for this ordeal in the story of Lady Godiva who was made to ride naked on a white horse (sacred to the Goddess) through the streets with only her long hair to cover her.

There is evidence of elements of the Cult in the world of pop music. The Rock group in particular often looked like a group of Celts with their coloured headbands, bare chests and long hair, not to mention tattoos and heavy jewellery of which the Celts were so fond. The focus of the Cult was the sexual prowess of the King because the cult was, above all, a fertility cult. We find just such a sexual focus in much pop music, particularly Rock and Roll.

Knowing of the godlike powers of the Sun King also explains the extraordinary emotionally hysterical reaction that pop stars like Elvis Presley, or groups such as The Beatles, aroused in teenage girls when the phenomenon re-surfaced. We were witnessing the reaction that the Sacred Sun King received from the community when he made one of his public appearances. Here was a man with superhuman powers whose energy and virility was gradually building up inside him to its climax at midsummer. That inner power could be fatal to ordinary men and women so there was the added frisson of the danger of being near such a man. In addition, women were also aware of his superhuman sexual powers. Little wonder that women swooned in the presence of such a man.

The punk phase, for example, in particular Sid Vicious, who mutilated and finally killed himself in a moment of maddened self-annihilation, as well as certain heavy rock bands, were recreating what had evolved into the Death Cult of the Sacred King. It resulted from those devotees of the Cult who, unbalanced by drugs and alcohol, were so besotted by the Sun King and his sacrificial death that it is likely they wished to share it with him in acts of self-destruction.

There is also a fashion in the pop world for a barbed wire tattoo around the upper arm. This marks the full extent of the sacred arm and where it would have been amputated. The barbed wire is the blackthorn which was sacred to the Goddess. A similar, thin black cord is worn around the neck to mark where the sacred head was struck off, as well as one around the wrist for the sacred hand.

More recently, with the emergence of Hip Hop, rap singers wear large baggy clothes which completely cover their bodies, including a woollen cap to cover the head. The trousers are very wide and long so as to completely cover the foot and the heavy gold jewellery also harks back to the Cult of the Sacred King and Celtic times which overlap that period. Most revealing of all are the hands of the rap singer, which you could say he uses in a most extraordinary way and which invites the question, from where does the idea come for these gesticulating hands thrust aggressively at an audience and with each finger heavily covered in rings? Why, also, do they show off the hand as if some of the fingers are missing? It is because this is how the Sacred King, as lead singer of the band, would have danced and the reason for the missing fingers is that some would have been cut off for ritual purposes? Just recently, pop music was playing in the background and the words "Don't let the sun go down on me" gradually sank in and Cassie thought that the Sacred King could very well have sung those words himself because, when the sun did sink low in the sky at midwinter, it signalled his sacrificial death.

Brief mention should be made here of the Cult of Celebrity which also harks back to the cult of human sacrifice. We are made to look up to people such as actors, football players and certain members of the media because their excessive wealth and/or media attention has put them in a world apart. We are given access to their lives through magazines such as 'Hello' and 'Heat', just as people were given access to the intimate life of the Sun King, Louis XIV. Then the assassination begins. On our behalf, the editorial begins criticising the figures, health, clothes and life styles of these demi-gods. Just as then, as onlookers in this spectator sport, we are partaking in a subliminal 'killing'. Perhaps such 'sport' should be compared with the popular public hangings of the Middle Ages.

The height of our quest coincided with a period in the English Conservative Party when they kept replacing their leaders in quick succession, before finally settling on David Cameron. The language often used for such a painful event – 'night of the long knives' or 'stabbed in the back' reveals how our subconscious interprets such disposals. The energies of the pagan cult have been cleared from ether and dimensions surrounding the planet: now it only remains for those memories lying in the subconscious mind to be accessed so they can be released, and many people healed.

APPENDIX X

Natural Laws

1. Acceptance of self totally - now

2. Non-judgementalism to everyone and everything

3. Accept our human limitations

4. Law of Correspondence

5. Until you are committed there is no movement at all

6. Every day is a new clean fresh day

7. No matter what happens give thanks

8. Every act has a consequence

9. You can only ever change yourself

10. Take full responsibility for your thoughts and actions

Bibliography

Bord, Janet and Colin Mysterious Britain (London, Thorsons, 1995)

Cunliffe, Barry Danebury: Anatomy of an Iron-Age Hillfort

Keatman, Martin & Graham Phillips The Green Stone (Neville Spearman, 1983)

Curry, Patrick Defending Middle-Earth Tolkien: Myth & Modernity (London, HarperCollins 1998)

Elurere, Christiane The Celts: First Masters of Europe (London, Thames and Hudson Ltd, 1992)

Gardner, Laurence Lost Secrets of the Sacred Ark (Element, 2003)

Gordon, E.O. Prehistoric London - Its Mounds and Circles (London, The Covenant Publishing Co., Ltd., 1932)

Graves, Robert The White Goddess (London, Faber and Faber Limited, 1961)

The Greek Myths (Penguin Books, 1992)

Hill Elder, Isabel Celt, Druid and Culdee (1973)

Joyce, P.W. Old Celtic Romances (Dublin, The Talbot Press Ltd, 1966 (1879))

Kilby, Clyde Tolkien and The Silmarillion (Lion Publishing, 1977)

Malory, Sir Thomas Le Morte D'Arthur (London, Penguin Books, 1986)

Miller, Hamish & Paul Broadhurst The Sun and the Serpent (Launceston, Pendragon Press, 1989)

Picard, Barbara Leonie Hero Tales from the British Isles (Penguin Books Ltd, 1966)

Pipe, Marian Northamptonshire Ghosts & Legends (Countryside Books, 1993)

Ross, Anne & Don Robbins the Life and Death of a Druid Prince (Rider & Co June 1989

Sutphen, Dick Finding your Answers Within (New York, Pocket Books, 1989)

Tolkien, J.R.R. The Lord of the Rings (London, Unwin Hyman Limited, 1966)

The Silmarillion (London, Harper Collins, 1994)

Unfinished Tales (London, Harper Collins, 1980)

The Hobbit (London, Harper Collins, 1990)

Sir Gawain and the Green Knight, Pear and Sir Orfeo (George Allen & Unwin Ltd, 1975)

Toulson, Shirley The Winter Solstice (Jill Norman & Hobhouse Ltd, 1981)

Wallis Budge, E.A. Egyptian Religion (London, Arkana Paperbacks, 1987 (1899))

Watkins, Alfred The Ley Hunter's Manual (The Aquarian Press, 1989)

ENDNOTES

1 At the end of the Second Age a terrible seven- year battle is waged against Sauron. Finally, Isildur kills Sauron in single combat on the slopes of the volcano and removes the Ring from Sauron's finger. He is urged to throw it then and there into the fires of the volcano but Isildur does not, for his will is quickly dominated by that of the Master Ring, and he finds it too 'fair' to destroy.

2 When Frodo enters the Forest of Lothlorien where the Elven folk live, he is keenly aware of the change in the atmosphere so that his surroundings seem more alive. There is no stain on that Land which is likened to the World as it was in the First Age, for it is under the power of an Elven Ring. Gandalf tells Aragorn that much will be lost at the end of the Third Age because the world is changing. The Elves will 'fade', i.e. they will become invisible to mortal eyes.

3 Sauron lost his physical body at the time of the destruction of the island of Numenor long ago at the end of the Second Age. Despite this loss he was still able to interact with the living world in a hideous guise, like the living dead, through the use of Black Magic. In the Third Age he creates the terrifying form of an eye. When the Ring falls into the fire with Gollum, Sauron's spirit leaves the world as a vast, black shape in the sky and we are told that he will never be able to take shape again.

4 The Seven Stones of Seeing were gifts from the Elves to the Numenoreans. The Stones were brought to Middle Earth by the faithful Numenoreans from over the seas. In the time of the story of the Fellowship of the Ring, the Stones had passed out of living knowledge but we learn that three have survived and are being used in secret by Sauron, Saruman and Denethor, Steward of Minas Tirith.

5 The powerful men who wore them were subverted and eventually controlled by Sauron's will, all except the dwarves. Only the Three Elven Rings were free as they had been forged in secret without Sauron's knowledge.

6 In his book *Prehistoric London*, (first published in 1914) E. O. Gordon mentions the other two sacred mounds in the "Port of

Londin" as the Llandin – Parliament Hill, and the Penton, both of which, being natural heights, would have been clearly visible as they rose above the surrounding moors, marshes and watery stretches that surrounded the pre-Christian capital. The Tothill was still standing in the reign of Queen Elizabeth I, as it is mentioned by Norden, topographer of Westminster at the time: "Tootehill Street, lying in the west part of the citie, taketh name of a hill near it which is called Toote-hill, in the great feyld near the street". A map of 1746 shows the Toothill Fields (map of 1746) at the bend in that ancient Causeway, the Horseferry Road.

Other well-known mounds are Silbury Hill, the Montem at Eton, the Windsor Round-Table Mound, the Mound at Oxford, Winton (St. Katherine's Hill, Winchester) and the Tot rearing high beside Totnes. Seventy Tot or Toot Hills are mentioned in Hones' *Year Book*, and many more might be added. He adds Tetbury (a corruption of Tot), Teterton Clee and Doddington Wood in Salop. This last has a height of 122 feet.

In the Welsh language Holy Hills or Mounds are called Gorsedds, which means "The Great Seat or throne of the Monarch". We were at once reminded of the Great Seat on the Hill of Seeing of the High Kings of the West in Tolkien's book. E.O. Gordon describes how far-reaching are the views from the summit of the Gorsedd at Totnes. The Great Seat stands on the highest point of the hill and is enclosed by a stone wall, which has never been roofed, like the Round-Table Mound at Windsor. The mound is artificial with the average dimensions of such "piled up", prehistoric Gorsedds, being 100 feet in diameter at the base, narrowing to about 80 at the top.

It is curious that the word 'Tot' (a sacred mound) should mean 'death' in German. Is it possibly because such sacred high places later became associated with human sacrifice? In Tolkien's story of Middle Earth, a precedent for human sacrifice is to be found in the Temple built by Sauron on the Sacred Heights of Numenor. There, the Faithful – those who were still friends of the Elves - were singled out for sacrifice.

Another point of interest is that Wickliffe, in his translation of the Bible applies the word Tot to Mount Zion (2 Sam.v. 7-9). Please see the Appendix on Brutus, the Trojan Prince.

[7] For sceptics of reincarnation as well as the idea that we can carry the memory of a past life trauma in the subconscious mind, we were very struck by the comment in a book called *Finding Your Answers Within* by the American writer Dick Sutphen. He related that when a past life trauma is triggered, you cannot <u>manufacture</u> those emotions of fear, sorrow or hatred.

[8] See Tolkien's *The Silmarillian*

[9] Frodo makes Gollum swear on The Ring that he will be a faithful guide and Gollum is delighted to do so if it means he can stay close to The Ring. But he can only be trusted up to a point as Samwise is only too aware.

[10] Aragorn captured Gollum in the Dead Marshes and because of his slippery ways, treated him harshly on the long journey they had together. No love was lost between them.

[11] There is a parallel in the story. Gollum found the bright eyes of the Elves and the tall Men of Numenor intolerable. Sauron's ambassador at the Gates of Mordor could not long hold Aragorn's eye and the power of the Lady Arwen's gaze pierced Frodo's heart.

[12] By appealing to his vanity, Bilbo had cleverly made the dragon roll over in the hope of finding a weak spot on his gem-encrusted underside. The thrush overhears him telling the dwarves about the bare yellow hollow over the dragon's heart. When all seems lost and the town is in flames, the thrush perches on Bard's shoulder and tells him to wait for the moon to appear and aim for the yellow patch on the dragon's belly with his remaining arrow as the dragon hurtles down on the beleaguered town, bent on total destruction.

[13] Beren gave the Silmaril to King Thingol in exchange for his daughter Luthien's hand in marriage. Bilbo gave the Arkenstone to both the Elven King and Bard to use as a bargaining counter in exchange for their rightful share of the dragon's treasure.

[14] The spiritual interpretation of the phenomenon known as "the diamond-ring effect", which occurs at the precise moment that the

moon covers the face of the sun at the time of an eclipse, is that it represents Nenya.

[15] from the original brothers, Elros and Elrond, the Half Elven. Elros chose to be human and Elrond became fully immortal as an Elf. Aragorn was descended from the Line of Elros and Arwen was the daughter of Elrond.

[17] Think Rachel Whiteread's inverted, transparent, resin cast of Trafalgar Square's fourth plinth, which had recently been placed on top of the real fourth plinth, and you will get the idea. The fourth plinth in Trafalgar Square has been used for the past couple of years for a changing exhibition of sculptures, while the authorities try and decide who in the twenty-first century should grace it permanently. At the moment, it appears to be a platform, both literally and metaphorically, for messages of darkness and light for those who have eyes to see. It is interesting that it is the *fourth* plinth. The translucent resin cast represents the fourth dimension resting on the solid, low vibrations of the third dimension.

[18] Peregrine Took, or Pippin.

[19] It was the badge of the House of Finarfin of the Noldorin Elves and had been made in the Blessed Land of the Valar, or Great Gods, before they returned to Middle Earth.

[20] Gresley is a Norman name and the family are related to William the Conqueror's Standard Bearer, Malahalshis. This meant that there could be a connection with the French noble family of de Guise and through them, to the Royal Line of David. Robert confirmed that this was so.

[21] The Sword is put to test for the first time in the Mines of Moria. A powerfully built Orc Chief is about to kill Frodo with his scimitar but, just in time, Aragorn uses Anduril to strike the orc's helmet and as he does so, a flash like a flame can be seen on impact. At the siege of Helm's Deep in the Land of the Horsemen, when Aragorn wields the Sword, a cry goes up from all the men manning the defences: 'Anduril! Anduril goes to war. The Blade that was Broken shines again'. As an inspirational piece of writing, Tolkien's work shows that the Light of the Sword really was visible in the days when energy levels were higher.

[22] Merlin was ensnared by the enchantress Nimue who imprisons him under a stone after learning all she can of his magic

[23] Like gold, its state could be altered using a high-spin alchemical process, which turns the metal to a fine white powder. The process involves a 44 per cent weight loss due to a part of the substance existing in a weightless state at a higher dimension. At the moment of transition there is a blinding flash of white light. The powder was ingested by those of the royal bloodline for it stimulated the pineal gland (gold) or, if the metal used was iridium, the pituitary gland (silver), so heightening the spiritual powers of the king, in addition to conferring longevity.

[24] Cirth Ungol is the Tower that guarded a little known entry into the Land of Mordor, the realm of the Dark Lord. It stood on the heights of the mountain range called the Ephel Duath, or the Mountains of Shadow. Guided by Gollum, Frodo and Samwise enter the ghostly Vale of Minas Morgul. They have only just climbed above the vapours of the valley, when lightening thunder appear around the evil fastness of Minas Morgul, at the head of the valley. An army marches out of its gates, at the head of which rides the black-cloaked General of Sauron's armies. War has broken at last and he is on his way to attack the chief City of the Western lands, Minas Tirith. As he makes his way down the valley he comes level with where the hobbits are crouching on the path running up the south side of the valley. When level with the Ringbearer, he halts for a brief moment before continuing. For the first time Frodo uses the crystal phial of Galadriel and the connection between Frodo and the ringwraith is broken. Frodo has had a narrow escape from detection.

From this point onwards, it can be worked out that the passage of time until the bursting of the two opposing gates - one in the East and the other in the West, is the same.

[25] One example would be the friction between England's King Henry II and the Archbishop, Thomas a Beckett and which led to the murder of the Archbishop in front of the alter by four of King Henry's knights..

[26] after the great-grandfather of King David.

[27] the high priest in the Temple of Jerusalem

[28] We see just such a union of the two powers in the Priest-Kings of the Sumerian civilisation. When the beautiful Temple of Solomon in Jerusalem was completed, the king called the nation together for the ceremony of dedication and led the procession to the Temple. When the Sacred Ark and other sacred things had been placed in the new building, King Solomon turned and blessed the people.

[29] It is because Jesus represented the qualities of true kingship that he aroused such fear and hatred – because he threatened the status quo. He was a threat to the power and authority of a rich and privileged priesthood and he posed a threat to Rome's puppet King, Herod Agrippa, who had been imposed upon the people of Israel. It had been no different for Aragorn. The ruling Steward Denethor would never voluntarily have given up his position to Aragorn. However, the important difference then was that the Stewards never presumed to call themselves 'king' because of the love and reverence in which the Royal Line was held. The Pharaoh Akhenaton also set about taking back the power and authority usurped by a power-hungry priesthood. But the opposition was too great, his mission failed, and the priests attempted to erase Akhenaton's name and deeds from history. European history of the past 2,000 years can be viewed in terms of the uneasy relationship between King and Church. Kingship was greatly weakened when the Church contrived that a Pope or Archbishop must anoint Kings. In addition, the Pope and Bishops encroached on the power of the king by living in palaces, owning land, being fabulously rich and even holding their own Courts of Law. History has shown us the terrible consequences that have arisen with the division of power because of the constant battle for supremacy between the two.

[30] Before the visit Caroline had also suddenly thought that this would be the place where the Golden and Silver Trees, Laurelin and Telperion, (later called Nimloth) from the Undying Land of Aman of the Great Gods could be united. Laurelin had been destroyed and was only present in the Silmarils, that is, at the Fourth dimension. In this way we would bring together the opposites of Gold and Silver, Masculine and Feminine. Finally, we brought them together: Laurelin, once more, a living tree, and

Telperion - the Golden and the Silver – the Masculine and the Feminine. This chimed with what came into Cassie's inner vision the instant she sounded the deep note from the horn. She saw the walls of the building (of 11 Kensington Place) come tumbling down (shades of the walls of Jericho falling by the same method!). An enormous pyramid-shaped tree sprang up in the open air. Instantly, around the immense tree there grew a tight circle of very much smaller trees. We thought it must be the Tree of Life but, nevertheless, ran it past Robert who replied that the pyramid tree is important as it may well be representative of the Tree of Life and Death? as above so below?

[31] The ancient crown of the Sea Kings, brought to Middle Earth by Elendil from the lost island of Numenor, was used at Aragorn's coronation. It was similar to the helms of the Guards of the Citadel of Minas Tirith save that it was taller and all white. There were wings at either side made of pearl and silver 'in the likeness of a sea-bird'. Seven diamonds were in the circlet and 'upon its summit was set a single jewel the light of which went up like a flame.'

[32] The rules for making a lexigram are quite precise. The word or phrase one is lexigramming should contain no more than four different vowels, and no more than fifteen different consonants. This is because, if they did, it would be possible to form most of the words in the dictionary! A letter in the original word or phrase can only be used once in each different word in the lexigram, unless it appears more than once in the original. It should be written in capital letters, but if necessary, a few words such as *a, the, at* , etc., may be added in lower case for better understanding of the meaning of the lexigram.

www.ingramcontent.com/pod-product-compliance
Lightning Source LLC
Chambersburg PA
CBHW031217290326
41931CB00034B/166